Stephen Martin SPRING 2020 V1.1

ANSELMS GIFT

I. BEGINNINGS

Anselm wasn't sure exactly how old he was. Time started from that day when he was found wandering the heath with no name and no history. Just how he got there he didn't know.

When the shepherd came upon him, he was stumbling like a new born lamb across the heath, the shock of the unknown staring from his blue-green eyes. There had been a late, brutal snap of cold that early March on the hilltops. Enough to see off some of the weaker lambs and more than enough to see off a boy without the insulation that Mother Nature had granted those lambs.

Yet there he was.

Anselm was unsure what to make of the shepherd. The old man's 'weather beaten face looked like the grain of one of the sandstone outcrops pushing through the pasture. Yet the shepherd moved. And he made sounds that Anselm could understand; soothing sounds of welcome. This was the first time he had heard a voice; it was the first time there had been any time.

The old man took the boy, bewildered, to a tumbledown, limestone-walled cottage perched on the valley side.

There he stood him in front of a log fire and clothed him in old trousers and a rough woollen top. He had the lean gangling physique of a teenager.

Anselm was a blank canvas. He had no re-collections of events before he was found by the shepherd. No memories to define him. None of the badges of a previous life. Yet he understood the shepherds words; enough at least to communicate his hunger.

The shepherd had lived on the hillside for as long as he could remember, an observer of the world of fleeting skies, ever shifting shadows, the bleating of lambs and smell of morning grass. The care of his flock filled his days. Like any good shepherd he let the flock find their way across the rugged pasture, take shelter under the sandstone rocks , find mates and give birth to young. He would simply watch over them, signal with his staff the time to move on and give a sense of safety through his presence.

The old man told the lad he could stay with him, learn the life of a shepherd and look after the flock and rolling hills. “This world can use two shepherds”. Now the shepherd would have someone with whom he could break his exile of aloneness.

The shepherd gave the boy the name ‘Anselm’.

Anselm showed an insatiable hunger to understand everything : “Where do the lambs come from? Can you understand what they say? What makes the rain? How do you know? Where does the stream end? What moves the sun and moon?"

The shepherd would explain patiently.

And so, things might have stayed , but the boy woke one morning and asked two questions, which changed everything:" Why am I here? What am I to do in life? "

It was then that the shepherd saw his own selfishness.

***

The Swinbournes lived in the village of Kirkmoor, to the north of York. Peter was , a professor of philosophy at York University and Martha the managing director of an on-line travel business. They lived together, apart, in pursuit of their careers. Theirs had become a ritual, kisses on the cheek 'partnership' without connection. Somewhere along the way, they had unconsciously signed an unwritten, unspoken contract that their passions would be their careers, each inaccessible to the other.

They had not been blessed with children. The doctor had said Martha was unable to conceive. Several specialist second opinions confirmed that diagnosis and there they let the matter rest. Though of course it never rested; it just lost its' voice and became buried deep beneath the minutes and hours of their working days.

Until one day, Peter came down to breakfast at his usual time to find Martha, eyes red, tear stained cheeks staring into the middle distance over a slice of abandoned toast and an open copy of the Gazette.

“What’s wrong hon .” he asked, the brevity of the word robbing it of any emotional content

She flickered a glance at him then immediately looked down at her breakfast plate.

“What is it?” he asked, the first bud of concern opening in his stomach.

“Nothing....... it's nothing.”

It was one of those ‘nothings’, which even the other-worldly Peter knew was code for a big ‘something’.

Peter tried further, inexpert coaxing but Martha wouldn’t be cornered. She jumped to her feet: “I’m going to be late; important meeting; the bankers are in this morning to discuss the re-financing. Got to go .....see you this evening.” All without drawing breath; a stream of automatic words building a bridge for her to get to the front door and out of the house before Peter could ask any more questions.

Peter’s life revolved around paradoxes and unresolved dilemmas. Action, cause and effect were some of the more problematic concepts in analytical philosophy. Peter had a mind which could see the paradoxes and difficulties in even the simplest of everyday things .A mind which grappled with Xeno's paradox of the tortoise and the hare, yet couldn't find the way of stopping his wife reaching the front door.

She had gone. No regulation peck on the cheek, such was her haste. What had thrown her?

Peter reached out for the Gazette, which Martha had closed and folded. Like putting something away. He flicked through and found the damp page with ink-runs.

'**Abandoned boy found on Heath,**' The page headline shouted above a picture of a young boy, maybe 14 or 15 years old. Peter scanned the article…'found by shepherd...name unknown...police and care authorities making appeal for anyone who knows boy to come forward...'

Peter's thoughts went back to that time of despair and unfaithful hope. A time when Martha finally accepted the opinions of so many doctors and she and Pete agreed to put the 'baby thing' behind them. For a while they had contemplated adoption and had approached the adoption agencies .Two professional people, comfortably well-off, churchgoing......... surely ideal material for adoptive parents. But nothing happened. They were reassured from time to time that they were top of the list but no suitable child had yet become available. As time wore on so, Martha's vision of herself as a mother seemed to fade until, one day, she could no longer imagine the house with a child in it.

Peter had been less sure about having children. Martha had made most of the running o that front. Yet, once it became clear Martha couldn't conceive, Peter began to feel a gnawing resent somewhere in his stomach. Sometimes, the resent leaked out in the form of irritation with Martha. The kind of irritation usually reserved for the less able, the imperfect, the ones who can't keep up. At root, Peter found it difficult to forgive Martha for not being able to give him something he didn't know that he needed.

***

The shepherd took Anselm into town. They waved down a lorry and the driver took them through crowded streets finally stopping outside a huge red brick building. The shepherd said something to someone sat behind a desk. They sat on a hard bench and waited.

The old man tried to explain to the boy that he couldn't stay in the hills. There were things to do in the world and it was a much larger place than the hills and pastures. Anselm didn't see why a bigger place was needed-until he arrived in town and saw the problem. He didn't think all those people wandering around on the hills would be such a good idea.

The shepherd said that Anselm would go to live with some people who could look after him, teach him and show him how to live in the world.

"But you could do that". Anselm had protested.

"That's not the way" was the old man's cryptic answer.

A lady appeared at the door. They were shown into a room. Two people were sat behind another desk. They asked the shepherd lots of questions.

“Where did you find the boy?”

“But where did he come from?”

“Surely he could tell you something about his parents ?How long has he been with you?”

The shepherd answered but his answers always seemed to draw another question. After a while they asked the same questions of Anselm who gave the same answers. He wondered why they needed to ask twice. The questioners faces seemed to get longer and harder as the meeting went on.

Anselm's bottom was getting numb on the hard, wooden bench. He shifted from side to side. After what, to his bottom, seemed a very long time the two people asking the questions left the room .

“Why did they ask the same questions twice?” asked Anselm.

“Because some people need to hear the truth more than once to recognise it”, the shepherd replied.

Anselm was on the verge of another ‘why when the two people re-appeared. “Well we must find him a place to live. There is a lady Mrs Stout who looks after our children before they are placed. We have a number of couples looking to adopt but we need to understand Anselm's background better before we look to find him a permanent home. Perhaps his real parents will come forward. The police will help in that”

“The boy doesn’t seem concerned about his situation” said one.

He hasn’t been around long enough to learn to worry about things”repled the shepherd.

Turning to Anselm the old man said in a whisper. “Now I must go. This is for the best.”

“Where are you going?”

“I’ll be right beside you-always.”

Anselm turned to look at the two people. He didn’t think he would want to stay with them; too many questions. But at least their faces had turned softer. He turned again to the shepherd, but the old man had gone. Anselm ran to the door and looked down a long corridor. Empty. He felt a heaviness in his chest.

***

Mrs Stout was a large lady. She wore soft shoes, a long, flowered dress and her hair was in a bun. Her kitchen smelled of a wet, sweet warmth which Anselm later found was a mixture of raspberry tarts and washing.

He was shown to his bedroom: the bottom section of a bunk bed. There didn't seem to be anyone using the top bunk.

"You'll be staying here for a week or two until we make some inquiries" said one of the faces from the big red building who had brought him to Mrs Stout's house.

"You'll be fine here lovely. Lots of children gone through my hands .There's football and a swing in the garden- though you look a bit big for the swing tells the truth. Anyway, you'll be fine."

The two big people went to the next room.

Anselm heard fragments of their conversation floating down the hallway. ".... just a week or two." "...don't seem worried... the boy."

The days in town seemed longer than they were in the country. Anselm thought of the hills a lot...it seemed like he could touch them and yet they stayed just out of reach.

Mrs Stout went about her business...which mostly seemed to be about making the kitchen hot, sweet and warm. She didn't have any questions of Anselm, but she did like to talk. She would rattle on about anything and everything..... "how the prices of things keep going up" and "the weather is so changeable these days..."

At first, Anselm didn't understand much of what she had to say. Yet, somehow, this big, bumbling woman unlocked a door in Anselm's mind; a door into a room filled with words, sentences, names...all sat patiently waiting to be used. Within a few short weeks he was talking her to a standstill...an experience unfamiliar to Mrs Stout. Everyday brought waves of questions from the boy to break on the rocks of Mrs Stout's ignorance of anything other than the commonplaces of human existence.

"I don't know the answer to that one, Anselm. Never really had much need to know them things. You do ask some funny questions my boy."

***

It was a few more days after the newspaper headline appeared before Martha told Peter what was on her mind.

"I want to try for adoption again," she announced in a tone that carried the steel of inevitability.

As soon as that transformational sentence was past her lips, things moved breathlessly fast and kettle-watch slow. Time had its foot simultaneously on both the accelerator and brake .

Until, one day, three months later, a middle-aged couple stood in front of a wide- eyed boy given the name of Anselm by a shepherd and said:

“Welcome to your new home; we really hope you will be happy here.”

Anselm was hesitant at first.

“Everything is unfamiliar to him,” said Peter to an anxious Martha.

‘Of course, I know that’ thought Martha. But there was something else about this boy that she couldn’t put her finger on. Something different; something unexpected.

Anselm seemed to have no understanding of what they meant when asking what happened ‘before’ he was found by the shepherd. He could remember now the hillside and its chattering streams, the sky changing white, blue, grey, black punctuated alternately by circling birds and shimmering lights. But all of this he reported as if it were a painting he had once seen, not a stage set on which he had acted.

He could speak but couldn’t remember ever having heard another human tongue before the day he was found. He ate the meals Martha put on his plate but seemed surprised each time they appeared. He slept soundly like any teenage boy and woke unsure where and who he was – like any teenage boy.

“It’s as if there was some immaculate conception amongst those hills,” said Peter. “He just sprung out of nowhere: a living, breathing teenage boy. But he’s checked into life without any baggage. No memories to speak of and just a basic understanding of language. A two, or three -year old's understanding of the world , held in an adolescents' body."

In the land of feelings Anselm was only partially sighted. Hunger, warmth, cold, and even fear he knew and, with help, could name. But anger, jealousy, hate and love meant nothing to him. These words didn't match anything in his short life experience. It would take him a while to 'know' such words which depend on the society of others to gain meaning.

The greatest surprise for Martha and Peter in the early days was Anselm's seeming assumption of the transience of things in the world. Like a kitten a few weeks old, if an object was removed from sight, Anselm acted as if it had ceased to exist. Getting dressed in the morning was a game of hit and miss until Anselm learnt that clothes put in a drawer the night before persisted unseen until the morning, ready to be discovered again. The longer things were out of sight, the more irretrievably they were out of mind. Peter reflected that Anselm shared this behaviour with many adults brought up in more conventional circumstances.

Gradually, Anselm grew more confident in the permanence of things, their reappearance happening consistently. Like many of us , he then started to take much of his new world for granted. Things that first wrapped themselves in surprise and mystery, in time, became de-frocked as commonplace. Anselm showed an insatiable desire to know everything there was to be known about the world.

This was a testing process for Peter and Martha. Each was committed to give the boy the education in life he hungered for. And each found themselves exhausted at end of day by Anselm's unceasing inquiries of the what, how, why and when of life.

Peter would often find himself in an infinite regress of 'why' questions, each more difficult to answer than the last. Like peeling the layers of an onion Anselm would pursue the truths nested inside each other until finally he would reach a kernel of "Why? Because it just is!" or "Because I say so!" Peter recognised the echoes of his own mother and father 's voices in this ultimate explanation of things in terms of parental fiat.

When they had first discussed Anselm, the people at the adoption agency stressed the boy's "learning difficulties". Within a few days , it became clear this was no ordinary boy. He had all the physical attributes of a teenage boy in early puberty but his emotional and learning development seemed hardly to have got off the ground.

Medical, psychiatric and behavioural tests said he was not autistic. He could communicate successfully albeit with a limited vocabulary at first. There were no signs of dysfunctional behaviour. He seemed at ease with himself and the frequent surprises the world had in store for him. 'Learning difficulties' was not the right term. Anselm learnt very quickly. He observed everything, short-circuiting the absent years through incessant questioning.

The agency probed Martha and Peter's motives for adoption at length. There were those who would have had Anselm stay much longer in care, not persuaded that he could operate 'outside'. But at last a conclusion was reached: only by living in the outside world, with his new parents, could Anselm hope to live a 'normal' life and get mental and physical development 'into sync'.

At times Martha and Peter's home seemed like a laboratory; Anselm experimenting with the basics of human existence. On the second day Martha came home from her office to find the TV at ear-shattering volume contesting the airwaves with the hi-fi. Anselm, seated in the middle of the floor, had his hands to his ears and a grimace on his face. He'd been examining the remote buttons. The more he pressed them, the louder things got and the more images of people and things leapt from the box.

Anselm seemed to have little understanding of cause and effect or, indeed, of the passing of time . Not until later when Martha showed him the effect of pressing certain buttons and repeating the process several times did he recognise there was some relationship between the buttons and events on the TV.

Peter observed that at least this proved that a grasp of all things electronic was not, after all, built into the DNA of every teenager.

Time was another difference in Anselm's perception of the world. He didn't make the clear distinction between past, present and future that we impose on life. The day after some of Peter's friends had been to the house for a few hours, Anselm would return to the dining room and express surprise that the visitors weren't there. It seemed that Anselm had them mentally parked in that space for all time.

For several days he exhibited this belief in a sort of co-existence of all moments. He assumed that each room in the house was an unchanging stage set where people and events played out on a kind of continuous video loop, forever there for him to interact with whenever he chose.

Anselm inhabited a permanent now, a continuum where all the events of his new life took place simultaneously. Life on-demand. But, gradually, he became accustomed to the fact that events disappeared from view and were not to be found again where he had first encountered them.

"I'm hungry. Where have you put my breakfast?" two hours after he had eaten his breakfast with gusto was a typical question in the first few days. When reminded he had eaten it he said "yes" suggesting the memory of the meal was there. "But where is it?"

One night, Martha heard sounds coming from his room around two in the morning. She found Anselm talking in his sleep. What he was saying was indecipherable but animated. She tucked him in and left him to his soliloquy.

For some weeks Anselm had difficulty drawing a boundary between his dreams and waking reality. He would often refer to things Peter and Martha had done, or said, of which they had no recollection. The couple began to fear Anselm had some psychological disorder, until they realised these phantom events were all nocturnal, taking place after Anselm had gone to bed.

When Martha explained to Anselm what a dream was, Anselm responded "But how am I to know the difference between the dream and being awake?" The dreams Anselm described seemed so vivid and detailed.

Peter explained. "One way to tell the difference is if you dream of your shepherd but, when you wake there's no trace of him. If you were to go see the shepherd , he would say he had never been to our house, although you dreamt of him being here. When we say, 'he was in your dream' that doesn't mean he was really physically present. It was just a series of images in your mind".

Anselm thought for a few moments. "So, when you say he was in my dream what you really mean is that he wasn't? Then how do I know I'm not dreaming now and when I wake up the shepherd will be here in the house with you two fast asleep upstairs?

"And you explained to me the other day (Anselm was making progress with the concept of time), "that some men thought that the true world only exists because men see it, touch it, hear it. Well I could see and touch and hear the shepherd. So, he was real, right?"

Martha smiled a knowing smile at Peter. Their eyes caught for a second. Peter blushed. She wondered whether the blush was a response to a glimpse of past connection or at being wrong-footed philosophically at breakfast by a teenager.

Of course, Peter had answers for Anselm's questions. These were the very questions that were his life's work. But he knew his answers just begged a whole series of other questions. A professor of philosophy is at least as happy to find a new question, as he is to find an answer. Without the next question there was no work to be done.

"Good questions Anselm," said Peter. "This is a subject generations of students of philosophy have spent a lot of time on. We will talk some more about it when I get back." With that he put on his tweed jacket to go to work.

"If generations have spent so much time on it you'd think they'd have come up with the answers by now", said Anselm. He was beginning to see a pattern in adult behaviour. When you don't know the answer then either just assert something to be so or say: "we'll talk about it later." Anselm thought momentarily that time was something invented by adults so they could park inconvenient questions, or things they had to do, somewhere in an ill-defined future.

***

The adoption agency had suggested the couple speak to some of the local junior schools to see whether they would take Anselm..

"Physically he's far too mature to join the infant school. He won't integrate socially. Better to try the junior school. Though he will be bigger than the other boys and girls, he will be better accepted there. But he'll need to start in the 'remedial' classes to have any chance of catching up," said the lady responsible for Anselm's placement.

"Remedial? Pah!" said Peter. "The boy's not going to start life with that badge. Over my dead body .He's brighter than any of the teachers. He just hasn't had the time in the world that other children have . Wherever, whenever he was before he was found, I don't know what happened but he's not going to be punished for his innocence."

Martha agreed and noted the embryonic father in Peter and the stirring mother in herself.

They found a private tutor. A retired teacher called Emily Watson agreed to come for five hours each week day. She had taught the school curriculum up to the age of sixteen. They discussed how they could arrange their own time to ensure one of them was at home and available to Anselm when Emily was not around. They agreed a pattern of when they could each work with Anselm to add to the teaching time Emily could provide.

Emily was in her late fifties with long silver hair tied up in a bun. An archetype, thought Peter. If there were a Platonic form representing 'retired lady teacher', then it would have the attributes of Emily. Time and the stubborn resistance to enlightenment of generations of pupils had not dulled her wit or her zeal for teaching. There was a sparkle in her eyes, which seemed to Martha to be shafts of light from the teacher's soul. She was undoubtedly the right person to teach Anselm.

For her part the opportunity, late in her career, to write in a book of empty pages and the potential of so many unknowns was beyond her hopes. She set about the task with the evangelical compassion of the missionary in the uncharted land that was this boy's mind and understanding.

Emily had never married. She had never dared to get too close to another person .It was too big a risk. What if that person didn't stay; what if having committed herself, s/he left. No ,it was safer to be alone; to live alone as she did in a small thatched cottage at the edge of the village.

Her pupils became her children by proxy. The irony was that all her 'children' left her when ready to leave school. She had placed herself in the path of the very thing she feared most...abandonment. An abandonment that recurred every year as every 'A' level class completed its last term and made ready for University.

Emily decided to start her teaching of Anselm with English ...grammar, reading and writing. He was rapidly filling out his vocabulary through his conversations with Peter and Martha and the hours he spent in front of the TV.

Anselm seemed to have an inherent understanding of the structure of language. His mind resembled a database with the linkages and relationships between words already embedded. Now he needed to populate that database with words that described the world and which others would recognize

He had learnt words for everyday things during the few weeks he lived with the shepherd. At least he had learnt the words for the few things the shepherd possessed. Peter and Martha's everyday things outnumbered those of the shepherd many times. Anselm wondered how people could understand each other when they had such different collections of words.

He learnt quickly ; this was not a two-year-old mind. It was the mind of a questioning teenager, a mind trying rapidly to catch up with his body age. Some adjectives he grasped without problem. The colours of the rainbow and hot, cold, fast, slow, light, dark were familiars. He could relate them to what he had seen and experienced on the heath. But the nouns that inhabited Peter and Martha's household seemed so many. 'No wonder they keep the book they call a 'dictionary' he thought.

He had more difficulty with what Emily described as 'possessive pronouns'; his, hers, theirs. She tried to explain the concept by example 'his shoes, his hands' and in terms of a special relationship between the person and the object. The notion of ownership was foreign to Anselm and whilst he seemed to grasp that there was a special relationship between 'he', Anselm, and a certain pair of hands, he was unable at first to extend that relationship to what Emily called 'his shoes'.

Emily went on to explain the rules that connected the different types of words into sentences. Again, Anselm was quick to learn. It was like turning on a faculty that he already had rather than learning from new.

His first homework was to report back to Emily what he had learnt in the previous session with he:.

“All things have a name ... a noun word.”

“All good nouns deserve a verb ... if they are going to make a sentence,” pronounced Anselm. “There should be no lazy nouns.They should all have a doing word attached to them.”

“Most nouns have a belonging word attached to them ... except some that belong to no-one ... like the Sun, stars and the Moon. When there is no belonging word then we have to have ‘the’ or ’a’ instead.”

“Pronouns like ‘he’, ‘she’, ‘it’ and ‘them’ are really special nouns saved for animals and people. ‘It’ is a pronoun too but you can use ‘it’ when you can't remember the noun.”

“Adjectives help us to tell similar nouns apart from each other. We could have had completely different noun words for green apples and red apples ... like greeples and redles ... but then it wouldn’t be clear from the words that we are really talking about the same kind of thing ...just different colours. I think adjectives are mostly about our senses ... sight, taste, smell, sound ... rough, smooth. Nouns on the other hand are about the object out there not about our sense of it ... I think”.

Anselm seemed less sure on the last point.

“Some verbs can only have a pronoun in front. Like ‘he thinks’ or ‘she runs’; but apples don’t think.”

“Sentences ending in a question mark usually need someone to say another sentence which doesn’t end in a question mark.

“If you use a lot of adjectives...you eventually get close to a noun. Like ‘green, hard, shiny, round, edible and tasty, altogether is very like ‘apple ‘.”

And his final learning point.....

“There don’t seem to be any ‘my’ things in this house.”

Emily noticed that Anselm's vocabulary or use of language showed some interesting gaps .He rapidly learnt verbs such as walk ,lift, run....things he could do himself, by himself. But verbs such as play, smile, ask...things one did with other people ...were more difficult for him. At first ,he would rarely start a sentence with ‘I’ as if his sense of self was too weak to support a verb.

The alphabet was learnt in ten minutes.“Why twenty six letters,” he asked. “Why not ten or fifty?”

“Well that’s just how language grew from the moment when people first began to talk to each other. You could say that ten might be too few to make all the different words we need, or want, to describe the world and to talk to each other. Maybe fifty would be just too many for people to learn."

"It might have been a very different world if we had a hundred letters in our alphabet. Probably there would have been far more things and colours and doings if we had so many letters we could mix together, don't you think?" Anselm asked.

"I'm not sure the world and its variety is driven by the content and structure of our language, Anselm.....but it's an interesting thought."

"Well if we only had two or three letters then we would have very few different things we could name.......or do...wouldn't we? I suppose then that life would be pretty boring; people wouldn't have much to say to each other... books would be very short and all much the same Learning about the world would be a very short process. That's really what I mean."

"I guess there's some truth in that. The French have only twenty-five letters in their alphabet...they don't have a 'k'; the Chinese have a very different structure to their written language with thousands of symbols...Arabic is different again. So other languages differ from English a lot but people in different countries generally learn the same things about how the world works.....well, more or less."

Emily realised she was on unsafe ground here.

"That must make things very difficult. How are the French, the English, Arabs and Chinese going to understand each other...or even understand the world in the same way?" asked Anselm.

"Good question. There have been a few problems on that front. We'll talk about that, perhaps, when we study geography, history and comparative religion," Emily replied, ducking the issue for another day.

***

"We have some friends coming to dinner tonight Anselm. They are looking forward to meeting you," said Peter.

"What are friends?" asked Anselm. Peter hesitated.

"They are people one likes a lot....people you are happy to be with....you like to talk to....people you are comfortable with..."

He caught himself not wanting to go too far with the description. Did John and Suzanne qualify? They had known the couple for maybe ten years now. John was a senior tutor in the Mathematics department. At times rather too cerebral even for Peters taste. The two men would occasionally play chess together, the nearest they came to any real meeting of minds. When the game was finished, John invariably having won, they would pass comment on the generally disappointing quality of that year's student intake and the inadequate pay of academics; then one of them would make his excuse to leave. The truth was it was Martha and Suzanne who had the real affinity for each other. The two husbands just made up the numbers and never felt at ease .

Peter tried to blot out the voice in his head " so who are your friends then? Who are you *comfortable* spending time with?" It was a critical voice, reproachful, pointing at his weakness.

"So, are you and Martha friends too ?" Anselm continued.

"Yes, I hope so."

"And you are my friends, aren't you?"

"Absolutely", said Peter, a young part of him was reassured just as much as Anselm by this confirmation.

***

Anselm was playing with his glass of diet coke; sucking the liquid up to near the top of the straw then letting it fall again. Even gravity seemed more entertaining than the dinner guests. The adults spent half their time talking about things he didn't really understand and the other half filling their mouths with food and drink as if to fill the silence.

"This year's intake seem a pretty dull bunch; even worse than last years", said John.

Peter wondered how much worse things could get since John had said the same thing every October for at least ten years running.

“Academic standards keep falling; whatever the government statistics say; the GCSE and A level exams are getting easier; that’s the only way to explain rising results and falling intellects. I’m having to go back over the fundamentals of calculus with this year’s freshers....it’ll be basic algebra next...”

Peter had drifted off; not for the first time.

....when education targets become a political football and we have one administrator for every teacher we’re in deep trouble, don’t you think Peter?”

Peter was well off his moorings by now, drifting on a sea of indifference some miles from the shoreline that was John's indignation with the education system.

A few moments passed. John saw the vacant look on Peter’s face.

Martha kicked Peter’s ankles beneath the table ,trying to jolt an answer out of her husband without announcing to John that his audience had left.

“What? What....yes, I’m sure...” Peter stuttered trying to rewind the tape in his head.

“Well I think it’s probably time for us to go; must be Anselm's bed-time soon I guess”. Suzanne jumped in to try to avoid a terminal level of embarrassment.

Martha shot a withering look at Peter.

Anselm held the coca-cola around half way up the straw, breath bated. There was something going on here but he wasn’t quite sure what. He didn’t think this was what the word ‘comfortable’ was supposed to mean. After all Martha and Peter had said they hoped he , Anselm, would be ‘comfortable’ when he first arrived.

“Very nice to meet you Anselm,” said Suzanne.

The women exchanged the usual promises : “We must do it again soon,” as jackets were retrieved and the two guests seen to the door. Peter fell over himself trying to redress his absence over dinner, effusive in his invitations to “come round again soon”, but conscious how false it sounded.

As the door shut, Martha looked at him and his eyes fell to the floor.

“Come ‘round again, indeed. There’s only one person who needs to come round, that’s you. You were unconscious throughout the meal. What is it with you? Where do you go? We don’t have people round much these days...couldn’t you make an effort ? A dinner for three with Banquo's ghost sat at the table is not my idea of fun... Well?”

"I'm sorry", said Peter, " but..."

" But what?"

"Well he's so boring; he sends me to sleep."

"It takes two to make a conversation."

"Exactly." replied Peter.

"Well you're not exactly the life and soul of the party yourself are you?"

"Thanks."

Martha looked at him again, head bowed like a naughty child. For a fleeting moment she felt a prick of compassion...or guilt. But anger put out the light.

"I'm going to bed."

Anselm heard the exchange from the dining room in between the rasping sounds of a straw sucking up the last drops of coca-cola. Peter seemed to have plenty to say to him when they were talking. Maybe sitting down isn't good for his brain. Anyway , these friends didn't seem likely to be visiting again in a hurry.

***

Weeks passed and Anselm's command of language grew exponentially. He began to speak and form arguments like a clever teenager. Emily decided to turn to the sciences.

Newton's mild concussion under the apple tree came as no great surprise to Anselm as he had observed things falling. The trees in the garden were shedding their leaves and he'd seen Martha drop a plate in the kitchen. Emily explained that these were due to gravity, an unseen force that attracted objects to each other.

The usual questioning then started."So, if gravity is an unseen force, how do we know it's really there?"

"Well, because we see things falling", said Emily.

"So ,when things aren't falling then there's no gravity?" asked Anselm. Emily thought there was some mischief in the question.

"No; gravity is there all the time and all around us", she explained.

"Ok, so gravity is there all the time and sometimes things fall but most of the time they don't. How does that work? Seems like this gravity stuff is a bit hit and miss."

Emily moved on to explain action and reaction, Newton's second law of thermodynamics and the resistance of solid things.

.

Anselm summarized again. "Ok, so things fall under gravity except when they are being held up by other things".

"Yes, that's the idea," said Emily pleased with this breakthrough.

"Then what's holding that thing up?" asked Anselm pointing up to the sun.
Emily could see she was not going to be able to compartmentalise her lessons with Anselm. They would have to go wherever his questions took them.

After half an hour on the structure of the solar system and planetary orbits illustrated by a piece of string with a cup tied to the end whirling above Emily's head, Anselm seemed satisfied that gravity had a role to play in the universe. It seemed at least a convenient label to use when certain things happened. But if you accepted that there was such a thing then it seemed to make a number of other situations more difficult to understand. For example, birds needed yet more explanation if one were to keep the idea of gravity intact whilst still allowing them to fly – as they obviously did.

It seemed strange to Anselm that an idea that was thought of to explain things like falling just made other things even more mysterious requiring a whole raft of other explanations. Emily admitted this was somewhat in the nature of what was called 'science'.

***

Anselm was getting used to the persistence of things. His bedroom, his bed, cupboard, all re-appeared consistently when he went back to his room. The dream- box was always there in the corner whenever he looked. He had tried averting his eyes and looking out the corner of them and turning around quickly. It was always there. Martha had shown him how to use the remote control. He concluded that this too must work by gravity, as its force was unseen.

The notion of keeping his room tidy was as alien to Anselm as to any teenager. Clothes would be left on the floor wherever they fell. Anselm tried using the new universal law of gravity as his excuse but it seemed not to cut much ice with Martha.

The universe was taking shape. Patterns of cause and effect and the permanence of objects were being installed in the teenager's perceptions of how the world worked. He felt he was learning things that others around him assumed as unquestionable. Or at least he did until one day he found out that other people were less sure of these 'facts'than they made out.

His science lessons progressed to Biology and the workings of the human eye along with Physics and the behaviour of light. What Emily had to say on these subjects was bewildering.

The table on which he rested his breakfast plate and through which he could not see the floor became a collection of tiny particles called 'atoms' separated by much larger spaces and held together by yet more unseen forces. Whilst he was told he couldn't see the atoms (they were "too small"), he could see the table; or so he thought with greater confidence than he had on most subjects. It seemed odd that he couldn't see one atom but he could see a collection of them plus even more empty space.

Martha explained that light reflected off the table, went through his eye, turned upside down, became 'electrical ' impulses and entered his brain at which point he 'saw' the table. Martha had given him a similar explanation of the dream box only the other way around.

Anselm was growing a little impatient with this stuff. Why was it necessary to invent such a complicated path of events to 'explain' something he had been perfectly comfortable with? The table was there. He saw it, yes, with his eyes, but that was plenty. There seemed to him to be other things more in need of explanation than this. In any case what kind of explanation was it that made something even more mysterious? When he asked where in his body the picture of the table ended up and what internal eye was used to look at this secondary image, the answers were deperately inadequate. After all these steps in seeing something, one final step seemed to be missing – that of 'seeing.'

Then Peter came along to cast even greater doubt on the simple matter of 'seeing' and even to go so far as to put a question mark over reality itself. The professor saw in Anselm's state of innocence many of the paradoxes and questions, which had occupied philosophers from Parmenides through to David Hume, Bishop Berkeley and Descartes.

They were sat together on the garden bench under the willow tree one dappled afternoon. The brook that meandered through the garden chattered over stones reminding Anselm of the streams that ran off the heath where once he was found. Anselm told Peter about his science lessons and said that the more facts he had the further from the truth he felt.

Peter asked Anselm to close his eyes. “Where is the garden?” asked Peter

“It’s here, all around us, “ said Anselm, firmly.

“How do you know that?” continued Peter.

“Because I just saw it with my eyes and I still hear the brook and the whisper of the willow tree.”

“Now open your eyes again,” said Peter.

“What is different from when you had your eyes closed?”

“I can see, of course!” replied Anselm with some impatience. “And what do you see?” asked Peter.

“I see the colours of the willow, the wood of this bench the blueness of the sky. I see your face.”

“David Hume would have replied that your eyes were receiving ‘sense-data’. Today we would say that what you were experiencing or ‘seeing’ was a result of electronic signals in your brain. Emily, your teacher, gave the correct scientific explanation.

“But there remains a problem,” Peter continued “Emily’s explanation of what a kitchen table is nothing like the thing you see. How can a collection of tiny particles too small to see with enormous spaces between them amount to the table at which you and I had breakfast this morning. But, worse than that, Hume would say that the table and this bench only exist by virtue of you seeing them. The things you ‘see’ depend for their existence on the very process of you seeing them since they are no more than the sum total of the images in your mind created by your senses. What is out there, if anything, is far removed from the seeing and hearing that you do. Indeed, when you closed your eyes didn’t the bench, the willow tree and I disappear? The thing you refer to as a bench, the clear image in your mind, ceased to exist didn’t it?”

“Well, if you were right,” retorted Anselm, “a blind man would inhabit an empty world. But blind men bump into things and hear things don’t they?” Anselm’s statement weakened into a question as he felt the rocks of reality give way slightly under his feet.

“No. Berkeley would say that the blind man has feeling and hearing sensations but this does not guarantee the existence of something outside him which provokes those iages .It could just as well be that those perceptions were due to someone playing aa virtual reality programme. The blind man assumes a table because of the sensation of hardness. Imagine then a man paralysed, without feeling and deaf and blind. What idea would he have of a table or a chattering brook?”

"Well, I can see such a man might have a problem experiencing the world. But you and I are not so badly off" said Anselm. "We have a pretty good idea what a table is because we have seen and felt one."

"What is it like when you dream, Anselm? Do you see, touch and hear things then? And do they exist in reality? You told me yesterday you dreamt of a Unicorn after the story Martha had read to you. But there are no Unicorns in the world. Did the Unicorn exist? I think not. And yet I don't doubt it was real enough for you in your dream."

Anselm went quiet. He looked intently at Peter, fully expecting him to turn into a Unicorn at any moment. The rocks beneath his feet now seemed to be in a landslide.

Peter saw the disconcerted look on the boy's face and the academic in him softened to fatherhood. "Let's turn the argument on its head. When we say there is a table, what we mean is we are having the sensations, which we refer to as a table. You have no doubt your sensations exist and so the table, which is synonymous with those sensations must exist. There you are, reality is re-instated.

"And as for dreams, well they are close to the real thing when you are in them but when you wake you can check with others whether the contents of your dream really happened.

"Other people can generally give you a reality check – so long as you believe those other people exist! So, let's give reality the benefit of the doubt. At least then we can avoid getting a lot of pain sense data from bumping into tables and life is bearable."

Anselm seemed relieved at the pragmatism of this new position on the subject of reality but did think that, for a serious man , Peter had a rather 'take it or leave it' attitude to reality.

He was interested to know more of Mr Hume and what Peter referred to as the school of British Empiricists. Peter told him of Bishop Berkeley's doubts about the existence of the tree in the quad at Cambridge and of Rene Descartes' attempted deduction of his own existence through the rather circular argument summed up as 'Cogito ergo sum'.

At the end of this brief tour of the philosophy of perception Anselm was puzzled as to how these highly intelligent gentlemen managed to live. He wondered why they even bothered to get up each morning and re-enter a reality so surrounded by a sea of doubt.

However, he did see some advantages in the denial of the existence of things in the outside world. Unfortunately, when later he tried his luck denying the existence of his clothes scattered on the bedroom floor, Martha insisted that he make a willing suspension of disbelief and put them away in the cupboard. Some sense data could be very persistent indeed. Martha insisted also on the objective existence of the shower and bar of soap and strongly suggested that Anselm should become acquainted with the related touch sensations.

***

That night Anselm dreamt that he observed a dialogue between the Bishop Berkeley and Descartes.

Berkeley: "Sir, though you are likely just a spectre, I nevertheless have a truth to convey to you. That truth is that there can be no proof of the existence of things outside of us. Our only experiences are based on sense – data which I maintain are as 'real' in hallucination or in dream as they are in what men refer to as true reality.

I conclude therefore that the occurrence of such sense data is no proof in itself of the existence of things and without proof we as philosophers must suspend belief. There is, for example, no proof sir that you exist and so we must assume you do not."

Descartes: "Your argument is repugnant to me, sir, and I think it is most readily shown to be false. My counter - argument is simply this: ' I think therefore I am.' It is beyond doubt that I am thinking and that very act of thinking is proof itself of my existence. For, how could I be conscious of these thoughts if I were not in fact to exist. Monsieur Berkeley you may have grave doubts about the world and I will concede that your own existence cannot be guaranteed, but I am assured of mine!"

At this point Berkeley was rather irritated by the superior air of the Frenchman.

Berkeley: "Sir, I extend to you no greater certainty of existence than all other things corporeal . You to to me are merely a collection of sense data. The act of your thinking is not visible to me sir nor do I deduce from your argument that any degree of rational thought is occurring on your part."

Descartes: "Well sir! Let me say that were you simply sense data evoked by my own mind, whether in hallucination or dream, I believe I would have conjured up an altogether more agreeable image and a dialogue which would have paid more respect to the undoubted merits of my position. And so sir, regrettably, I have to conclude that you must exist independently of my perception as my most perverse imaginations would not have created one such as you."

Berkeley: "Well thank you sir. I am heartily pleased that you grant me my existence but must report that I am not in a position to reciprocate. For as for your statement 'I think therefore I am', the premise of your statement is assumed in the very first word. By using the word 'I' you have already ,invalidly, assumed your conclusion.

And so sir, I, to whose existence you so conclusively have testified, take my leave of you who remain, as I always knew, a figment of my imagination.

In the blink of an eye Descartes disappeared and Anselm awoke from his fitful sleep.

***

II -PICTURES CAUGHT IN TIME

It was Tuesday morning. Martha had already left for work. Peter lingered with Anselm over the remains of breakfast.

"Where did you come from?" asked Anselm.

Peter wondered if this was some sort of existential test but decided on giving a more commonplace answer.

"I was brought up in Birmingham a city about a hundred miles from here"

"No, I mean ...how did you come into this world? Where were you found?

"I wasn't found Anselm. I was born. My mother gave birth to me....in Birmingham."

Peter hadn't quite prepared himself for a 'birds and bees' talk. Perhaps he had been hoping Emily would cover this in Biology. There couldn't be many fifteen-year olds to whom this was a mystery...but it was to Anselm.

"Born?"

"Well, the way people come into the world normally...er, usually, is as a result of their mothers and fathers coming together...er..." Peter could feel the skin on his face prickle, " the mother provides the egg and the father the sperm and when the two combine they create an embryo..."

Peter had no idea what level of knowledge to assume on Anselm's part; whether any of this would make any sense to the boy. He had found it implausible enough himself as an adolescent...and pretty much ever since. Not having been through the full process it still seemed somewhat theoretical to him.

"And the embryo...er...the baby grows inside the mother's womb until, after about nine months, it's ready to come out...to be born. At that stage the baby needs a lot of looking after, unable to walk or talk or to feed itself. So, the parents do the looking after until the baby grows, learns how the world works and learns how to look after itself..."

Peter tailed off as he noticed a wide-eyed look of astonishment on Anselm's face. For a moment he felt a lightning bolt of panic as he imagined the raft of supplementary questions he might face on this topic.

Anselm was quiet for a few moments.

“I don’t understand everything you said but it seems like you got here, other people got here, in a very different way to me...unless my mother grew me then left me on the heath. But if she did, how come I don’t remember her? How come I got so big without the beginning bit...the baby bit you described?”

“We don’t know the answer to that Anselm.”

“ These people who made you....your mother and father, where did they come from?

“They had mothers and fathers too...same process. They were what we call ‘grandparents’.”

“So, everybody arrives that way. Except me.?”

“Yes, Anselm.”

Anselm didn’t know what to make of this; but his body didn’t seem to like the news; he felt a weight inside his chest as if some great stone had lodged there. “Tell me about them....your mother and father...what were they like?

Peter stopped for a moment as an image of his father came to mind. “Well, Dad was a builder...someone who built houses for people. He had his own business, just him and two other guys...

Peter remembered the roughness of his father's hands and the wrestling matches he and his brother would have on the lounge floor with 'Dad' when he came home.

"It seemed to me he'd built half the houses in West Birmingham," Peter smiled.

"Was he a philosopher too?"

"Of sorts . Yes, you could say that. He didn't study; left school at fourteen to become a bricklayer's apprentice. Didn't have much choice in those days; the family didn't have much money...needed my Dad to go out to work and bring in a wage. So, he didn't have much time for Hume and Descartes . Didn't like French people much anyway...though I am not sure he'd ever met one. But he was wise...he was a practical philosopher and he was always interested in the world, science in particular...liked to understand how things worked, but always kept a space in his heart for mystery."

"Did he teach you to build houses?"

"Goodness, no. Last thing in the world he wanted for me and my brother. He always drummed into us that we had to get an education. 'Soft hands like yours lad are no good for the trowel...be bleeding in no time.'

"He worked very hard; left the house long before we went to school; home for tea- time at six and then often in his work shed in the evening...used to let me go in there to watch him sometimes and to pass him his tools as he needed them..."

“Where was your Mum?

“Oh, Mum kept the house and she had a part-time job at the mill ...a place for making cloth. She ran the home on a tight schedule...liked to have everything in its place ,on-time, including me and my brother. She’d be glad to be rid of us in the evening...out in the work shed where we could ‘make as much mess as we liked.’

Peter also remembered the rows .His mother would start them; or so it seemed to him. Small things which seemed to explode. If his father was home late by half an hour... “your dinner’s spoilt; it’s in the oven”, or if he wore his boots into the house... “look at the mess you’re making”.

His father was the quiet type but on these occasions would snap back “shut up woman; I’ll do as I like. Who do you think pays the bills around here?”

Peter and his brother would try to stay out of the way until it blew over. That wasn’t easy in a ‘two-up two down’ terrace house with walls of cardboard.

“And your brother came from the same place as you?”

“Yes, he did Anselm. Five years after me.”

“That’s a long time.”

“Yes; but it meant I was the king of the castle and had the undivided attention of my parents...when they were there.”

"So, are you like your Mum and Dad?"

"I don't know really....Martha might be able to tell you that easier than I can...I guess I must be in some ways; we all are...chips of the old block; I must have pieces of them in me."

He remembered his mother combing his hair before school. "Why can't you get your tie straight?" She was a funny mix of tearfulness and scolding. Things needed to be just so or she would seem to lose her bearings. Most of all he remembered her nagging of his father 'when are you going to fix the kitchen door ? You spend all your time fixing other people's homes and can't be bothered to do the smallest job around here.'

As a young boy these outbursts just seemed disconnected storms which he and his brother had to weather, hands clapped to ears. Now, from a distance, he could see his mother's insecurity and the terrible irony of it all. The more his mother tried to get his father's attention, the more critical she became, the more he retreated. She needed him more than he could bear. Every half hour late for tea was an abandonment for a girl whose own father had left for war one day and never returned.

" I wonder who I am like", said Anselm.

***

Anselm did not use the words 'before' and 'after', 'yesterday', 'today', 'tomorrow' when he arrived in Martha and Peter's home. There had been no need to measure time until now. But his few weeks in that world had vested him with some memories.

He found he could direct his mind towards these memories. He had some influence over when they came and went which he did not seem to have when dreaming. He would remember the warmth of the shepherd's fire and the smell of the grass on the heath after rain, and smile. Anselm thought of the discussion between Berkeley and Descartes. He rather sided with Descartes as he, Anselm, had a growing sense of 'I-ness', an identity to whom others spoke, a 'me' who remembered and increasingly imagined things.

What was less clear to him was the difference between these experiences: remembering, seeing, dreaming, imagining. Each could absorb him and each could play tricks. Peter had shown him how a stick would bend in the water of the brook. When he first caught sight of himself in the mirror he thought it was a dream-box until he found he could control the reflection in a way he could not control the image on the TV. These' mirror' pictures seemed to be something else, not memories, dreams, or imaginings.

Gradually, he learnt the quality of memories and to distinguish them from 'seeing' something. He could bring up a memory in a similar way to making his hand move. He would turn his attention to an inner place and a weaker version of the picture on the dream-box would appear. The picture was stronger if he closed his eyes but still without the sharpness or depth of colour he saw on the dream-box.

He knew this picture was of something that happened to him. However,these memory images were unstable, easily breaking up or being replaced by others as if the things remembered had only a shadowy, weak existence.

One Saturday evening he asked Martha and Peter whether they could see such pictures.

“Memories” said Martha. “These are memories Anselm. They are in your mind and a kind of replay of things that happened ‘before’. Can you remember having dinner together yesterday evening?”

Anselm paused, closed his eyes and said, “I can see you and Peter at the dinner table and the white table cloth...”

“You are ‘remembering’,” said Peter “as I am too, now you have reminded me.”

He understood that these memories were feint copies of the ‘real’ dinner, the one he didn’t make- up, the one with an independent life of its’ own, which he couldn’t switch off. These feint copies they called ‘memories’ and the word ‘before’ seemed to describe the position of the real dinner to the memory dinner. He thought this word ‘before’ must mean something like ‘stronger’ or ‘clearer’, more ‘out there’

.

Martha got out from the bottom drawer of the bookcase a big book which, when opened, revealed lots of pictures carefully mounted in the yellow vellum pages.

"Anselm, these are family photographs of Peter and I when we were younger and of our parents, brothers and sisters."

Anselm was totally absorbed as Martha explained the relationships between the people in the 'photographs' and the 'where', 'when' and 'who' of each. As she spoke he began to see the photograph album as a kind of storybook and to understand these photos as pieces of memory, somewhere between his 'memories' and the pictures on the dream-box.

He began to understand the words 'before', 'now', 'after' and 'later' from the way Martha used them to position different photographs relative to each other.

Anselm noticed that in the earlier pages Peter had more hair and a thinner face than in the later pages and asked why this was.

"All those 'now's' in the photographs change us. We grow older Anselm and our bodies gradually wear out like old clothes."

The older photographs at the beginning of the book were of younger people, and yet were more faded. These sepia tints of Peter and Martha's grandparents seemed more like memories than the bright colours he saw later.

"And this is a photo of me at about the same age you are now," said Martha. "I was at high school; this is my brother beside me."

Martha at fifteen was long-legged with cascading auburn curls and emerald eyes which turned the head of many a teenage boy . Anselm looked at her now, so many pages turned and saw the auburn hair now flecked with grey and eyes, somehow more distant than the photo. Anselm felt himself exhale and something in his chest sank.

"I met Peter at University," she continued. "He was the best-looking bloke on campus. But he had his head in the clouds, you know, studying Philosophy. He never noticed me but that just made me more determined to catch him."

"I did notice you. How could I not? But I was irredeemably shy. You know that," blurted Peter.

"You lived, no *live*, in another world. One of paradoxes, logic and analysis. A world full of concepts with no space for the trivia of feelings." There was a sharpness in Martha's tone bordering on accusation. It was not the first time he had heard it. Yet she had pursued him and found a way to unlock his heart. Long enough at least for the wedding photographs to be taken.

Anselm studied the photograph of the couple with Peter looking into Martha's eyes as if the two of them were trapped by some invisible force. 'Gravity?' wondered Anselm. He saw that force between the two in other photographs as they leafed through the early pages of the book. Their faces were softer, then. But as the pages made their way towards the present there were fewer pictures of the two of them together. Other people entered the frame: friends, colleagues from work. Martha and

Peter's attention seemed go somewhere else, no longer on each other.

Anselm caught himself exhaling and felt that stone in his chest sink again.

Hours passed as the three of them worked through the album and Martha and Peter each took it in turn to tell Anselm about the people and places frozen in the amber of those pages. Sometimes, one of them seemed to fade and then to grow brighter again like flickering oil lamps. As one picked up the story the other would grow quiet. The eyes once locked together found it difficult now to look at each other's memories.

- ***

Early the next morning Anselm crept on tiptoes downstairs, opened the drawer in the bookcase and retrieved the 'memory book'. He flicked through the pages and felt a sense of relief that the pictures were still there, complete and looking just as they had the previous night. He wondered how he would capture his own memories. Would he have such a book and who else might be in it? Have things past gone forever or could he in some way go find them and make a record stronger than memories?

When Peter and Martha came down to breakfast, Anselm seemed very agitated. The book lay before him open at the last page.

"Where am I?" he asked . "Where am I?"

“You weren’t here when these photographs were taken, Anselm,” explained Peter. “But wait here until I fetch the camera.”

Martha knew Peter had missed the point of Anselm’s question. The question was a lament for what might have been . It was a grieving for a history that had not been written; for memories beyond reach and a life whose time had started late.

Peter clicked his old Instamatic and the image of a wistful Anselm took form and colour from the air. He tore off the picture and mounted it in the book. Anselm looked longingly at the picture and ran his fingers over it. He thought briefly of all those pages before ‘now’, exhaled and then announced: “Today my memories begin.”

Throughout the next few days Anselm would report to Peter, Martha or Emily things he had done just half an hour before. Each sentence would begin with “I remember.....” It was as if he was banking as many memories as possible as quickly as he could.

Then on Tuesday evening, out of the blue, he said to Peter “’Now’ isn’t a real place you know.”

“What do you mean, Anselm?” asked Peter.

“Well as soon as you took that picture of me in the ‘now’ ,it had already passed. As soon as I say here we are ‘now’ it’s no longer true. ‘Now’ becomes ‘then’ before you can even say the word. The moment before you say it ‘now’ is in the future. But as soon as you say it....or even think it ‘now’ is in the past. ‘Now’ doesn’t stick around even as long as it takes your camera to flash.”

Peter was amused . A ready-made fifteen-year old, found on a heath, with few memories with which to anchor the concept of time was now leap-frogging several hundred years of academic philosophical thought to pose a paradox which still divided philosophers in the twenty-first century.

“I remember the water boatman you showed me in the pond near the brook. It’s feet touching but not breaking the surface of the still water. You explained to me the ‘meniscus’, the boundary between the water and the air. Not something separate in itself, just the boundary between two other things. Well maybe ‘now’ is just like that meniscus, the boundary between past and future,” said the boy.

Anselm went on further, “But if there is really no such thing as now, then there is no past or future. You have explained them to me as a succession of ‘now's’. Seems to me the river called ‘time’ has just dried up!”

Peter knew these arguments well but was nevertheless amazed to hear them from the lips of this boy. “Anselm you are right. The idea of time carries its problems and apparent contradictions. You have put your finger on the paradoxes. Let me give you another to ponder. Imagine again a person born deaf, blind and so paralysed to have no sense of touch. They also have neither sense of smell or taste. What experience then would such a person have of the world? He would see, hear, feel, smell, taste, nothing from the beginning; no experience of the world we know. No images of, or interaction with, things. An event-less, empty, nothingness .What memories could such a person have? Surely none? For we know memories to be a recollection of some past experience. What of dreams or imagination? Well I cannot think that this person would have any of the building blocks from which dreams or visions are made – can you?"

Anselm shook his head, wondering what all this leading up to.

.

"So without memory or any sequence of experiences, how can we say this person is conscious .What thoughts could they possibly have and what idea could they have, therefore, of the passage of time. Surely such a person would exist in a timeless, nothingness with no content in their mind. So the concept of time depends on the human mind for its meaning. Without minds there is no time. There's no objective 'out there' passing of time like the river. Time is purely a thing of the human mind invented to give dimensions to our experiences. When the last person in the world dies, so does time."

At that moment it seemed to Anselm that the two of them had conclusively buried time or at least made its' existence totally dependent on the existence of a human observer. But he wasn't satisfied fully by Peter's argument, which left time with some sort of secondary existence. He couldn't fit this together with his own argument which collapsed time into one very, very .....very long, single moment. How to square this with changes in the world, the existence of the photographs in the memory book, the sequence of day and night.

He did see some practical sense in the argument Peter had put. After all, if there were absolutely nobody around what would be the use of time droning on? And he had noticed in everyday life that when time was watched, for example when he was waiting for Peter or Martha to come home or longing for his boring French lessons to finish, then it ran much, much more slowly.

Peter had originally explained ***time*** to him as something that went in a straight line, in one direction and at an even speed. But he, Anselm, thought that time often zigzagged, taking shorter or longer paths to the future depending on what he was doing. So yes, perhaps time is something that depends on people doing stuff.

He explained his thinking to Peter: " since people in the world do different things, they must have different times. Some sleep longer than others, some do Maths (he liked maths) while others are learning French. Some are waiting whilst others are busy and being waited for."

"Well ,there was a man called Einstein who proved just that. He used mathematics to show that time depends on the position of the observer and the relative speed at which the observer is moving. For example, a man travels in a spaceship at near the speed of light and travels for what, for him, is just a few days. If he then return to his starting point, the family he left behind would be many years older. Time would have run at different speeds for him and for his family.

Anselm liked this idea, though he wondered what Einstein's mathematics would have said about his interminable French lessons. Perhaps the fact that they went so slow was the reason Emily looked so old. What would happen to him then if he had too many French lessons?

"So, let me summarize," said Anselm, mimicking the professorial air that Peter adopted in their discussions. "Time depends on people, not vice-versa. Without us time would come to a full stop. With us it doesn't always go in a straight line; the direction and speed at which it moves depends on what you're doing and the faster I go the slower time goes. And since people do different things at different speeds we are all in different times.

"Emily told me in Geography that there are such things as time zones and that Americans are in the past whilst the people in China are in the future relative to us here in England. But you and I are also in different times since we live life at different speeds. I don't know whether you are in my future right now or in my past. Although you appear 'here' you almost certainly are not 'now'. In which case you are either a memory or a vision of the future and it will be a pure coincidence of speed if we two ever meet up for real."

"Well done Anselm. It's difficult to argue with your conclusions. Anyway, you would probably pay little attention to someone so obviously lacking in substance as I" Peter smiled and his face softened to a younger time. Anselm caught a look in Peter's eyes like the one he had shared with Martha in those early pages of the memory book.

***

It was later that evening, whilst waiting for Martha to come home, that Peter introduced Anselm to the ***measurement*** of time. This was the day that Martha was due to finalise the rights issue pricing with the company's bankers. She had said she would be late and that he and Anselm should eat the pizzas stored in the freezer . "I should be home by nine if things go according to plan," she had forecast.

After the pizzas Peter drew Anselm's attention to the calendar on the wall. He started with today's date, the 26th of September 2020 explaining first that a day was the time between two sunrises and that there were generally 30 days in what was called a month – except when there were 31 or 28 or periodically 29. Already Anselm was wondering who had invented this system and was this just another example of the elasticity of time?

Twelve months made a year and he, Peter, had lived for fifty-one years. Anselm tried to figure out how many days that was but his mental arithmetic wasn't up to it – yet. Almost as an aside, Peter said that a year was the time it took the earth to rotate around the sun. He saw immediately the look on Anselm's face which was about to trigger them headlong into a Copernican/Galilean debate and he quickly jumped in with "Trust me!"

Then turning to the clock Peter explained that a day was made up of 24 hours and broke down further into minutes and seconds. As he spoke Anselm felt his chest tighten as if he were in a cage whose bars were getting closer and closer together. “So, what are seconds made up of,” the boy asked.

”Nothing.....well.... er.... I mean, that’s it; we don’t measure time in any smaller amounts....not in everyday life anyway.”

Anselm looked at the second hand on the clock. It seemed to move so fast past each second that there was hardly time to catch one’s breath. He couldn’t see how anyone could do anything worthwhile in one second and frankly minutes might have been a more sensible place to stop breaking time into bits.

Maybe one second was like a ‘now’. Maybe now came in small packets like this and this is how time made progress.

“So that’s the way time is measured then,” said he. “If I want to measure how many seconds (or now's) you have lived I just have to multiply 60 times 60 times 24 times 30(or maybe 31, 28 or 29) times 12 times 51. Could have been a bit more convenient, couldn’t it?” Anselm teased. “I guess if there had been twice as many hours in the day then you would only have been around 25 years old now. Would you have had more hair left in that case?”

Peter was never sure where the boundary line was between naivety and sarcasm with Anselm. The boy certainly had a sense of humour and somewhere he had learnt to dress it up in mock seriousness.

Anselm resolved to check the length of his Maths and French lessons by reference to the clock. When he did so, the clock said one hour in both cases. He could only conclude that the world to which the clock was attached had been spinning at a very fast speed during the French lesson – like the spaceship – whilst he and Emily had been left on a French shore getting old and bored.

"And one day time runs out for each of us," said Peter. "Whether we live sixty, seventy years or more .Eventually we die. Our bodies, and for some of us, our minds wear out."

"What do you mean?" asked Anselm.

"We all have difficulty in imagining how it would be to *not* be; to no longer exist. But that's what dying is; rather we stop existing in the way we do now; our bodies are laid to rest and decay. Martha believes that something else called our spirit or soul continues . Christians believe that it is the soul which is the essence of who we are. It continues in an afterlife in a different place that Christians refer to as heaven.

"It doesn't seem so strange to me," said Anselm. "I popped out of nowhere so I can easily believe I might pop back there one day."

"The idea of us exiting without our bodies throws up all sorts of philosophical conundrums," said Peter. "People tend to think of themselves as indestructible and continuing after death, as still being able to see events, to communicate with others, to touch and to feel, all of which in this life are reliant on our physical senses. But these senses surely don't work in a 'disembodied' existence. How would we know where 'we' were; how could we get our bearings; how would others encounter us?"

"I can see your problem," said Anselm, as if the dilemma were peculiar to Peter. "We couldn't appear in any more photographs , either," he continued. "The book would run out....like the photographs of your's and Martha's parents. The photographs of you and Martha would run out too, wouldn't they? How long do you think it will be before that happens Peter?"

"Quite some time yet, I hope; though none of us know excactly how long."

"You mean it can happen any time, this dying thing?"

"Yes. Some people die from accidents, some from illness, some from old age. Living is a dangerous pursuit."

"But that means some people get to stick around longer than others ;it means some get to do and see less. Doesn't seem very fair."

Anselm went silent for a few moments.

"It means, for example, that you and Martha might die at different times ; one leaving the other behind. So, when you said ‘Marriage’ was a promise to stay together it depends on death.”

“Yes, some wedding ceremonies even talk of ‘till death us do part.’”

“How would that be, Peter, if Martha died and left you behind. Who would make the roast potatoes? Wouldn’t you want to follow her? Wouldn’t you give up your body to go to the same place as Martha?” There was an urgency in Anselm's voice.

“I don’t know what I would do; we are all tied very strongly to our earthly selves. But lovers sometimes feel so strongly connected that they end their lives at the same time in an attempt to be sure of spending eternity together.”

“And do you and Martha feel that way?”

“As one gets older that romantic idea weakens. It tends to be at the beginning of a relationship you feel the most connected; or maybe not so much connected as confused ; yes, confusing yourself with being part of a couple. No, even that’s not right. It varies between couples, I think. Young lovers are so identified with their romantic love that they find it almost unbearable to be separated from each other. And yet, I’m not sure they are truly connected in the way that more mature couples might be, couples who have experienced the ups and downs of life, together. When you have appeared in many photos together in many different times and places it can form a bond that is very strong."

"And how is it with you and Martha?" Anselm persisted.

Peter went quiet. He didn't know where to start in answering Anselm's question. It had been too long since he'd asked himself the same. He imagined two people connected in very different ways in the beginning and later years . He and Martha seemed to be lost somewhere in the middle. The separation after the romantic phase had happened but they had not found each other again in their mid-life.

Suddenly, a pit of loneliness yawned in front of him and a moment of panic snatched his breath. It was that loneliness we all try to pack away underneath busy lives; not the loneliness of boredom but the loneliness which wakes at three a.m. when the world is totally empty; when we know that nothing , least of all us, lasts forever and we imagine other people going about their business-without us .Then we realise that another person ,however loved , can never truly fill that void.

"Peter? Are you still here?" asked Anselm.

"Yes ...sorry; I was thinking about your question and realising that I don't know the answer."

The clock chimed ten.

"Wow, it's your bed time young man. Time flies when you are measuring it," said Peter.

“Not in my experience” rebutted Anselm. He had been hoping to see Martha. Dissecting time had made the waiting seem longer. She had said nine. He wondered if she was on a different time zone Reluctantly he went off to his room, hoping to dream.

***

Martha finally opened the bedroom door at just before midnight. She’d checked first on Anselm who seemed dead to the world. She was surprised to find Peter still awake reading by the bedside light.

“Hi, I’m sorry I’m so late. Those bankers and lawyers can argue about the number of angels you can fit on a pin-head.”

Martha recognised Peter’s silence as reproach. He never spoke it. That was part of the distance between them.

“What did you two do tonight?”

“We talked,” he said, economically.

“About what?” she pressed.

“About time.”

“About time what?”

"What?"

"It's about time what?" she said defensively. She imagined he was working up to a criticism of her lateness.

"No, we talked about time, you know, past, present, future, calendars, clocks," he explained.

"Oh. Was he interested in that?"

"More than that .The boy's a revelation. He's fifteen going on seventy-five. He's several leagues ahead of many of my students."

Martha felt left out though she knew it had been her choice of priorities to deal with the bankers. Still ,she felt a bud of resentment . Peter was spending a lot of time with their son. Surely that was good...particularly over the last week when things had been crazy for her at work.

"I wonder if the cerebral world of philosophy is really where Anselm should be spending his time when there is so much else he needs to learn about the world." She wanted to swallow the words again the moment they had left her lips, but too late.

"Other things to learn like how to play the stock market, I guess" retorted Peter..

For years now there had been a sheet of glass between the two of them. One that got thicker and more opaque, as the years went by. They could see each other but not touch.

Another millimetre's thickness of glass was added that night. She undressed in the bathroom. Peter switched off his bedside light and turned to face the window. He thought of Anselm's theory that everyone lived in a different time. That was surely true of he and Martha. Their careers had conspired to run to different clocks. A second's distance grew to hours then to days imperceptibly. Neither of them conscious of the gap growing between them until it reached the point where it seemed unbridgeable, too high an emotional risk to make the leap back to find each other.

Ten minutes later Martha slid between the sheets knowing him still to be awake, but behaving as if not to disturb him. They often collaborated in this ritual .

***

Anselm woke with a start. The bedclothes were on the floor. He lay there in the striped pyjamas Martha had bought him, covered in sweat. He had dreamt, but he didn't like this dream. Usually he could remember his dreams for a while quite vividly but of this one he could only bring back fragments and a feeling he couldn't name. The feeling was like the stone sinking in his chest but there was something else there too.

He could recall a wide, dark river running fast. On each bank of the river was a person. They had no faces. They seemed to want to cross the river but were afraid of the torrent. They stood there full of wanting; unable to move. And then their faces became his face, each in turn and he knew their wanting and he knew their fear of the river. And each time as he looked across the angry flow he saw the other figure, faceless and felt the stone drag him down into the muddy bank to his ankles, then his knees and fear became panic.

It was then he woke. He lay there for a while trying to recover other fragments of the dream but they seemed to have been carried away by the river.

Anselm went downstairs for a glass of water to quench his thirst. He saw light leaking beneath the closed door to the kitchen. Fingers hesitant around the doorknob he turned it, afraid to break the silence .He pushed it slowly ajar, screwing up his eyes to shield against the light. Sat at the kitchen table was a hunched figure, back to the door, motionless. He recognised the dressing gown as Martha's.

He made to make a sound but all that came out was a long "Mmmm..." Whether it was the dryness of his throat or his falling between 'Martha' and 'Mother' he wasn't sure, but it was enough to turn her around. As she turned she closed a large book lying in front of her.

"Hello darling. What's wrong , can't sleep?" she asked with a tenderness that surprised her.

"I had a dream which I didn't like," said Anselm.

"A nightmare , son. It's called a nightmare."

Anselm shrugged his shoulders. Giving it a name didn't make it any more friendly . "Do you want to tell me about it?"

He took a glass of water, and sat down beside her seeing the book was the 'memory book'. He opened his mouth to say something about the dream.....but what? Those fragments that had stuck around just after he woke had also disappeared now. He knew he had been afraid but it was the kind of memory that lived in his head, like the debates with Peter. The stone in his chest had gone.

Instead he asked Martha what she had been looking at in the book. She opened the page to one with photographs of a young couple, the man's arms around the woman; she dressed in long white and he in a dark blue suit, both smiling wide, both in the same moment in time. He recognised the woman's emerald eyes and the philosopher's beard.

***

The sun had made long, morning shadows from the trees when, finally, Martha closed the book. Anselm had wanted to start at the beginning and wouldn't let her close until they had reached the very last page. Not that she was in a hurry. Sometimes life seems episodic without a thread to connect the different people we are each passing year. Martha felt at one and the same time both removed from, but familiar with, that twenty-two year old in the wedding dress .It was as if she were looking now at some younger sister emigrated to Australia years ago.

The twenty-two- year old was an open-faced girl ,recently graduated in English literature at Cambridge. Anselm looked at her now. Her hair was shorter and her emeralds had lost some of their sparkle but he knew this was the same person. Martha was less sure. Anselm said she looked now like her mother.

"Peter told me about getting born, about having real parents. His Dad was a builder. What about your Mum and Dad?" asked Anselm.

Martha was taken by surprise .She thought about her parents still, but without siblings or children of her own there had been no one around to remind her. No one to say 'remember when'. So they had become private shadows of a past that seemed less and less real as the years passed. Like the imaginary friends she had as a girl. No one else could testify to their being ...except Peter; but Peter testified to little.

My father was in the Army...a soldier .I remember he was away from home a lot, travelling. Sometimes we went with him .We lived in Singapore then in Cyprus for a few years. We got used to moving ...but then came back to live in England when I was ten...so I could go to school here.

Again, she was surprised, at where she had started her description. "What was he like?" asked Anselm.

"He was tall; a big man with a big voice. He used to play with me when I was young...piggy backs or on his shoulders. I would feel on top of the world...he was very strong... When he laughed it seemed like the windows and cups would rattle; it was thunder."

" Did he laugh a lot?"

"Yes, at first when he came home. But he was very stern too. He expected me to come top of the class at school and if I didn't...well, the thunder would roll again but in a less pleasant way. "

"Were you afraid of him?"

"I suppose I was .Sometimes he seemed like a stranger; I didn't know what to expect, what mood he would be in. He was never horrible to me, just distant and hard; he never seemed satisfied. Always wanted me to do better at school...even when I did come top of the class. That seemed unfair to me...like I got criticised however well I did."

"What about your Mum?"

"Oh, she was very different. She would just tell me "just do your best darling, that's all any of us can do". She enjoyed people; very outgoing and sociable. She seemed to have lots of friends who would drop by the house and she liked to go to parties. It seemed like she had to drag my father along with her at times. Mum was so different to him. She was soft and warm and physically loving; she was always giving me hugs. The only time I touched my father was when he picked me up onto his shoulders."

Martha's voice was growing quieter, more distant.

“What did your Mum do?”

“She was at home until I was eleven and going to secondary school. Then she took a supply teaching job. She liked being with people.... young and old. Getting that job gave her a bit of independence, I think... she didn’t have to rely on Dad for money for example.”

“Was she like Emily?”

“ I don’t know. I think Emily’s a quieter type.”

Anselm had an image of two people looking at each other, one smiling, one serious.

Martha remembered the quiet, solemn dinner times. Her mother would serve the food....always more than enough, and try to make conversation. But her father’s answers seemed to become increasingly monosyllabic as she, Martha , got older. Occasionally, he would become animated about some subject of the day, usually politics or events in some far- off place which Martha had never heard of. On such subjects Martha's father always had a view firmly held, unassailable and presented as fact in a booming voice of authority. “Mark my words....”preceded every verdict on the rights and wrongs of any situation. Martha and her mother knew better than to argue.

“It does sound like your Mum and Dad were very different to each other”

“Yes. But that often happens with people who are attracted to each other. It’s a bit like the North and South pole of a magnet. I think my mother liked Dads strength; he always seemed in control of a situation; knew what to do; and Dad liked my Mums energy and warmth...she was a great talker and at ease meeting new people. Dad was shy ,and found it difficult to make conversation, to get to know people.

They seemed somehow to complement each other as Martha described the two of them. One brought what the other lacked or needed. Her mother was a bird flying, wheeling and diving in the breeze but needed her father as a home base, someone to ground her and keep her safely in touch with reality. She was daring in a different way to him, He, a man who was fearless in the face of physical danger but lost in a social gathering.

At least that’s how things seemed to have started out.

The very things that attracted them to the other eventually became the things that kept them apart. Martha's father became jealous and critical of her mother spending more and more time with her friends. He would retreat into sullen disapproval. The more he absented himself, the less his wife found safety with him; the more she closed off and so the less he got the intimacy he craved. The things they most needed from each other to feel complete became the very forces which pulled them apart.

Martha saw this only in hindsight. As a teenager she was aware of the growing distance between them but she didn’t know why; perhaps this was just what happened to all couples who had been together a long time she had thought. She never asked her mother how she felt about her father. All families have taboos and this was theirs. The biggest secrets are the ones every-one knows about but dare not name.

Anselm had noticed that half way through the book the images of Martha's Mum and Dad had stopped . "Where are they now?" he asked.

"They died, nearly ten years ago, son," replied Martha looking out the window as if something in their garden had caught her attention.
'Died'. This was the first time Anselm had heard the word. Martha explained as best she could. But after her explanation and a few moments of puzzled reflection, Anselm asked again. "But where are they now?"

Martha paused. She seemed to Anselm to be struggling to breathe; and then he saw a raindrop make its' way down her cheek, falling onto the vellum page.

"They've gone to a better place....I hope," she said finally. "Together?"

"Yes, that's what I believe," said Martha in a whisper. But she didn't know what the implication was of her words. Anselm wondered where this place could be which was better....but he was afraid to ask lest Martha could not breathe. What he understood from her explanation was that dying must be like the deaf, blind man without sensations which Peter had asked him to imagine. It seemed clear that she did not expect to see them again. For them time had reached its' full stop and it was left for Martha and others to keep time alive.

"They came to the end of their time," said Martha unsolicited. "Will you and Peter run out of time?" he asked.
"Yes." She was conscious of the clock on the wall.

"And me?"
"We all do, someday, Anselm."

"And then all that's left of me will be the memories in a book which might be left unseen in a bottom drawer?"

"And the memories in the hearts of those who love you , Anselm. We don't need photographs to remember."

He wasn't listening. He was thinking what a horrible tease this was. Something he had no need of and he thought Peter and he had argued out of existence now seemed to have the power to make people disappear, including him. Why would people keep calendars and watches? Wasn't it enough to know you would have to leave some time without watching the second hand eat life away? He preferred to believe in the forever 'now'. Without a future we cannot reach the end, he thought.

"Where have you gone Anselm?" she asked again in a whisper.

"I'm not going anywhere. I'm here and now and that's where I'm staying. And I want you and Peter to stay here and now too. This is the best place I've been."

***

III -STOLEN PROMISES

It was Friday. Martha had decided to take the day off and make a long weekend. Anselm didn't really know what Martha did the other days of the week. She went to a place called the 'office' where she 'worked'. Peter 'worked' too at the University but not such long hours.

But today they were both at home and he, Anselm, was the centre of attention. He liked this. No Emily today either. This was one of the days she didn't come to their house. She taught other children on Fridays. In a moment of mischief, Anselm hoped they were doing French.

He had risen early and squatted in front of the dream-box. He did this most mornings flicking the remote between channels until Emily arrived and made the screen go black saying "you'll get square eyes."

Many of the images on the dream-box didn't make much sense to Anselm at first. They were moving but that wasn't all; many of the pictures were of things he hadn't seen anywhere else in the house or in those few weeks on the heath with the shepherd.

He liked 'Loony Tunes' which seemed to be an altogether different world of highly coloured creatures with elastic limbs and eyes that lost contact with their bodies when some disaster was about to happen. And disasters often happened. One of the creatures would be squashed flat like the 'pressed flowers' Emily had him collect from the garden during his Biology lesson. But the creature didn't stay pressed for long. It was soon up and running frantically after the other to go through the same cycle, time and again.

Anselm pressed the button on the remote.

A man wearing a suit and no smile appeared. Peter had told him this was the 'News' man reporting what was happening in different parts of the world. The man hardly ever smiled except at the end. Anselm assumed that was because he could stop talking about things which clearly made him unhappy. He wondered why everything in this world was so serious.

He pressed the button again .Now the screen flicked itself between different images

every thirty seconds or so. These images were of familiar things Anselm could find in, and around , the house: washing up liquid, garden furniture, hair shampoo, coffee, breakfast cereal. For each one there was a voice claiming great things. How such ordinary things could attract such energy was beyond Anselm.

Around 9.00 am Martha appeared at the door to the lounge saying, "Turn the TV off Anselm, we are going out for the day."

"Where are we going?"

“Down to Gull Cove . You are going to see the sea.”

Anselm had heard of the sea in his Geography lessons. Emily had promised him a ‘field trip’; perhaps this was it. Gull Cove was just thirty minutes by car from Martha and Peter’s house. Peter wove his old Volkswagen down the country lanes whilst Anselm tried to look at every blade of grass in the countryside whizzing past his window like the dream-box on fast forward.

The whole trip was a kaleidoscope of ‘firsts’ for Anselm. His first time in the car; his first bout of travel sickness; his first hearing of ‘b...ard!’ as someone ‘cut’ Peter up on a roundabout; his first bite of a toffee apple; his first footprint in the sand and his first sighting of the sea. The sea . Nothing had prepared Anselm for this. Gull Cove was a giant’s bite taken from a marshmallow. The crumbling cliffs fell vertically to a strand of gold and endless green waves. And the wheeling, diving, piping seagulls echoing off the cliffs, huddling on the ledges or hanging motionless in mid-air perfectly in balance with the headwind.

They took the steep path winding down the cliff face to reach the strand. Shoes and socks came off and all three planted their footprints at the water’s edge, like Hollywood starlets in wet cement, and then watched the incoming tide erase them.

“So much for fame,” said Martha.

It was early October. Gold leaf was falling from the trees in the copses above their heads and restless pewter skies mixed in the sea's blue and green palette. White horses surfed and broke on the rocks sending spray twenty feet into the air and filling Anselm's nostrils with the musty smell of kelp and brine. Martha's hair whipped round her eyes and cheeks like the cars windscreen wipers broken loose in the gathering wind.

Peter taught him the lucky dip delights of beach combing. They zigzagged around the cove discovering seaweed that snapped, crackled and popped when you jumped on it; empty crab shells – either cast off as a size too small or victim to the ever-hungry gulls; bleached wood, gnarled into faces and hands and every size and shape of sea-shell. Half a bikini, a bucket sans spade, remnants of a fisherman's net and a faded plastic sun-tan lotion pack- all in memory of summer holiday crowds now departed back to their jobs and schools in the city.

The three of them scrambled across rocks into a great wave-cut hall of limestone dripping with the last high tide . A cathedral cave running dark into the cliff-face..

"Haaallllloooo", Peter mouthed the syllables slowly through cupped hands giving the sound time to ricochet off the cave walls and welcome him back. Anselm was agog and immediately followed suit, delighted to get a response to his greeting too from the cave. And then the rock pools; miniature seas in their own right replete with anemones shy to the touch, crabs hiding, blushing under stones and shrimps with frantic legs racing for cover.

The hours flew. Geography lessons would never be the same dry textbook theory again. Nor would Anselm's concept of time and space . Martha explained how the sea over millions of years licking at the cliffs had made the sand upon the beach; how sea creatures had used the sand to make their shells and then given back their shells to the waves to add again to the cliffs and beach. It seemed so clear to him that the sea, the beach and these cliffs had been and would be, here forever.

Anselm decided he preferred this version of reality.

They explored every nook and cranny of Gull Cove that afternoon till, trouser legs rolled up, arms linked, they stood ankle deep in the infinite sea and watched it gradually extinguish the sun.

***

That evening they ate in a restaurant in the village above Gull Cove. Peter insisted on fish and chips.

Anselm wanted a description of each type of fish before choosing and rather stretched Peter and Martha's marine knowledge....hake, halibut, cod, haddock, skate, rock eel may be readily distinguishable to a trawler man but not to a professor of philosophy and a Managing Director of a 'dot com' business.

He settled on four C's – cod, chips and `Coca Cola and asked for three more as a desert – chocolate chip cookies. "Well after all we're at the 'C'-side," quipped Peter to a groan from Martha .

Peter asked for the bill and paid with his credit card. Anselm immediately asked what the card was and the beginnings of the answer occupied the whole of their car journey home. Peter decided an explanation of the banking system leading onto the principles of capitalism was best left to Martha while he kept his attention on the road.

"So let me summarise," said Anselm twenty minutes into his interrogation of Martha. Peter smiled; he knew what was coming was one of Anselm's naïve, or was it tongue in cheek, resumes.

"Peter's plastic card is used to buy things . He lets the waiter have the card for a few minutes and then puts a secret number in a machine held by the waiter....and that's it. Or rather that's the beginning of it . We walk out of the restaurant and go home whilst the restaurant sends a message to the bank to add numbers to a record on the computer which tells them how much Peter has spent on various other things. And then at the end of the month they list the whole lot out on a 'statement and either put it in an envelope or an e-mail, and send it back to us. Peter opens the mail, sees the numbers, checks they are ok.

" If they aren't right Peter rings the bank and listens to some music for a long time getting irritated If the music doesn't stop. Peter and takes out another piece of paper,on which he writes his name and number, puts it in an envelope and sends it back to the bank. And then the bank checks that Peter has enough money again and finally Peter gets another piece of paper called a statement showing that he has paid and how much money he has left paid."

"And overdrawn", piped up Peter.

"It does seem to me that an awful lot of things could go wrong," opined Anselm. "For example, what if someone added the numbers up wrong ."

"Well," said Martha, "there are thousands of people in the banks checking things and running computer systems to make sure that doesn't happen."

Anselm frowned for a few moments in intense puzzlement, then exclaimed "Well all I can say is that there were a lot of people involved in us getting the meal we ate tonight."

Martha then attempted an explanation of division of labour in an industrialised society and the use of 'money' as a store of value that people could exchange for goods. Anselm began to see that even more people were involved in providing their fish and chip meal than he had first suspected. There was the fisherman and his boat builder and then the farmer who provided the potatoes and the oil in which to cook things. There was the cook in the kitchen whom Anselm had not seen and the waiter who brought the food to the table. But more, there was the man who owned the restaurant building and the people who took the rubbish away; the people in factories who made the plates, the knives and forks and on and on. And then there were all the people who made the clothes, the houses and furniture which all these people used. It was endless. It seemed like everyone in the world had been involved in making this meal.

And all these people had bank accounts and secret numbers to pay for things they needed so others had to work in checking the adds and the minuses and so on. The whole world seemed to be connected to each other and all had worked hard to play their part in bringing that simple fish and ship meal to them. Anselm felt a rush of humility though he couldn't name it.

Martha took out from her purse a ten-pound note to show Anselm. "This is paper money, Anselm. We use this to pay for things as an alternative to the plastic card. So, we could have given some of this form of money to the waiter in the restaurant. He could then have given it to his boss who would break it down into smaller notes and give some to the fisherman, some to the cook and some back to the waiter and so on....., as she spoke she was struck by the absurdity of the whole process.

Anselm scrutinised the note and asked about the lady whose face appeared on it.

"That's the Queen," said Martha. "But we'll talk about her another day," she said hastily heading off a lesson on history and the English constitution.

"I promise to pay the bearer on demand the sum of Ten Pounds," Anselm read out loud from the small print. He asked Martha when the Queen had given this promise.

"This is what is called a 'promissory note' and it is issued by the Bank of England which is kind of the bank of all banks. What it means is that if you give this note to the Bank of England, they would see it as if you were calling in a promise from the Bank which it has made to you as the person carrying the note......and the bank would give you Ten pounds."Again. Martha could feel herself sliding towards the absurd.

"But I thought you said this piece of paper ***is*** 'Ten Pounds'. Now you're telling me it's just a promise. So, what will the Bank of England give you if you take this promise to them and ask them to keep their promise?" he asked.

"Well, I guess they would just give you another Ten Pound note. Once upon a time you could have asked for gold but nowadays, 'Ten Pounds' means one of these or a 'credit' on your bank statement."

Anselm thought this was a very trusting world where the Bank of England issued promises and people exchanged these promises for meals and all sorts of other things even though, if they went to the Bank and asked them to make good the promise, all you would get was yet another promise. He had understood from Emily that making a 'promise' was saying you would do something for sure in the future, something which if you didn't do it then the person to whom you made the promise would feel upset and let down.

It struck him that a promise was much less real than a memory or a dream- as it was something about the future. He had already established with Peter that the future was a bit of a wobbly, uncertain thing. So, for all these people to trust the Bank of England in this way seemed to him to show they had a lot of belief in the future and in the Bank of England's ability to make sure the future happened. He wondered what else the Bank knew about the future.

By the time the wheels of the car made a crunching sound on the gravel drive to their house it was gone eleven – well past Anselm's normal bed time.

As he lay in his bed waiting for sleep he could hear the faint murmur of Peter and Martha talking in their bedroom just down the hall. He couldn't hear the words but the sound was soft and comforting. He fell asleep to images of those early photographs of the couple in the memory book.

***

The next morning Anselm took up his usual lotus position in front of the TV. He was tuned to the News channel.

"The 'Footsie' closed at a twelve- month high following a strong run yesterday on Wall Street.......tech stocks forging ahead. The Bank of England raises interest rates a quarter point on fears of inflationary pressures......high street spending still strong..........twelve percent increase in house prices on an annualised basis...... three thousand jobs moving to India......."

Anselm couldn't make much sense of all this but his ears pricked up on the mention of the Bank of England.

Feeling hungry he went into the kitchen. It was nine o'clock and no sign of Peter and Martha yet. Breakfast was overdue.

Along the black marble surface under the cupboards was a row of earthenware jars marked up coffee, tea, rice, and biscuits. He went fishing for his favourite chocolate chip cookies and tried the biscuit jar, but it was empty bar a few crumbs. Saturday was Martha's usual shopping day.

He tried another unmarked jar and to his surprise found inside a bundle of ten and twenty- pound notes. He had seen Martha often put money in the jar and sometimes take it back out and give it to Emily. But he didn't have any of these promises of his own. He took out a ten-pound note.....and then a twenty, thinking there were several more left in the jar so there should be plenty for Martha and Emily. Putting the notes carefully in his pocket he went back to the T.V. room, hoping Martha or Peter would come down soon for breakfast.

"..........drought in Somalia . The failure of the maize crop is leaving millions of people without food. Relief agencies are mobilising....but it will take several weeks to get supply lines in place.........meanwhile these children face the very real prospect of starvation.....Aid workers worried about the spread of disease in the tented cities due to poor sanitation....."

Things had taken a turn for the worse on the News programme. Anselm sat frozen looking at hairless black heads and swollen bellies with stick-thin arms and legs... and eyes crying without water. And flies, thousands of flies............ "without much needed medical supplies........"

He thought of the fish and chips, the plastic card, ten-pound notes and Bank of England and wondered why these people had no promises.

Peter and Martha appeared for breakfast half an hour later. Anselm felt a mild form of anger at their lateness but got over it quickly when the toast and marmalade hit his plate. Odd how close hunger and anger are to each other. He thought those people on the TV must be very angry inside and wondered if they might show that anger one day. He felt strangely uncomfortable as if someone, soon, might be angry with him because he was eating toast and marmalade....and maybe because he had promises in his pocket.

Breakfast finished, Martha said she was going to do the shopping and asked if Anselm wanted to come with her.

He nodded, and then watched her as she went to the unmarked earthenware jar, took off the lid and slipped in her hand. She took out some of the notes and put them in a purse then replaced the lid. She didn't seem to notice the absence of the two notes which now hid in Anselm's pocket. He thought of telling her he had some of the 'promissory' notes but something unseen, unnamed held him back. His hand went to his pocket and felt the outline of the notes through the denim. “”She doesn’t need them,” said a reassuring voice in his head.

Tesco was a throng of people, navigating trolleys up and down the aisles oblivious of each other, totally focussed on the packets, jars and bottles on the shelves. Each seemed to fill their trolley or basket with a different mixture of things; some had trolleys piled high and others stood with baskets in the queue marked ‘5 items or less.’ Anselm concluded some people were hungrier than others.

“Do the people in Somalia have supermarkets like this one?” he asked Martha.

She was a little thrown by the question. She didn’t know Anselm had ever heard of Somalia. “I don’t think so Anselm. Somalia is a very poor country. They grow their own food.”

“Well they don’t have enough to eat,” he said . “I saw it on the TV this morning. Everyone is hungry. Perhaps we could send them some of this food,” he pointed to the cornucopia on the shelves.

“That’s a good idea, Anselm. Problem is Somalia is a long way away and the food would take a long time to get there. The little food we could send wouldn’t go far. But the government and charities are raising money to help and we could give some money and help that way, if you would like.”

Anselm nodded. He couldn't quite see how money was going to help if the people in Somalia didn't have anywhere to shop but Martha seemed to think it would be useful.

"Why don't they have money of their own?" Anselm continued.

"When I say it's a poor country it's because they don't have lots of services or factories that make things which they can sell to each other and to people outside their country. Without factories and other places of work then there is nothing for people to do to earn money which they can spend on things. Then, if no-one is spending, there is no point in people making things. It's a 'vicious circle'.

Imagine if Peter and I hadn't any money. Then we couldn't have bought dinner in the restaurant last night and, in turn, the restaurant owner could not have paid the fisherman and the cook – so they wouldn't have been able to go to the supermarket on Saturday morning. 'Not an entirely bad thing', thought Martha as she found herself in a shopping trolley gridlock half way down the bread and pasta aisle.

"Why can't they make things or go fishing?" persisted Anselm. Martha was starting to find driving a trolley, which seemed to have its' own sense of direction opposite to hers, and searching for Peter's favourite bow-tie pasta whilst under relentless interrogation by Anselm, a little stressful.

"Why don't you read what it says on each of the packets we've picked up Anselm and see if you can find what country each of them has come from."?

Her tone was more of an instruction that a question, but the diversionary tactic worked.....at least for a few minutes.

Rice from Thailand .Pasta from Italy .Tea from India . Coffee from Brazil . Bacon from Denmark . Water and jam from France. Nothing from Somalia . Nothing from England for that matter.

As far as Anselm was concerned the mystery was just getting deeper."I can see what you mean about Somalia. There's nothing here from Somalia.....because they haven't got any food to spare I guess. But I can't see anything from England. We seem to have to get all our food from other countries. What happens if they run out? And what is it that we make here in England to get the money we need to pay all these other countries for their food?"

"We make other things which we sell to those other countries and that gives us the money we need to pay for food imports," answered Martha. "And if we need more money, well.....the Bank of England prints some more," she caught herself cheating, but justified it to herself on the basis that right now getting out of the gridlock was a higher priority than giving Anselm a full lesson in international trade and the UK balance of payments.

Anselm took to examining other things on the shelves once Martha had extricated the trolley from the pasta. He lingered in the hardware section looking at the labels. TV's – made in 'Japan'. Toasters 'Made in Taiwan.' And so it continued.

He could find nothing made in England. It seemed that the only thing made here was 'money' or promises. 'If the other countries lost their trust in the Bank of England and didn't believe in its promises any more, we could very soon end up like Somalia,' he thought. He decided not to mention this to Martha as it might worry her.

They finally got to the checkout queue. The fat lady in front who clearly didn't need any of the food piled high on the check-out, was using her plastic card. He heard her say, "Can I have fifty-pound cash-back please?" As the ten-pound notes were counted out and given to the fat lady, Anselm thought the plastic seemed even more powerful than the notes because using it you get both food and notes. He wondered where he might get a plastic card; just in case the Bank of England ever started breaking its' promises.

***

All the domestic chores got done on Saturday and Sunday. Martha had a cleaner who came to the house during the week but there were always things she "never got around to." The washing basket was full of dirty clothes.

After lunch Martha sent Peter and Anselm out for a long walk while she reverted to her housewife persona and launched herself at the laundry task. Before the two of them could get to the door she insisted Anselm change his trousers. The denims had a salty tide mark from the paddle at Gull Cove the day before. Anselm peeled them off quickly, stood in the middle of the kitchen and put on his second favourite, a tracksuit bottom that had belonged to Peter in a younger age.

"We should be back in a couple of hours or so," said Peter.

"No rush," replied Martha. Doing the washing was therapeutic for a busy managing director. She was in total control; no need to explain her actions to others; no debate or attempt at committee decisions from the clothes, the washing machine or the iron; they all knew their place and performed unquestioningly.

Peter suggested they walk alongside the brook which ran through their garden then on into the woodlands at the edge of the village. They went through the gate at the bottom of the garden and picked up the footpath that snaked along the banks of the brook.

"What does it mean when two people are 'married'?" asked Anselm.

Peter looked at him, wondering where this question had come from and where to start.

“It’s when two people, a man and a woman...generally....make a special commitment to each other .When they love each other and want to spend their lives together. Then they usually get married...become husband and wife.”

“Martha’s your wife…and you are her husband…right?”

“Yes”.

“She is yours and you are hers...like each one belongs to the other?”

“Well that’s how we speak about husband and wife...but no person belongs to another like a possession. We aren’t property .When I say ‘my wife’ it’s not like ‘my car’. Instead of saying I own something I’m saying I have a special relationship to that person...and only that one person... er......generally”

“You can only have one wife....one special person?”

“Yes , only one at a time...at least in most societies that is true. There are some where a man can have more than one wife...but not here in England.”

“Strange ,” said Anselm. He decided not to pursue discussion of where men have more than one wife, thinking this must be a very complicated arrangement.

“So, you decide on who is the special person and then.....then what? You get a house together?”

“There’s usually a bit more to it than that. First you fall in love. You have feelings for the other person.. You find you want to be with them as much as you can. You feel happy around them...like the best of friends...but more so. They become the most important person in your life...and you want to be close to them...”

Peters face was turning red and a dew drop of sweat formed on his forehead. Anselm noticed the change in colour but wasn’t sure what to make of it.

Anselm wasn’t sure about some of the words..... ‘love’ , ‘feelings’, ‘commitment’. “So, if I meet someone I want to be with then I’ll be married too?”

“Well it works better if both people feel the same way. If they do and decide to be together then they usually get married. Getting married isn’t something you just decide ; it’s something you do. You go through a special ceremony where you make promises to each other. It often takes place in a church in front of your family and friends. That’s how it was with Martha and me. You promise to love each other. To look after each other and to stay together.”

“Like the Bank of England's promises?”

“Not quite. The Bank of England's promises are money which you can give to anyone. Marriage promises are only given to that one special person....they're no use to anyone else.," Peter replied, wondering if he was right.

"And 'love'. What is it....where does it come from?"

"I'm not sure how to describe it There are different types of love...between a man and a woman its maybe ... a kind of wanting; a really strong kind of wanting; wanting the other person, to be with them and to be special to them. It's also about caring for that person...they are very important; you want them, above all others, to be happy. Where it comes from, I'm not sure anyone knows the answer. It seems to just happen ; often suddenly. You just meet someone and they are different; somehow they fit."

Peter wasn't very satisfied with his explanation. He hadn't given love much attention for quite some time.

"I don't see how you can promise to love someone if you don't understand what you are talking about. How can you promise to love them tomorrow. What happens if you wake up in the morning and love has disappeared"

"Well....that's another story."

"Do you love Martha?"

"Yes.......yes, of course."

"When did you start loving her?"

"When we first met. Or very soon afterwards. When we were at University .Some friends introduced us. I thought she was the most beautiful person I'd ever met. She was so warm and lively and easy to talk to .She seemed to understand me; understand how I felt about things. We talked a lot, in those days. I remember it took me a little while to pluck up the courage to ask her out on a date..."

Peter was conscious of Anselm's intense scrutiny and wondered how much of this he was 'getting'.

"We walked for hours along the riverbank near the University. The time seemed to go in a flash. It wasn't like being with anyone else. There just seemed to be the two of us in the world and...it was like I had found something that had been missing... like a piece of myself; it was as if I had known her all my life."

"And she loved you, straight away?"

"Maybe not straight away; but soon...I think. She told me on our third date she was falling in love."

"Falling?"

"Just a figure of speech .Anyway ,it all seemed to happen very fast. And then..... then she went away for a summer to her parent's house in Italy. I couldn't go...my exams were coming up. So, we wrote to each other. No mobile phones then. We wrote every two or three days for six weeks. I remember checking the mail box every day, twice a day, and the disappointment if there was no letter; the absolute joy if there was one.

“That’s what love can do to you. And I used to worry that she would stop loving me; she would meet someone else while she was away. “

“Sounds horrible.”

“Yes...I guess that’s the other thing about love; or at least about that stage of romantic love. It can feel like an illness; like you are in the grip of something and nothing else in life matters; you can think of nothing else but the other person and being without them is ...well....torture.”

Anselm was beginning to think this love thing was a rather mixed blessing. He wasn’t at all sure he wanted to ‘fall’, but since this was something boys seemed to do with girls then he, fortunately, didn’t see much prospect of it happening to him right now. The only females in his life were Martha and Emily. Martha had already made her promises and if Emily was going to she would have done so by now, surely. Anyway, he was happy to buy some time as there was clearly more to all this than met the eye.

”So, do you still miss Martha....when she is out at work? It seems like you have both chosen to be apart most of the time during the day....maybe love isn’t as strong as it was at the beginning?”

“You find out eventually that even two people who love each other need other things, other people in their lives, and need some purpose , something to do with themselves. Besides we have to go to work. We have to earn a living....to earn those promises from the Bank of England. "

"Seems like earning one type of promise means it's difficult to keep another kind of promise," said Anselm.

Peter heard the words...but didn't want to let them in.

***

IV ELUSIVE SELF

Following the path, they came to a place where the stream widened out into a dark, glassy pool overarched by a canopy of trees. Willows, oak and sycamore . Anselm stopped and gazed at the surface of the pool seeing the reflection of the trees and their many greens.

"It's like the mirror in my room," he said.

"You can see the 'reflection' of the trees," said Peter. "The light from the trees is bouncing off the surface of the water into your eyes," he continued as amateur scientist.

Anselm picked up a small stone from the path and plopped it into the pool, watching as the concentric circles echoed outwards. He saw the trees lose their straightness and branches lose contact with the trunk. He was reminded of the argument of Messrs Berkeley and Descartes in his dream.

The reflection has gone wobbly, but the real trees haven't," observed Anselm. "Maybe that's a way I can tell real trees from pretend ones. But in my dreams it's more difficult. I don't seem to throw stones in my dreams to check whether I am asleep or awake. But you can see the trees too, right?"

"Yes, of course."

“So if we both see them then they must really be there, mustn’t they?”

“Well, that would seem to be rather better evidence than with the example of a dream It ‘s rare for two people to have the same dream at the same time. But wait a moment, let’s both close our eyes. Now what do you see?”

“Nothing much, just blackness with some fuzzy splashes of light coming and going .”

“Well that’s pretty much what I ‘see’ too. Are we to conclude they are the same fuzzy splashes of light and that they are real too? And what happened to the trees? If our evidence for their real existence was because we were both seeing them then what has happened to them now?”

“But if I open my eyes again I see them again still standing there and if you did the same you would too,” replied Anselm.

“Maybe, but since I still have my eyes closed your evidence seems to have weakened a bit and , in any case, how do we know they were still there when we both had our eyes closed ....just because they reappear when we open them?”

Anselm thought that things so large were unlikely to flick in and out of existence just because of the opening and closing of people’s eyes, however many people were involved in the experiment. However, he admitted the logic of Peter's argument without for one moment losing faith in the trees. He was getting used to Peter's mind games and was grateful that Peter could separate the doubting philosopher in him from the husband and father who drove the car to and from Gull Cove yesterday.

"So, you see that's why Descartes looked for something that was beyond doubt; something he could be absolutely certain of; a rock on which he could later build other certainties and reinstate the world. And he decided the one thing he could be absolutely sure of was that he himself existed. 'Cogito ergo sum': 'I think therefore I am'" recounted Peter. He said it in Latin. Odd for a Frenchman.

"I think therefore I am," declared Anselm.

"Well, you might conclude that but I cannot be sure," teased Peter.

"No, you think therefore you am ...er...are" said Anselm generously aiming to extend the same existential certainty to Peter.

"What I meant was that you may conclude you exist from your own process of thinking, as might I, but neither of us can be sure the other exists. We are just like the trees," explained Peter.

"So 'I' people exist but 'you' people are not so sure?" Anselm embellished.

“Yes, sort of.” Peter thought he must take Anselm along to one of his tutorials, the boy would really plunge the students into an existential crisis.....which he had no doubt would be good for their development and humility .

Then the lens of reality started to fog up again.

“Ok, so I exist and you are not so sure. So, what am I?”

“Well, I am Peter. I am a professor of philosophy. I am six foot tall. I am the husband of Martha and father of Anselm” replied Peter.

“And I am Anselm. I am fifteen (I think). I am the son of Martha and Peter. I am hungry,” responded Anselm. “So, it seems to me that ‘I’ is a lot of things, including being a fifteen year-old, six foot tall professor of philosophy who is both the son of Martha and married to her and is looking forward to lunch. This ‘I’ is a rather mixed up person.”

“Hah. That’s because you and me are both referring to different persons when we used the word ‘I’. But more importantly when I said what ‘I’ was I gave my name, my job, my role in the family and my size ...all descriptions of me but surely not the same as ‘me’. So, you are right to ask the question ‘What am I ?”

Anselm waited , assuming that Peter was going to go on and reveal all. But Peter didn’t answer, so Anselm continued:“Well, I think I am a sort of observer. The thing that does the looking, hearing, touching, smelling ....and, hopefully tasting soon. I am the one who saw the reflection of the trees; I am the one who threw the stone into the pool and I am the one talking to you now telling you what I am."

"But surely Anselm that's not you, it's your body doing those things. Your eyes, your arms, your mouth and voice . Are you just the sum of the parts of your body?"

"No, I am different, separate from my body. I am the one who tells my body what to do. I am the one who can stand quietly, eyes closed and think; the one who dreams. Usually, my body isn't in my dreams, or at least I can't see it."

He used the word usually as, a couple of nihts ago he had a dream in which his body had been fully involved.....with that of another...a girl he had seen on the TV holiday programme. He had been stroking her body and she had stroked his.

"We talk about 'thinking' and 'dreaming' as somehow taking place in what we call the 'mind'," Peter jolted him back to unreality.

"The mind ? Is there only one?"

"No, we each have a mind, quite separate from each other's," said Peter conscious that even this statement would be denied by a Buddhist.

"And where or what is this mind?" searched Anselm.

"Some would say it is the same as, or is in , your brain," replied Peter.

Emily had taught Anselm about the brain, along with the heart, lungs, skeleton and other parts of the human body, in his first Biology lessons. She said the working of the brain was still a mystery but it had something to do with an invisible force called 'electricity', a bit like the TV. Probably that's why both make pictures he had thought .She had said that the brain was what you think with and feel pain, hot or cold with.

"Ok, so I know the brain is a bit like a TV except it doesn't just have pictures and sound it also has feelings of smoothness, roughness, the taste of fish and chips and the smell of the sea and other things. But if you are arguing that when I say "I'm hungry" it's my mind in my brain that's hungry, then what's this ***'me'*** that combines a mind and brain?"

"Good question, Anselm."

Anselm sensed a patronising cop out on its way, but was surprised and impressed when Peter continued: "Your point is that these I, my, me words refer to an identity that is more than your body, brain or mind. Perhaps we could say it is all of these together or it is the thing to which all your perceptions, experiences, feelings, memories attach. It's what all of these things have one thing in common... that they happen to you. So perhaps the self isn't something you can go looking for, or point at, but it is a quality attaching to all these experiences. For example, you don't feel another persons' pain do you?"

"No, I don't think so." Anselm was hesitant.

"So, when you are aware of pain, it's your pain; the very fact of your awareness of it means it's you who is feeling the pain. So with everything 'you' see, hear feel... it's like these things are all painted blue they have an unmistakable quality of 'youness'. But we don't talk of blue existing on its' own, separately. There are just blue things.

What a strange world if that 'I' quality did not exist Anselm and there was just a kind of pea soup of mixed feelings, perceptions not attached to any selves or identities. Who then would own them or even be able to report on them?"

Anselm had gotten lost when Peter arrived at the 'blue' analogy. He felt his 'self' to be something rather more than a colour, a texture....something more substantive. more wilful. Yes, that was it. His 'self' wasn't a sort of label on his experiences it was an active force that made things happen. He lifted his arm and then let it drop by his side just by way of confirmation. Peter was startled for a moment and wondered if the boy was about to have a fit. Was this all too much for him?

Then Anselm re-engaged.

"I don't think there would be a ***me*** if things weren't ***happening*** 'to' me or if I weren't able to make things happen."

“Ah!” said Peter as if something had struck him in the ribs. “Now we are in the territory of Immanuel Kant. Kant said that the ‘I’ is the point of view from which interpretation of experience is made. Thinking in terms of ‘I’ is necessary for us to be able to link experiences and events and to be able to understand how the will impacts the world around. ‘I’ is the golden thread that connects the experiences, events and actions which fill our consciousness.

“Suppose one had no memory, just a blank. Suppose from second to second the blackboard of your memory was rubbed clean and no memories stuck. Surely then the golden thread would be broken into atoms. There would be no continuing ‘I’ or self to link these experiences, just a lot of flickering , unconnected images and sounds like when you flick the TV channels with the remote control. Or, suppose there was a single point of time in the past before which there were no experiences, perceptions, actions.”

Anselm looked a little shocked: “Then what you say means that, before that time ‘I’ did not exist. Well, I guess that’s how it was with me , until the moment when the shepherd found me. I can’t remember anything before that, no matter how hard I try. Does that mean I didn’t exist until that moment? And if I didn’t......how did I get to be there.........and how did I get so big?”

Anselm’s tone was getting desperate. He had just collided with the nightmare that he had ,for weeks, been shutting out of his mind :the idea that only a few weeks ago he didn't exist and he was very different to other human beings.

Peter saw the boy's distress and put his hand on Anselm's shoulder. He spoke quietly. "We don't know where you came from son,and perhaps we never will. But Martha and I bless the day you appeared and everyday you are with us. You are the answer to a prayer. Perhaps some higher power saw our loneliness and decided that there was no time to be lost. Had Martha been able to give birth at the time we saw the doctor then that child would have been fifteen years old today. And here you are."

Anselm did not understand the reference to the 'higher power' but nevertheless felt comforted by what Peter had said..... and to know that wherever his 'I' had come from it was wanted so much.

They retraced their steps along the course of the brook arm in arm.They arrived back at the house at dusk.

"You two were a long time," observed Martha.

"Discovering one's self can take a while," said Peter. Anselm smiled. Martha shrugged and continued with the ironing.

Anselm decided to go up to his bedroom. Martha had bought him an iPod and laoeup some music. She had downloaded Sibelius, Eminem, Taylor Swift, The Beatles and Miles Davis to discover what type of music he might like. It turned out he liked them all in different ways for different reasons. He liked Sibelius because the music took him to imaginary worlds where he imagined no human being had ever set foot or uttered a syllable; like the heath before time began. Whereas Eminem was all words, fast and furious, too fast for Anselm to hang on to but somehow still telling their stories through the tone of his voice. Much of what he said was unfamiliar to Anselm but how he said it reminded Anselm of that stone sinking in his chest.

Downstairs Martha shattered the peace of the afternoon with a discovery.

"I found these in Anselm's pocket." She threw onto the kitchen table a twenty- pound and a ten- pound note.

"Where would he have gotten those from?" asked Peter.

"I wondered if you had given them to him. "

"I didn't."

"If you didn't then the only place he could have gotten them is from the housekeeping money I keep in the jar to pay Emily and for odds 'n sods. He must have stolen the notes from there," she said.

The word 'stolen' hung in the air between them.

"I don't think the boy would know what stealing is. If he took the notes from the jar he would have been treating them like the chocolate cookies...something that's there for him to take if and when he wants.

“But we didn’t give him permission to take the notes,” argued Martha.

“That’s true, but I still don’t think the boy would have seen it as wrong to take the notes. You guys had been talking a lot in the car last night about the use of money, the Bank of England and all that. My guess is he was curious and just wanted to have some notes of his own.” countered Peter

”His own ? The whole point is they don’t belong to him and we need to make sure he understands that it’s wrong to take things without permission. Whether we call it stealing or not ,it’s not something we can overlook . If Anselm is to operate normally in society he can’t simply go around taking other people’s things because he’s curious.” Martha felt a wave of irritation rise up in her chest and catch at her breath. She was surprised at her own response to the incident. She could well understand that Anselm would have no notion of stealing but the more Peter defended the boys’ action, the more she dug in her heels and pressed the point.

“I think you’re making a mountain out of a molehill. The boy has still very little understanding the rules you and I ,and society live by. If your point is we should teach him right from wrong then of course I agree. But you seem to be getting all hot and bothered about this as if it were some sort of original sin,” said Peter with a tone of reprimand.

If it was Peter’s intention that this should calm Martha down he was to be disappointed. His cold logic now, as often, had the opposite effect - pouring petrol on the flames of her more emotional response .

“You’re complacent. We need to nip this in the bud now or goodness knows what he might get up to. No one has drawn boundaries for him as to what is right and wrong, what is acceptable and unacceptable behaviour. If we don’t others will, with much less sensitivity. Perhaps you should spend less time debating the irrelevant backwaters of British Empiricist philosophy and more on practical morality and economics.”

“Yes, why not . Let’s ensure he understands the workings of capitalism, the banking system, insurance , capital markets and how to borrow from the poor to pay the rich. That will surely equip him for life and the pursuit of happiness!”

They each knew how to press each other’s buttons. The most effective button of them all was the one marked ‘career.’ A few acerbic lines would relegate each other’s life’s work to the dustbin of irrelevance suggesting their chosen path ‘missed the point’ or, worse, was positively harmful. Their careers had become the thing that defined them. Peter was first and foremost a Professor of Philosophy ; Martha the MD of ‘Gothere.com’. The people who earlier in life had been the son and daughter of their respective parents and then husband and wife of each other were now... a couple of job.

Their jobs or rather their job titles, Professor and Managing Director seemed somehow more permanent than anything else and described their relationship to the people with whom they spent most of their time. So, each knew at some level that denial of value in each other's job and its belief system was denying value in the person and all that they stood for. It was a kind of verbal annihilation.

Words you would never utter against a stranger seemed to come tumbling out without any editorial intervention when they having an argument. Neither had any firewall. Criticisms. sent by the other always got through, , and, like an Internet virus, proved nigh impossible to 'delete' once opened.

"Well at least if he understands the idea of property and theft, the boy may stay out of jail long enough to have the chance of happiness," replied Martha melodramatically.

"Property is theft ?"snorted Peter taking a sarcastic refuge in Proudhon and Marxism.

Martha wasn't listening. She was struggling to find her equilibrium. These days there was rarely a heated word between her and Peter but ,when it happened, it was over some household trivia or abstract debate. The anger never seemed to be in the right place. It was as if a well of the stuff had been sunk underground and then capped off. Every now and again something would come along and puncture the sides of the well and a spurt of anger would leak to the surface often some distance away from where the original well had been sunk. And when it did, she knew it was she who usually had cast the first stone.

Peter was the passive type, and that in itself could be infuriating. This time she knew she was right about 'the principle' but was completely overreacting. She couldn't help it and wasn't going to back down. She also knew that this anger had little or nothing to do with Anselm.

"Well?"

"Well what?"

"Well, what are we going to do?" asked Martha.

The thought that we would be about to do anything together, seemed a highly improbable one to Peter based on the last ten minutes . But perhaps this was an olive branch. If so Peter would take it, he didn't like confrontation and still less did he like Martha's sulks. 'Anything for a quiet life' was the motto on the Swinbourn coat of arms.

"I suppose we had better talk to him. I do agree he needs to understand that he shouldn't just take things without asking. But I also think we need to keep the whole incident in some perspective."

Peter offered his own version of an olive branch......without too many leaves on it and a few strings attached but nevertheless recognisably an olive branch.

"Ok," said Martha, hand loosely grasping the branch. "We both need to be involved and need to be in a good space. I suggest we leave it until tomorrow morning."

***

Dinner was passed with chatting about family and friends. Just by listening, Anselm got a little more colouring in of the figures in the memory book. When dinner was finished he went into the TV room, took up his usual position and watched a quiz show. As the prize money doubled each time the contestant chose the right answer Anselm thought to that maybe the lessons with Emily might come in useful, one day.

Martha and Peter each retired to separate rooms to read or to lick their wounds. Peter often 'went to ground' in his study where the book-lined walls provided insulation against the rest of the world in general and Martha's disapproval in particular.

Martha took a detective novel up to their en-suite, ran a hot bath and then soaked for an hour.

As she lay there she went back over her upset with Peter and wondered where it had all come from. Couldn't they just have agreed at the beginning as they had at the end? She felt ,at some level, that she had been looking for a fight. As soon as Peter had sprung to the boy's defence her hackles went up. This was the perfect opportunity to engage with Peter, to get a reaction. Any reaction would do and he rose to the bait, at least briefly.

When they had first met at University, Peter was in his post-graduate year and she in her second year of English. Peter had an unworldly and distracted air. It took Martha some time to catch the shy and introverted young man's attention. But when she did, marriage seemed an inevitable consequence. In the centre of each of them was a loneliness that the other appeared to extinguish.

In those much younger days. the idealist in Peter fitted to the romantic in Martha like pieces of a jigsaw puzzle. They would talk into the early hours, she listening to his heroism as he fed the starving, emancipated the oppressed, disarmed the superpowers and robbed the rich to pay the poor.

"You can't get a cigarette paper between the two of them," friends would say, so close were they, always in each other's company. The world was Copernican, revolving around the two of them. Sometimes it seemed that all others were merely 'extras' in their two-person drama.

It was a romantic love, in that 'Can't do without you',' no-one else understands' sense. And all the things they had never told anyone else, they told each other. Hours flew by in blink as they emptied their chests of hopes and fears.

The wedding was morning suits and church. Martha's mother had been insistent that it was to be a full family affair with all the bells and whistles.

"Only happens once, my dear; least it does in our family."

Peter had wanted a quieter ceremony, immediate family and close friends only; but this was never going to be enough for Martha's family who took over the event as if it were a regimental re-union rather than a union of two.

Perhaps that was the first time the world intruded on their dreams.

Peter was always going to stay in academia but Martha wanted to" run something". Three more years of exams followed for her as she qualified as an accountant and then moved into a management role. Peter continued to 'challenge the obvious' as Martha's mother had unsympathetically described his philosophical studies.

The obsession of romance and youth gave them momentum for the first few years.

But ,as time passed ,their worlds separated .The change was imperceptible; just like falling asleep. Neither of them could say when it happened and neither could break the fall. Day by day their time spent with each other waned and careers filled the space. Which came first, their estrangement from each other or the demands of their work , wasn't clear either. But their worlds were very different. Her's the deadlines and endless meetings with bankers, lawyers and management teams which left her 'peopled out' at end of day. His, the introversion, reflection and the effort of will needed to teach. The cadence of their lives diverged; they became sine and cosine.

The intimacy they had shared in those early years built on total absorption with, and in, each other had slowly evaporated. As their lives diverged, neither could find new ground on which they could meet. Each seemed to inhabit a world foreign to the other and...gradually...each began to collude with this separation to keep their two worlds apart. Martha stopped bringing business contacts home for dinner; Peter started to find excuses not to attend functions at the University. Non-attendance became a habit; excuses were no longer needed.

The hopeful idealists at University, raw-skinned with hearts on sleeves gave way to thirty-something, then forty-something, pragmatists, hearts buried deep beneath the silt of neglect. To talk of their relationship was taboo. Any attempt by one of them would inevitably be seen as a criticism by the other drawing a stinging response followed by further hibernation. And so ,the sheet of glass between them thickened.

Martha stepped out of the bath and pulled on her robe. It was 9.30 pm Well before their normal bedtime but the hot bath had drained her. Peter was still downstairs in his study. He would be there until midnight. She crossed the hall and found Anselm asleep on top of the duvet. Carefully she folded him into the bed and switched off the TV.

She lay in bed for a while feeling the cool linen on her bath-hot skin, waiting to slide into the anaesthesia of sleep. She was surprised to feel a small green shoot open in her chest. The heated argument with Peter was out of the ordinary being just that ... .heated. Most of their exchanges these days were so matter of fact. Somewhere, she knew then that she would rather fight with him than be without him.

***

V RULES

“Anselm, Peter and I would like to talk to you,” announced Martha in an unfamiliar tone. They had just finished breakfast and filed the dirty plates into the dishwasher. Anselm was in his starting blocks to make for the TV and Sunday morning cartoons when Martha changed the course of the morning.”

“What about?” he replied, curious and a little nervous. He hadn’t encountered this kind of pre-booking of a conversation before. When people wanted to talk to him they usually just did so. Whatever she wanted to talk about Martha had a look similar to the one she wore when Anselm’s room was untidy. But this one looked more than one untidy room’s worth.

“Yes,” said Peter, “we need to have a chat young man.”

Both of them. ? Peter didn’t usually get involved in the untidy bedroom situations. Anselm thought Peter was probably pretty untidy himself. So ,this must be something else.

Martha gestured for Anselm to sit down again at the table.”I found these in your trouser pocket yesterday Anselm when I was doing the washing. Can you tell me where you got them from .... son?”

The ‘son’ word seemed an afterthought. It wasn’t yet automatic with Martha and this time she’d consciously added it to sweeten what might have seemed like some kind of kangaroo court. Anselm looked at the two notes. He had forgotten all about them until now. Now he felt that confusion again. Martha had taken the shopping money from the jar and something had stopped him from telling her that he had taken two of the promises. That same something now seemed to rob him of his voice for what seemed like several minutes .

“Well?” asked Martha.

“I found them in the jar over there,” said Anselm pointing to the sideboard.

“But who said you could take them, Anselm?”

“Er....no one,” Anselm thought as soon as the words were out that his probably wasn’t the best of answers.

“You and Peter weren’t here. I don’t have any promises and there were so many in the jar. What if I need to buy something? No one tells me when I can take cookies. I was going to tell you that I had them......” Anselm gabbled, looking for a sentence that would get Martha and Peter to relax their stares. Peter was shifting his weight from one foot to another and finding it difficult to know where to put his hands. His discomfort was only marginally behind Anselm’s. But, he daren’t intercede with a defence of the boy for fear of being seen by Martha as breaking ranks and provoking an even worse outcome, for both of them.

“Don’t worry, darling. Nothing bad is going to happen.” Suddenly Martha’s tone softened as she saw the worry in Anselm’s eyes. “But it’s important you understand that you can’t just take things which don’t belong to you. This is a lot of money. We keep it here to buy things for the house and to pay Emily. If you need something you should ask me or Peter and we will get it for you. Taking money is wrong...people call it stealing..."

Martha's explanation tailed off as she saw the anxious look give way to one of puzzlement which reminded her of how far this boy still had to travel in understanding the world. The kitchen went quiet, save the ticking of the clock on the wall, and the three of them hung there in suspense, each afraid to break the moment.

Finally, Peter said, in belated support, "Your mother's right, Anselm," followed quickly by a conciliatory: "I guess you didn't know it was wrong to take the money". Peter was clearly concerned not to put the boy into another tailspin. Peter felt redundant. Martha was calling the shots .Some part of him wished she'd make up her mind. Was she going to be angry and righteous ,like earlier, or would she stay the concerned parent, as now. He wasn't sure which he preferred.

The clock ticked ...

"Why?" Anselm at last found a question to rescue him from this most uncomfortable of 'now's'.

"Why what?" asked Martha.

"Why is it bad for me to take the money?"

"Well...because it's stealing, as I said."

“But why is stealing bad?” persisted Anselm.

.

“It’s against the law. We have laws against stealing. If people steal money from others then they may go to prison or, at the very least, they will be made to pay the money back.”

Anselm hadn’t heard the word ‘prison’ before but guessed it was probably a place that people didn’t like.

“What is the law?”

Martha and Peter looked at each other with a look that said simultaneously, ‘where on earth do we start’....and...’over to you’. They both sat down, elbows on the kitchen table, ready to attempt an explanation to justify their view on the ethics of the situation.

Peter picked up the baton, “When we talk about the law we mean a collection of rules that people in society live by. These rules tell us what it’s ok to do and what not to do in different situations.”

“Like the rules in the game of chess you were teaching me the other day,” said Anselm trying to help.

“A bit like that, “said a momentarily grateful Peter.

“But you didn’t send me to prison when I moved the knight the wrong way, did you?”

“No, the law is more serious than the rules of a game like chess. People pass laws to.....er........protect themselves ....er.......from each other.”

“What do they think is going to happen to them?”

Peter thought it wise to try approaching the issue from a different angle. “Let me give you a better example. Suppose someone were to come into the kitchen, pick up that knife and stab me with it. I think you would agree that would be a very bad thing to do, wouldn’t you?”

Anselm nodded. He had fallen down the steps to the garden and grazed his knee a few days ago and knew the sharp feeling of ‘pain’ that came with a cut. He’d also seen Martha cut her finger peeling potatoes and how her face had screwed up in pain. So ,he could readily see that getting a knife pushed into one would be a very disagreeable experience. But he couldn’t for the life of him think why anyone would want to do that. He thought he’d wait to see if things became clearer as Peter went on.

Peter wasn’t entirely satisfied with Anselm’s nod. “Stabbing someone or hurting another person in any way and causing them pain is a VERRRRY BAD THING to do, Anselm,” he said, drumming home the point with an elongated adjective.

“So, we have laws against people doing that kind of thing. Hurting someone else is against the law and if a person is found doing so then they are punished. ....they are sent to prison where they are locked up, away from other people so they can't do it again."

'A bit late!' thought Anselm. He couldn't quite see what all this had to do with promises from the Bank of England.

"So that's an example of the laws people make to protect themselves from other people doing bad things," Peter continued. "There are also rules, or laws, against people taking things, which belong to others. We have decided that 'stealing' or taking someone else's things is bad and have made laws to make it clear to people that they shouldn't steal and, if they do so, they will be punished."

Anselm wondered who this 'we' was that had decided that taking things was bad. Was it Martha and Peter or some others who got to decide on such things? He decided to let this pass for the time being as there was something rather more pressing that he hadn't understood.

"So, taking other people's things has been decided to be bad?"

"Yes."

"The people who 'took' the photographs in the memory books...are they in prison? And when Emily takes my time going over French grammar.....is that against the law? And when I take cookies from the jar..?"

“No. When I say taking things I’m really talking about other kinds of things which are owned by someone else, which have value to them and where someone takes them without the owner’s permission.”

Anselm wasn’t clear about this word ‘own’. Peter explained it in terms of things one said , like, ***my*** car, ***my*** house, ***my*** money, ***my*** trousers. Anselm noted that he didn’t really seem to have any of these ‘***my***things’......they all seemed to be Martha and Peter’s things, some of which they let him use, some of which, like the bank notes, they didn’t want him to have.

“So really, whether I am doing a bad thing by taking something depends pretty much on how you or Martha feel about it,” Anselm summarised.

“To some extent yes,” said Peter. “It depends on whether we say: “yes it’s ok for you to take the thing”, like the cookies, or whether we haven’t said ‘yes’. If we haven’t said “yes” we haven’t given permission.......and that’s how it is with money.”

Anselm was now convinced that Emily was breaking the law by forcing him to do his French lessons.

“It also depends a bit on how valuable the thing is that is taken and the circumstances in which it is taken,” Martha chipped in, breaking her silence. Peter let out a groan; he could almost hear the lid of Pandora’s box creak as it opened wide.

Anselm thought this was getting very complicated. If you were to play chess like this, making up the rules according to how one of the players felt or the 'circumstances', it would be very difficult to win.

"So, for example," continued Martha digging the hole deeper, "the pencil Peter has in his top pocket is one he has taken from the University. He has brought it home and uses it to make notes for the book he is writing. The pencil belongs to the University and I don't suppose he asked permission to bring it home but we don't see this as stealing because..."She flailed the air with her arms as if trying to catch some gossamer truth...." it's a very small thing, not very valuable and he is using it in his work...which is something the University encourages."

Martha heaved a sigh of relief ,as if having just completed a very tricky landing of a light aircraft in heavy crosswinds. Gathering strength, she continued. "Whereas, if Peter were to bring home boxes and boxes of pencils and paper and, maybe, to sell them to other people to make money, we would see that as stealing and the University would be quite within its rights to use the law to stop Peter from doing so."

Anselm looked quizzically at Peter, who seemed to be shifting uncomfortably in his seat and unwilling to meet Anselm's eyes.

Anselm overlooked the question of who exactly this University person was that owned all these pencils which were now such desirable property. Stranger still was the idea that the act of taking something was' good' or 'bad' depending on the number of things taken and what you did with them afterwards.

"So, when does it become bad to take pencils...when you take two, three, four, five... how many before you are breaking the law. And suppose Peter took lots of pencils but gave them away afterwards to people who didn't have any....would that still be bad?"

The adults fell silent again.

"It depends," said Martha with a weak attempt at finality.

"On what?" pestered Anselm. Peter thought he saw a flash of mischief cross Anselm's face.

"I suppose it depends partly on whether Peter was trying to make personal gain out of taking the pencils; whether they would be missed by the University; whether other people would be short of pencils as a result..." She regretted using the example.

Peter stepped in to try and get Martha out of a hole: "Philosophers have tried for thousands of years to define what is good and what is bad and I have to admit that there are still differences of view. But, we need rules to live by and ,generally, people are agreed on most of the rules we have today. It's just that when you start to examine them at the edges, they get a bit blurred, like trying to point to where fog begins and ends.

" Some philosophers have tried to define 'bad' or 'wrong' in terms of actions, which we wouldn't want to be general practice. So, for example, I wouldn't like someone to take my possessions without my permission. Or, worse ,I wouldn't like someone to hit me with a cricket bat. The 'Golden rule' or 'Categorical Imperative' says we should only do those things which we would be happy to have as a universal law . We shouldn't do things which we wouldn't be happy to become general behaviour. 'Do unto others as you would have them do unto you'. This is quite a good rule of thumb to live life by, Anselm.

Other thinkers have tried to define 'bad' actions as those which result in more unhappiness than happiness....and 'good' is vice-versa. So, if the people who are affected by my action are made happier as a result then, generally, we say my action is 'good'. If, however, my action makes more unhappy than are made happy....or, to be more precise, if the total unhappiness created outweighs the happiness, then my action is seen as bad. A man called John Stuart Mill had this idea and called it the 'Utility Principle'."

"So, what about the pencils?" asked Anselm.

Peter felt himself somewhat trapped in Martha's analogy but ,through a sense of loyalty,persevered.

"Well, if I were to take one pencil, " began Peter,...

"You did, There it is peeping out of your pocket," Anselm reminded him.

.

"Yes, well if I were in the shoes of the University I think

I would not mind the loss of one pencil to a professor who will almost certainly use the pencil to write on matters philosophical. So, I conclude, using the Golden Rule, that my taking the pencil was ok.......it was not a bad action."

Anselm noticed Peter had pretended to be the University and had not answered the question of how he would feel if it had been his own pencil . "Also , if we think apply the Utility Principle, then I think we get the same result," said Peter more confidently.

"The University will not miss one pencil amongst many and I am happy to have the use of the pencil for my work. The net score is one happy professor and one indifferent University....so we can conclude this is a good action."

Martha shot a glance of charmed reproach as she watched Peter short-circuit Anselm's moral education. Anselm wondered just how happy anyone could be about one pencil. He also thought that his parents' reaction to the missing promise notes didn't fit very well with Peter's definition of 'bad'. After all a pencil is useful, and it wasn't clear that the notes were.

"So, taking one or two pencils ,which the University didn't miss because it has plenty of others, is ok then," summarised Anselm.

"Yes, that's about it," replied Peter pleased with himself.

“So ,what’s the difference between a pencil or two and a couple of promise notes?” asked Anselm with what seemed to Martha exaggerated innocence.

“The notes are much more valuable Anselm. For example, we could buy a lot of pencils with thirty pounds. So, we would be losing much, much more.” Martha replied confident that this would put enough distance between the two acts.

“But you didn’t miss them. When you looked in the tin for the money for the supermarket you didn’t say there were some notes missing. You were surprised when you found them in my pocket. In fact, you didn’t seem to be unhappy ***until*** you f***ound*** them again. It’s like the University not missing the pencils. Nobody ended up unhappy and I was very happy to have some promises.”

Anselm didn’t much like the idea of going to prison. He didn’t really think Martha and Peter would do that to him...but why take chances? It seemed to him that the adults had made rules to suit them; he hadn’t had any say in deciding what would be called good or bad and there seemed to be different rules for different people. Anyway, given that philosophers had spent thousands of years trying to decide what’s good and bad, how was he supposed to know . He decided to try the Golden Rule as his defence.

“I wouldn’t mind if it had been my jar and someone took two of the notes, particularly if that someone was going to use the notes to buy food for the people in Somalia.I would be very happy for that to be a universal law – you are allowed to take money to buy food for Somalia!"

The couple were running out of ideas to explain or justify what they had, thought of as self-evident. "It's good you wanted to help out those people in Somalia. If you had asked for the money to give to them, we would have been pleased to help. It's just that there are rules in the world and this house about not taking things without permission. Sometimes the rules may not make sense but, by and large, they are a way of creating order so we know where we stand and what we can expect of each other."

Martha made the best fist she could of being conciliatory whilst still trying to keep the boundary line clear.

They agreed that was more than enough on 'right' and 'wrong' for one day. Martha looked at her watch. "Whoops, I'm going to be late." She always went to mass on Sundays. Peter didn't; he was a practising atheist "until somebody comes up with a solution to the problem of evil."

Peter suggested a kick around with a football in the garden and Anselm readily agreed. He felt a surge through his right leg. Kicking a football, hard, seemed a very good idea indeed .

Over the coming months Anselm learnt more about what counted as 'wrong' and 'right'. He learnt that wrongs came in different sizes. Some small ones, like passing wind or picking one's nose, were only wrong if they were done in front of adults but were funny if done in the company of teenagers. Others were wrong only if Martha was around .... like kicking the football in the kitchen or leaving his room untidy. Then there were those which drew the disapproval of both Martha and Peter. Drawing the picture of the naked woman on his bedroom wall seemed to come into that category. Even though he'd learnt from Emily that a man called Leonardo was celebrated for doing just that kind of thing. One truth became very clear through his process of trial and error: a thing was generally wrong only if someone else found out about it and didn't like it.

***,

When Martha returned from Church she found Peter and Anselm draped over the garden chairs at the edge of the dappled shade cast by the apple tree. Late September and the fruit had fallen, been peeled, boiled, baked and now frozen in apple pies and chutneys. The watery light of an autumn, Sunday afternoon played on tenacious leaves still clinging to the branches....reluctant to let go of summer.

Both of them were red in the face and still panting for breath. Martha detected a male bonding had been under way, with the football being a sort of go- between.

The garden was a large, two hundred yards long falling gently to the brook at its' southern boundary. It was fifty yards wide bounded on one side by the neighbour's fence and on the other by a line of shrubs. Beyond was common land marking the edge of the village.

They had bought the house fifteen years earlier. Four bedrooms, three bathrooms were rather more than they'd ever needed but Martha wanted the space as the hope of a family still flickered. Peter was drawn to the garden and to the study/library whose French doors gave out to the herb garden and whose high ceilings gave "space for ideas to bloom." His first act had been to paint the library in pastel shades and then deck out his philosophy books on bookcases against three of the walls. This was his nesting instinct. Kant, Popper, Plato, Aristotle, Hume were the twigs and down which made his eyrie.

As each box of books was emptied and the shelves filled, he felt the room become a home for his own thoughts and the quiet reflections of these immortals. Here, every significant argument, paradox, fallacy of Western thought was within arms-reach. Here Plato, Locke and Russell could sit shoulder-to-shoulder, front to back, prologue to epilogue, no longer separated by centuries. Here, Peter was amongst the closest of friends; men who understood his dilemmas because they had grappled with them too; men who had lived at twenty thousand feet, lungs straining to catch the rarefied air of ideas and problems that never exercised the majority. Those men whose legacy was never obsolete and was still read....if only by other students of philosophy; men who stood apart from the world as observers and analysts rather than participants..... men like him.

Martha had gladly surrendered the library to Peter at first. It seemed a small price to pay to get the house she wanted. Georgian, once a rectory, it was the style of her parents' house, one she had always loved right down to the cellar, the pantry/scullery and the stubborn sash windows. But as the years passed, barren, she became more aware of the unused space, the closed doors of spare bedrooms and the cold spots where radiators were turned off. Peter and she could not fill the house; they couldn't give off enough warmth to make it feel fully lived in.

Peter would spend much of his time in his study and she in her office or meeting rooms in the City. 'Home' became a kitchen, a study, one bedroom and, occasionally, with guests, one of the three reception rooms. She had wondered lately about selling the house and them moving into something much smaller,. It would be more practical, more suited to a middle-aged couple. But to do so meant admitting something she hadn't wanted to give voice to. Peter knew, but kept quiet too. Many of their greatest collaborations were done silently.

So, the house stood two thirds empty with Peter and Martha occupying only its hinterland, like hotel guests who never unpacked their suitcases .

Until Anselm came along .

Within days of Anselm's arrival, the house was opened up. An inquisitive fifteen -year old changes the ecosystem. First he has a bedroom and a bathroom; next the TV room gets switched on; the smallest reception room becomes his 'classroom' for working with Emily; then footballs, clothes, sneakers and all those other essential accumulations of teenagers start to infest the once closed spaces. A teenager can colonise a four-bedroom, three- bathroom house very rapidly. Now 'The Rectory' cast off that austerity taken on from vicars, philosophers, business people. It cast off its incompleteness and became the 'family home' estate agents had once so hopefully described.

"Come and sit down, it's a beautiful day," said Peter. He'd seen Martha hesitate to break the spell of maleness in the air, binding him and Anselm.

"I should start to prepare lunch," said Martha.

"Not yet. Let's sit out for a while. A few more weeks and it'll be too cool to do this. Besides Anselm hasn't quite finished on the fundamental questions of rules and right and wrong," Peter winked at him.

Anselm had tried to continue the debate whilst they were playing football but Peter had pleaded shortage of breath. At the age of fifty-one and with a largely sedentary life, playing uphill against a fifteen-year old took all of his wind and concentration.

Martha took another chair, vaguely pleased, for once, not to be relegated to the housewife role.

"What is it you want to ask, Anselm?"

"I was wondering who it was that made all the rules. You know, you were talking about laws and said that the people made the laws to protect themselves. Which people made the laws; who decided what would be right and what would be wrong?"

“Laws are made by the Government,” said Peter, “which is made up of a small number of people who represent the interests of the wider population. The Government is a bit like the referee in a football side. The rest of the team might decide who will be the referee and then look to that person for guidance on when things arewithin the rules and when they are not. For example, he decides on fouls, offsides, free-kicks and can even send a player off the pitch if they keep breaking the rules.”

Anselm had seen the referees on the TV. They had whistles and didn’t seem to be very popular with the players. Still, he could understand that the referee decided right and wrong even if at least half the players usually disagreed with him whenever he blew his whistle.

Martha continued. “Well a government isn’t usually just one person. There are different types of government in the world. A few do depend on one person, but in this country, and many others, we have a form of government, which we call ‘democracy’. That means the government is made up of people chosen by the population as a whole.....or at least those who are allowed to vote.” Martha decided to skate over this last point.

“Every few years we have a vote when the people say who they want to have in the Government. We each get one choice....generally. The people chosen then get together and form the Government. I’m oversimplifying a bit because, when we vote, we are choosing people who belong to one of several groups called ‘parties .It is the party with the greatest number of votes who form the

Government. The others form what's called 'the opposition'."

"Like two football teams playing against each other." chimed Anselm.

"Yes, sort of ."

"So, the 'party' that forms the Government is not only the referee but is also one of the sides playing in the match. I bet they win most of the matches!"

"It's not quite like that....but I take your point Anselm. Peter's analogy of the football match doesn't quite stretch that far," said Martha. Peter wasn't so sure.

"So, once we have a Government they elect a leader called the Prime Minister and get down to making some laws . They write laws and then, in turn. vote to decide which ones should be .....er.....made law. This has happened over hundreds of years. So, the laws we have today are an accumulation of laws passed by many governments over the centuries. When a new Government comes into power they may create additional laws or amend some of the old ones."

"Why didn't the earlier Governments finish the job properly?" asked Anselm.

"Well, the world changes and so does the type of laws you need with it."

"So, laws can change. Perhaps if you waited long enough, something that was once wrong might become right" mused Anselm. "Problem is you might have spent all the time in between in prison."

"How many people are there in the Government usually?" he asked.

"In this country there are about six hundred people in what is called the House of Commons. Three hundred might be members of the party in power which forms the Government . It is these six hundred who make laws," explained Peter."

"And how many people are there altogether in this country?" asked Anselm. He thought he had seen more than five hundred people at the football matches on the TV...but things never stood still long enough for him to count.

"Sixty million ."

" Wow" Anselm gasped. "And only six hundred get a say as to what's going to be right or wrong?"

"Well, no. We get our say by choosing these people in the first place. That's the meaning of democracy. We the people as a whole get to choose the lawmakers and if we don't like what they get up to then we can change them.....after five years." Peter was starting to feel apologetic.

“I’ve got it, I think,” said Anselm. “Sixty million people vote to find six hundred. That’s.......one for each hundred thousand. Those six hundred are supposed to represent the rest.The six hundredare split into two or more teams and argue about what should be law and what shouldn’t....and then they take a vote which is usually won by the team which is the biggest – the Government... which is led by one man...a bit like a referee or a captain, maybe. So, after all this, one man probably makes most of the decisions.”

“Well, hopefully not,” said Peter. “The six hundred should be strong willed individuals who won’t let one person or even a small group of people dominate matters too much. Otherwise we might just as well have only a King or Queen or some dictator.”

“So, when will I be asked who I want in the Government ?”

“Not until you are eighteen years old. People younger than that are not allowed to vote .”

Anselm was not very surprised. He had suspected for a while that his business of making rules was really designed for the convenience of only a limited number of people. There didn’t seem to be any rules about looking after the people in Somalia for example

“How many people are there who are younger than 18?”

“About fifteen million .”

“And are there any others who aren’t allowed to vote?”

“Well, people in prison having broken the law can’t vote. And nor can those who are said to be ‘insane’,” said Peter.

“The people who broke the rules don’t get a say in deciding who makes the rules. No wonder they go around breaking them....nobody asked their opinion

Martha giggled.

“From the people who are allowed to vote, there’s maybe only just over half who actually cast their vote in the election There’s no guarantee they’ll get the person they voted for into the House of Commons and even then he or she may not be part of the Government. And even if they are, the person who voted them in will probably spend the next five years criticising them and will vote for someone else when the next chance comes.” Peter warmed to the theme.

By this stage Anselm was beginning to wonder whether Peter and Martha were making all of this up....just to justify the rules that they had made. But then he thought surely they would have come up with a more believable explanation.

“Well it’s interesting to know that I have the same level of input to this whole process as the people you call criminal or insane,” said Anselm with more than a hint of reproach. “If I can’t vote for others, maybe people could vote for me to join the Government?”

“Not until you are eighteen, I’m afraid.”

Anselm thought this business of rule-making was maybe one he should find a way of getting involved in. How else was he going to stay out of prison?

“What kind of people get chosen to join the House of Commons? asked Anselm. “How come they get chosen, are they smarter than the rest of us or just more ‘good’ ?”

Peter saw a chance to express a few more personal prejudices. “They are what we call politicians. Generally, they have a point of view on most things. That point of view is developed so it is popular with as many people as possible so those people are more likely to vote for that politician when the election comes around. There are some things that people generally agree on and on which politicians have the same view. For example, causing physical harm to someone else – most people ..”

“Except the criminal and insane,” chirped Anselm.

“.....agree that is a bad thing and against the law. But there are other things on which there are a variety of views.For example, which groups of people should pay what rate of tax. On these things politicians have to choose a view they represent. They will choose a popular view to maximise the votes they can attract, usually arguing that it is really good for everyone. If it looks like too many people are against what they propose then the politician will either change their position or, more likely, they will make it so vague that everyone concludes it is good for them And, where in doubt, a spot of lying is standard political practice."

A new word. Lying .Or rather a different way of using it. Anselm would lie on his bed but he was sure Peter didn't mean the politicians just lay around.

"What does lying mean?" he asked.

Martha responded: "Telling untruths . Saying something which is not true, not factual .Usually when people lie it's in orderto mislead someone else; to get them believing something is the case when it's not. For example ,if I said Peter is ninety -hree years old I would be telling a lie....not a very serious one, but a lie all the same because I know it's not true. More seriously, if you had said to me ,when I found the thirty pounds in your pocket, that you didn't put it there.....you would have been lying. Telling lies is another rule, certainly in this house. We don't do it."

Martha's strong Catholic upbringing was on the front foot. Anselm had been hoping that there would be no more mention of the notes he had taken. If he'd known that lying had been an option he might have been tempted to use it. But he hadn't. Probably a good job as two wrongs might have really gotten him into trouble. Why anyone would lie about his or her age or anyone else's was not clear to him.

Anselm went quiet. He had a sense that opening his mouth right at that moment might be risky. Peter did so instead and, to Anselm's relief, deflected the conversation back to the politicians who seemed to Anselm in any event to have a lot more to answer for.

"I have to say that in my view a lot of politicians, if not the majority, bend the truth or are economical with it and some are out and out liars," said Peter continuing his character assassination.

Anselm didn't understand 'bend the truth' or 'economical' but got the general idea that Peter wasn't 'friendly' with many politicians. He also got the sense that there were lies and there were nearl-ies and he wondered at what point you got to a full lie. Was it like the fractions that Emily had been teaching him. Two halves made a whole one maybe.

"I don't agree with Peter that all of politicians are cast in the same mould," said Martha. "You make all politicians sound like liars just grasping for power, Peter. Don't you think there's at least an element of principle....or are we dumb voters hoodwinked all the time?"

"I don't vote, for that very reason. We are presented with a choice, yes, choosing the lesser of several evils. I'd rather abstain. It's in the nature of people who like to stand on soap-boxes, kiss strange babies heads and make grandiose promises that they are not to be trusted. Why should I be forced to choose one liar over another?"

"Well at least they live in the real world rather than one filled with doubt," Martha retorted taking a simultaneous dig at Peter and Descartes. She didn't like Peters black and white tone.

“Real world? The world politicians inhabit is one where we can’t feed our poor, heal our sick or keep our elderly warm because we are too busy invading countries who don’t share our real world, Western ‘values’”

The temperature was rising. Politics and social justice were subjects that evoked Peter’s dormant, undergraduate idealist. Academic philosophy comprised ‘safe’ subjects like existential doubt-which, paradoxically, even Peter couldn’t get emotionally worked up about.

“I think we should stop there. I don’t want Anselm to catch your cynicism. He will come to his own views in time , no doubt.”

“My cynicism? Once upon a time you called it idealism. Funny how the passage of time can turn heroes into villains.” Peter’s face was red and his voice trembling.

Martha realised the stakes in the conversation had been raised too high and tried to get back to the relative calm of explaining society’s system of rules to Anselm.

“Okay. Perhaps you were just exaggerating to make a point, I don’t know” said Martha.

Anselm wondered if ‘exaggerating’ meant Peter was telling the truth, a lie or somewhere in between. He had watched the two of them throughout this exchange. For some reason he was reminded of the dream dialogue between Berkeley and Descartes. They seemed to be arguing about one thing but the real difference between them was something else; something unsaid.

"I'd better get on with lunch," said Martha taking the opportunity to draw a line under social ethics for the time being.

"Can I have some volunteers for potato peeling, please?"

***

VI MORE RULES

Mondays was Maths and Science. Anselm enjoyed these subjects the most. They seemed somehow to be more real for him. He didn't want to live in France so speaking French didn't seem much of a priority and he had little interest in the History of things that happened tens or hundreds of years ago. There was enough to learn about the ' here and now or' what might happen in the near future without examining things you can't change.

Emily had tried to justify the History lessons on the basis that one could learn from the past – its' successes and failures- and that to really understand today's world one had to know where our institutions, cultures and way of life had come from. Anselm couldn't see how the love affairs of Kings and Queens in the middle ages or the Roman's long extinguished occupancy of France was of any relevance to his life.

There were plenty of other things he needed to have a better understanding of. Having made some progress on identifying his 'self', making a willing suspension of disbelief in the existence of the physical world and starting to learn some rules he thought he had better concentrate on Geography and Science since these were the subjects which seemed to have most to say on reality and the laws that govern it.

So, when Emily arrived, punctual as always, on Monday morning, Anselm was eager and full of questions. She had taught him already about the law of gravity, about the speed of light (VERY fast), about electricity, temperatures , freezing and melting points; about atoms, neutrons, electrons; about human anatomy and some basic chemical reactions. Throughout all this she had talked about the 'laws' of nature. Fresh from his conversations with Martha and Peter about the 'do not steal' kind of laws, he wondered whether nature's laws were the similar.

"Was Isaac Newton the Prime Minister?" he asked. "Why would you think that? Replied Emily, intrigued .

Anselm didn't like this habit of adults, replying to ones questions with a question of their own. How did anyone ever get an answer instead of going around in circles with question and counter question...like a game of 'dare'.

"He was the guy who made the law about gravity. Martha and Peter have explained that laws are made by the Government....and the main person in the Government is the Prime Minister..."Anselm summarised.

Emily chuckled. The notion of a politician making the laws of the Universe didn't really bear thinking of. What a strange world we might then live in. Things would fall down or up according to what was politically convenient. Light would travel at varying speeds according to which was most popular with the voters . Ships would float or sink depending on Government trade policies and embargoes. We could lose the moon from its orbit , and worse, if the Government decided Plank's Constant needed revision. It might of course be much easier and a smaller drain on the U.S. economy to put a man on Mars....so there was some upside from new governance arrangements for the Universe...but ,on balance...

"The laws of the Universe are rather different to those of men," explained Emily. She thought for a moment trying to conjure up an explanation for this rather bald assertion.

"The laws of men are standards to live by, based on what is seen as right and wrong; good and bad. The laws of the Universe are not about people's behaviour or what's morally right or wrong. Instead they describe the rules by which the Universe or nature operates.

"Like the rules of a game?" asked Anselm. He remembered having asked Peter that the day before.

"A bit like that....but, then again not really," replied Emily getting a bit vague. "Men invent the rules of games but discover the laws of the Universe. These laws are a set of rules which determine the workings of the Universe...why it is how it is,... and they don't change. They are not made by men , they just are what they are, and,scientists spend much of their time trying to discover what they are."

Anselm understood this distinction and was reassured that the process Peter had described about electing Governments was not necessary to keep the kettle boiling.This need to discover what they are sounded like a mystery game on the net.

Still he found the answer “laws of the Universe” just “are” a little unsatisfying. Something seemed to be missing. “If the laws ‘just are’, why aren’t they just... .different. Surely somehow these laws were chosen from amongst others as the most suitable way to have the Universe tick along. “

He knew enough about electricity and conductors ; that the element in the kettle needed to be made of metal, not wood, if it was going to heat up the water. The person who designed the kettle decided to design it that way, knowing that was the best choice if he wanted a cup of tea. Surely someone had chosen how the Universe should be constructed and to what rules....so that it would work well?

Anselm put this argument to Emily.

“Well, there are many people who would say that there is a ‘person’ who made the laws of the Universe and that that person is ‘God’” said Emily.

“Who?” asked Anselm somewhat disingenuously as he had heard Martha speak of God and the Church before. When he had quizzed Martha he had found that God was a rather mysterious being, unseen, unheard but present everywhere and was ‘the maker of all things.’ The notion had seemed implausible to Anselm and he had decided not to spend any more time on it, although Martha had said she wanted to talk more God in the future. She had said it in a similar way to the way she asked for volunteers for potato peeling.

"Well, God is the maker of all things, he is eternal and though you can't see him, he is all powerful. He created the Universe and its' laws," said Emily.

Nothing new there then thought Anselm . "So, God made the Universe, then?" he said.

"Yes."

"So, who made God?"

"Nobody ."

"Nobody ?"

"No, God is timeless. He neither started nor will He end. He is eternal. He had no beginning and so wasn't 'made' by anyone or anything ." Emily's answers seemed to be very much in line with those of Martha and just as bizarre. There was clearly some room for debate about God because when he had asked Peter for his view on the guy and his origin, Peter had simply muttered, "Case unproven" and then scuttled away from Martha's disapproving look.

"So, God has been around forever and at some point he decided to make the Universe and a bunch of laws. What was he doing before he made the Universe then?" asked Anselm.

"To be honest, I don't know. I guess he had other things to think about." Emily was feeling out of her depth.

“I don’t see what else he could have been doing or even thinking about. If the Universe includes everything then before he made it there would have been nothing around. I’m not sure what he could have been busy with...other than maybe just thinking and about what.”

“Well I guess he could have been thinking about what he wanted the world ...er... .the Universe to be like. He could have been planning things,” ventured Emily unconvincingly.

“That’s an awful lot of planning. And I’m not sure it’s paid off. Seems to me quite a lot of things could have been improved on. Anyway, I’m not sure it would have taken someone as smart and powerful as God, at least as Martha explained him to me, forever less fifteen billion years to come up with a plan for a Big Bang and a set of laws.”

Emily realised Anselm was rather better informed on cosmology and God’s attributes than he would have her think.

“There are plenty of people who don’t believe in God. They don’t believe that such a divine maker exists. Some of those people believe that the Universe either has existed by itself forever and naturally moved in line with laws which themselves have applied forever with no beginning. Others might say the Universe did start with the ‘Big Bang’ before which there was just....nothingness, continued Emily.

“What do you believe? “ asked Anselm.

“I believe there is a God, that He created the Universe, that He is good and He is concerned with the world of men and women and watches over how we conduct our lives....how we distinguish between right and wrong, good and evil...and He wants us to pursue the path of goodness,” confessed Emily.

Anselm thought for a few moments.

“Well I don’t know how anyone is ever going to settle the argument since even you and Martha, who believe in Him ,agree that we can’t see, hear or touch him in our normal lives. I guess even if we could see some candidates for the position of God, we would have difficulty in checking out that person’s qualifications. Who is going to check that this God has lived forever? Even with a time machine or God doing us a favour by speeding up light a fair bit that’s a long journey.”

“For me it’s not a question of seeing Him. I experience Him every day in my life. I’m aware of His presence. You could say I ‘see’ Him with my heart,” replied Emily.

‘Some anatomical inconsistencies here,’ thought Anselm, but he let it pass as he sensed this was a very serious subject for Emily.

He switched tack.

“I’m not sure right now what to think about God. It’s difficult to see how the Universe and its laws could have started by themselves. But if God started things off, who made God? The answer seems to be He was always there or just popped up ut of nowhere. If that's the best explanation we can find, we might as well just believe the Universe was there forever or just popped up....bringing in God seems to just double the mystery."

"It i*s* a mystery and no-one has all the answers", Emily responded. " But those who believe do so out of faith and a feeling of God's presence rather than some scientific or logical proof. Talk to Martha and Peter some more about this . I think maybe we need to get on with the science lessons," she said, a little conscious that Religious Education wasn't on the syllabus she had agreed with the couple.

Anselm agreed to move on, somewhat reluctantly. It seemed to him that learning how the Universe worked was all well and good but it involved a lot of trial and error. Getting a better understanding of God and his intentions in making all this stuff and the rules that drove it ought to be a better route....but he admitted to himself he couldn't quite see how to do that right now.

Emily continued the lesson she had started last time around on the properties of light. She told him about light waves, reflection and refraction. She explained the principles of the human eye, how a prism split light into its' different colours and how rainbows were made.

Throughout, Anselm was attentive and engaged but at the back of his mind was this question of what God had in mind with all this.

He summarised what she had told him about how the eye worked, and how people 'saw' things.

"So light waves , or particles , depending, come from the sun, ninety-three million miles away and they bounce off the billions of atoms that make up objects. Then the waves , or paritlcles go into my eye where they go through the lens and get focussed, upside down, on the back of my eye. This sets off some electric signals which travel through my optic nerve into my brain which is a collection of cells with lots of different pathways to carry these signals and then.....I see the table, the right way up."

"That's it," affirmed Emily.

"Well it's a good job light travels very fast indeed otherwise by the time I saw something it would be history. Imagine, if it was much slower, I might be seeing you and talking to you after you've left to go to your next appointment. It's a good job also that the speed of light and the speed of sound are such that I don't notice a big gap between you drawing on the flip chart and you saying something about the angle of the light rays in the diagram."

"Well of course there is a big difference in speeds but over short distances you don't notice it. Next time there is a rainstorm, count the seconds between seeing the lightening and hearing the thunder," explained Emily.

"And I suppose it's a good job my brain turns the table the right way up," Anselm continued, "or I suppose it is.

But then if everything, including my hands and my body were upside down, then it would look the right way up wouldn't it?" His head was spinning with trying to envisage a world in which everything looked upside down including himself. Surely everything would look the same?

"What exactly happens when the electrical signals go into my brain? You say that's when we 'see' but when I see this table it seems to be here in front of me....not in my head, and 'seeing' something doesn't seem like electricity....which is invisible, right?" Anselm was far from convinced of Emily's explanation at all. It didn't leave him feeling he understood any better how he 'saw' something Okay, the process of the light bouncing around and going into his eye he could live with, but there seemed to be a step missing when things reached the brain.

She had told him about the workings of the ear and also how people smell things. These processes also seemed to have a missing step. Just how was it that the smell which was in the coffee got into his brain....he didn't have bits of coffee swilling around in his head.

Emily tried the analogy with the TV set. The camera taking pictures turned them into a different language...electrical impulses....which were stored and then transmitted as radio signals ("a bit like light waves but invisible to humans") which were then used to reform the original picture on the screen so we could watch. She suggested Anselm think of the act of seeing as if there were a screen somewhere receiving signals from the outside world and reconstituting the image.

Anselm could see Emily was trying hard but this just begged the question of where the screen was and anyway it just delayed the problem; it didn't solve it. However the TV pictures got onto the screen, there was still the issue of how we see them. This act of seeing seemed entirely different to him to having a projector and screen somewhere in his head. Even if there was room up there and a nice image of the table on the screen, he would then still have to look at it and 'see' it.

He was beginning to think Bishop Berkeley had a point about the existence, or rather non-existence, of the physical world. We seem to take all our comfort that the world exists from our senses....from seeing, hearing, touching, smelling...but there was a big gap in the process which Emily was at a loss to explain.

"That last step of seeing is still something that puzzles scientists and philosophers, like Peter. It's about the difference between mind and body. Your mind is a different kind of 'place'....or rather, not really a place at all. When we talk about seeing or hearing something we sort of mix the two up. The something we think of as a physical, material thing 'out there' whereas the act of seeing or hearing is a mental process; one that takes place in the mind."

"But the mind isn't a place, you said," corrected Anselm.

“I’m sorry. Even our language tricks us. No, I was using the word ‘place’ in a metaphorical sense....really there isn’t a proper answer to the question “where do I see?” because it’s not a proper question” said Emily.

Anselm thought this was another of the last hiding places of adults. If you don’t know the answer to a question, then just rubbish the question. He was surprised at Emily but could see she didn’t have the answers.

Emily saw the disappointed look in his eyes....and fleetingly thought that the notion of seeing ‘a look in his eyes’ was somewhat of a paradox of mind body interaction in itself.

“I’m reaching the limits of what I can teach you here Anselm. I think Peter may be better placed to take this discussion further with you. Why don’t you ask him about the mind and what we know of it?”

“I will” complied Anselm, conscious that Peter himself exhibited a significant degree of confusion over reality.

He returned to an earlier topic. “When we say that something is a law of nature, what exactly do we mean? I can see it’s not the same as men’s laws but are these ***rules*** that nature has to obey and if so how do we know they are laws? For example, what if I woke up one morning, found the sun shining on a warm July day but the brook at the end of our garden was frozen over? Who says that couldn’t happen?

Emily felt a sense of relief to be back on more familiar ground.

"Well, assuming a warm day means well above 0°C and there hadn't been a recent drop in temperatures, then we know the river couldn't freeze over a because water only freezes at that temperature. That's a law of nature....just as water only boils at 100°C....at least it does if it's pure and is at normal sea-level, atmospheric pressure."

Suddenly a 'law' had become an 'if'. Anselm ignored the caveats but noted that what started off as a certainty had now become a little doubtful.

"But how do we know water always freezes at 0°C and never above that temperature?" he probed.

"Through observation .By seeing water freeze on many occasions and always finding that this happens and only happens at temperatures of 0°C or below .This is the fundamental basis of all science and the discovery of nature's laws – 'empirical' observation. When we see that one event always follows another we link the two and say the first event 'causes' the second. By observing water at different temperatures scientists discovered that water always freezes when the temperature drops to 0°C or below. More than that, we say the reduction in temperature 'causes' freezing.

"Similarly , men found that physical bodies attract other physical objects; the earth attracts the raindrop and the sun attracts the earth and vice versa.

“ Newton went further and discovered the ‘law’ of gravity, which says that all bodies attract each other with a force proportional to their masses. This was then described through a mathematical formula which allows us to calculate the force acting on a raindrop or on a stone making it fall to earth.”

“So,” she continued, “not only do we know that when we drop a stone from the top of a building, or indeed when an apple falls from a tree, that it will fall directly to the earth’s surface but Newton discovered the equation which governs the force and therefore the speed with which the stone will fall .Here it is; she drew in Anselm's exercise book :-

$$F= Gm_1\ m_2\ r^2$$

.........which basically says the force of attraction between two objects depends on how far they are apart (r) and their masses (m1,m2). The bigger and closer they are the stronger the force of attraction.”

For a fleeting moment Anselm wondered if the law applied to people ...Martha and Peter were bigger than him and lived in the same house but if anything seemed to push each other away. They seemed more like two North poles, remembering his lesson on magnetism.

Anselm had already done some basic algebra with Emily in his Maths lessons. He seemed to have an immediate grasp of mathematical concepts, which didn’t rely on his limited experience of the world. But this equation was a bit more complex that the ones he had met thus far.

“What does ‘G’ stand for?” he asked.

“Ah, that’s the gravitational constant,” replied Emily. “It’s one of the universal constants-the same anywhere in the universe”

“So, we can test that these equations do represent a Universal law by doing experiments where, for example, we take differing objects at different distances and measure the force of gravity ‘between them ‘,” said Emily. And we find always that the equation holds true. That’s the genius of Newton’s discovery. It enabled him to predict the movement of the planets in the solar system and the moon’s orbit around the earth.”

“Just how did he go about weighing the moon and measuring its distance from the earth?” wondered Anselm, not really expecting an answer.

“He found the distance by trigonometry, in fact, others had done that before him. We looked at that in Maths, if you remember.”

Anselm thought it was one thing to measure how far up a wall a ladder might reach and another thing altogether to calculate that the sun was ninety-three million miles away. Who’s to say that rules that hold true over a few feet do so over millions of miles . And if they don’t, would we ever be any the wiser?

“So, a law of nature is not just the fact that one event is linked to, or causes, another event consistently, but it’s where there is some underlying connection, some rule that links them. And if we can discover that rule then we can predict how things will behave, like stones falling, planets orbiting, water freezing or light bending through a prism. All of these have physical laws which explain and predict what will happen in certain situations," continued Emily.

"I've noticed that whenever I have a bath at some point I lose the soap and it always takes me ages to find it again. Is that one of the laws of nature and is there a formula which predicts the position of the soap? If there was it would be awfully useful , although I guess it might mean having a ruler and calculator ready at hand in the bathroom?"

"Wel there are some physical laws operating when that happens, yes, including the laws of friction, or lack of it, and gravity, itself. But just because it always happens doesn't mean it's bound to happen ....it's dependent on you being a 'butter-fingers!' So, we wouldn't say that 'every time Anselm gets in the bath he loses the soap' is a law of the universe, however regularly it happens. There is no underlying cause which makes it inevitable. Frankly when people are involved it is difficult to discover any universal laws governing what happens because they often act arbitrarily or have accidents."

"What about 'every time I get in the bath I get wet,' how's that for a physical law?"

"Yes, I suppose so....it's nearer to one; actually , there are a number of physical laws happening there but, yes, that's a situation where wetness follows with certainty due to the operation of physical laws."

"Only if I've turned the taps on . Just like light goes in straight lines...except when it doesn't!" retorted Anselm with that mischievous light in his eyes.

"Going back to gravity, I understand that Maths can help us predict how things move and that we use the word gravity to refer to objects attracting each other; but how does gravity work? You've told me how we might calculate the effect it has on something but how does it actually work? What is doing the pulling and with what?"

"We are getting somewhat ahead of ourselves. That's a question for advanced physics. A long time ago men thought that this force resulted from particles moving between two objects; more recently Einstein said that physical bodies with mass bend space- time and that was what really gave rise to the motions of the planets. Astronomers have found that light from a distant star bends when it passes planets in our solar system and other experiments support the idea now that gravity isn't some kind of attraction between objects so much as a following of a path in space time."

"Wow," said Anselm, "another example of bendy light ...and space too? Does that mean Newton got it wrong?"

"Well I suppose you could say he got it approximately right. His equations work on most scales; it's just that when you observe something the scale of the Universe or as small as the atom, you test the limits of his laws and his equations. Einstein and others discovered new laws that more accurately predict events at a sub-atomic or... .astronomic scale," replied Emily.

"Not bad, getting a knighthood for being nearly right. Wonder if you will let me off in my Maths test if I get things nearly right."

"We have to remember that before Newton there was little or no understanding of the laws that govern the motion of objects. He made major breakthroughs in man's understanding. But the process of scientific discovery and refining our understanding of the workings of the world never ends. No doubt in another hundred years we'll look back at Einstein in the same way and say – 'good try'," replied Emily, feeling Newton in need of some defence from the irreverence of a teenager.

"Well, all I can say is that if there is a God , and it was God who is responsible for all these complicated laws of the Universe, then I can well see he would have needed a lot of time to plan things. He must be an ace mathematician too since it's taken all these brilliant minds to, almost figure out what the rules are. It does make you wonder why God made it so difficult. It's a bit like a game of hide and seek."

Anselm was becoming rather agitated.

"God invents a bunch of rules, creates a very small, very dense bit of stuff from nothing and then kicks off the game. Several billion years later through an amazing series of accidents you described as evolution, man arrives on the scene scratching his collective head, wondering what it's all about and how everything works. It's a bit like if you came to our lessons and you said to me "now please speak French", when you hadn't taught me a word and you insisted on keeping all the textbooks closed. I hope God knows what he's up to because as far as I can see he is wasting a lot of people's time. But then I guess since he invented time it's for him to give or take it as he pleases. People might just run out of patience though, you know..."

Emily was unsure whether this was real or feigned outrage from Anselm but the boy certainly gave the impression that he had a bone to pick with the Divinity. Her religious faith was not affronted by Anselm's secular remonstrations. She rather admired the spark in a boy to whom so much was unfamiliar and everything, but everything, was open to question and cross-examination. She had never had such a pupil so bright and enquiring. Never one with this mix of sophistication in language and thought yet total naivety which questioned all that humans took for granted.

"....and stop trying to figure out how things work. We might just stick at a few approximations and say :"that'll do," no point in looking any further because every time we do it it's like peeling another layer off some kind of infinite onion. The more 'nearly' answers we find, the more questions there are hidden under the rocks of the answers. So, we are giving up now Mr God. We'll make do with what we've got. Most of us are not interested in the next rash of sub-atomic particles some sad scientist might find deep inside a mountain side; we've got far too many already to handle and just because we haven't 'seen' them separately we don't seem to have any problem with our tables falling to bits.

"No, this is where we're drawing the line; we have other pressing things to concentrate on like Somalia and making sure promises are kept. So any more laws you've got up your sleeve God, well you can just keep them there or maybe go off and create another Universe somewhere where you can make some more inquisitive species evolve, so you can watch them wandering around trying to figure out the what, how and who of everything. We , the human race, have had enough!

What is he going to do then?" Anselm continued. "He's got all these undiscovered laws and mysteries of the Universe, galaxies, particles which he has taken time to dream up, all just left on his hands...'cos no-one's interested any more..."

Anselm's voice tailed off. He became conscious of Emily just sitting there, dumbfounded as his voice got louder and more hoarse .And he was shaking; he wasn't cold so what was this? He fell quiet.

A few moments passed.

"Well Anselm, you certainly feel strongly about this. Do you know why?" She left a space for Anselm to answer ,but he just looked down at the table.

"I can see your point of view but I tend to give God the benefit of the doubt. I know him as a loving force for good in the world. Though his ways are mysterious my faith tells me He is benevolent and isn't just playing games with us like hamsters in a cage. But I think you are angry....do you know why you feel that way?" asked Emily, softly.

He hadn't felt this before. Emily calls it 'angry'. All he knew was that the world was far too complicated. He didn't know what else he was supposed to be doing but trying to understand this complicated piece of machinery and to catch up with everybody else on the planet suddenly just seemed too much.

Since time started on the heath it seemed to have been accelerating....maybe the force of gravity pulls on the days and hours too...and they fall faster and faster... towards what?

"I don't know," he said.

***

Emily left at 3.30 pm She had a sandwich lunch with Anselm and they had done some work on trigonometry. He had been very quiet after his outburst.

Martha arrived home early at 4.30 pm She had finished her last meeting of the day much earlier than scheduled. Some of her staff had brought a presentation to her on the three-year plan which she had pulled to pieces, telling them to go back and "do their homework". 'Anselm would have made a better job of it', she thought as she opened the front door to the house.

"Anselm. I'm home." She took off her coa, opened her mobile and looked at her e- mails. Bills....and an Instagram postcard from friends holidaying in the South of France . "Still warm here .Nathalie swimming a lot; John and I gorging ourselves on tourist menus. My French just good enough to ensure we don't eat anything too unusual. Love to you and Peter."

Anselm hadn't answered. Normally he would come to meet her, flooding her with questions about her day before she could even get her coat off.

She went to the TV room hearing the sound of late afternoon cartoons. Anselm was curled up in a ball a few feet away from the TV with the sound at a level only teenagers can tolerate . He looked comatose.

She knelt behind him, touching his shoulder. He didn't move; eyes open he was fixed on the TV screen where a cat was racing after a mouse, hammer in hand.

"Anselm, are you OK? What's the matter?" she asked with rising anxiety.

He didn't respond. She shook him gently by the shoulder. His eyes flickered and then shot a glance at her out of their corners.

What is it...darling?" She still wasn't accustomed to that or any other term of endearment. Martha's maternal instincts didn't know how to express themselves with confidence yet. She knew they were there....under the layers of past disappointment, but their language wasn't yet fluent.

A tear started out of the corner of Anselm's eye, slowly tracking across the bridge of his nose and falling to the carpet.

"Anselm, what is it?" She put her other arm under his neck and rolled him towards her lap. A moment's resistance gave way and he turned, laid his head on her thigh and started to sob. She held him as the tears soaked into the trousers of her business suit, wanting to move but not daring to. She didn't know what else to do but stroke his hair and wipe the tears with her thumb.

He didn't want to look at her. Minutes passed, the sobbing abated and his jaw dropped to find air. She took out a handkerchief and pinched it round his nose. "Blow".

He took a great gulp and blew as if his life depended on it, making a rasping noise that brought simultaneous peels of laughter from the two of them. His eyes found hers. Whatever was in the way had been dismantled by the laughter.

Martha turned the TV off.

"Come sit with me on the settee and let's find out what's been upsetting you" she said, coaxing as if with some frightened animal that might bolt with one move too sudden.

He lay facing her looking up, head on her lap.

"Do you want to tell me what happened?" She gazed at him. Every part of her focussed on him. When she had arrived home she was carrying all the tension of the day and on automatic pilot, head full of three- year plans, product launches, analyst presentations .Now these were gone, as if in some previous life, her whole attention now fixed on this boy .This teenager, this son of who knows who and when .She waited.

"I don't like this world," he started.

She felt a flush in her cheeks and a catch in her throat

.

"Don't you like it here...with Peter and me?" she asked, hardly daring..and stopped breathing.

He looked at her for a moment...the longest moment she had ever lived.

" No. I like it right here with you. I like being with Peter. I like talking to Emily.....and the house, the garden."

Suddenly he felt the need to mention everyone, everything important lest if he left them out they would be taken away.

Martha began to breathe again. "Then what is it that you don't like?"

“Rules. Rules I don’t know about. God playing tricks .People in charge making rules; telling lies .Dreams .... I don’t know where they begin or end. Light that goes straight one day, then bends the next. Promises that belong only to other people ... .like memories....” he blurted.

She recognised some of this jumble and imagined the other threads must have come from talking to Peter or Emily.

“What else?” she asked.

“Me.”

“What about you?”

“I’m different. I don’t come from anywhere. I don’t go to school like others of my age. And how old am I? I saw the babies and the younger children when we went to Gull Cove and I’ve seen them on the TV, but I’m not like them. And I’m not like you and Peter or Emily. And I can’t remember anything before the shepherd. Is everyone such a stranger in this world, like me? I don’t think so.”

Martha cupped his face with her hands.

“You are different Anselm....and beautifully so. Other people come into the world, crying for air and shocked....tiny, fragile, unable to tell us how they feel, still less able to ask questions of the world. You, you came into the world, our world, like ... like a jumping bean...." She struggled for the words...."fizzing up and down and sideways with raw energy and a thousand, ten thousand questions. You came into the world, a fifteen-year-old boy with fifteen years to catch up on, racing, exploring, going into places that many adults never visit and taking us with you. You are special Anselm and that's far, far better than just plain different."

The tears started to fall again. From two pairs of eyes. Anselm felt the stone buried in his chest seem to dissolve with the salty trickle falling down his cheeks and a warm, calmness spread inside like the feeling from a hot bath. Unknown to him the same feeling was flooding through Martha, like ink on blotting paper. He felt the edge of his face blur into her lap, melt into her warmth. She felt herself passing from guardian into mother. Anselm's tears were welcome now on her trousers; the more the better. With each drop she claimed him, closer and closer as a son.

The minutes passed, neither speaking, neither wanting to break the spell. Martha thought she could hear the kitchen clock ticking through the wall rhyming with the splash of Anselm's tears. She smelt his warmth. Every sense was tuned to wavelengths beyond the visible spectrum.

"I don't know why I'm here," he said finally .

"What do you mean, Anselm?"

"Well, all the other boys and girls in the world were born because their mothers and fathers wanted them and ***made*** them. Emily taught me; they come from the man and woman mixing together. They start life so small and are protected from the world. They grow gradually and learn things step by step; to walk, to talk...word by word... And eventually they go to school. So ,they know why they are here."

"Why?

"They are here because of their mothers and fathers; because they wished them here. And they are here to grow and one day have children too. That's what Emily told me as a law of nature."

"But you are here because Peter and I wanted you so much....I haven't told you how much I wished for you Anselm, but I did....and Peter too. And when you grow up I'm sure you will have children too. You have a head start on the rest."

Anselm wore that attentive, but doubting, look on his face as he stared up into Martha's eyes.

"It's not the same. You and Peter didn't make me, you ...sort of... found me. We don't know who made me. I don't know if I will be able to make children. Emily said the 'genes' pass down through each generation. How do I know I have some to pass on if I don't know where or who I came from . I don't remember ever being a baby, or learning to walk and talk. I don't remember being so small. Will I be able to teach my child something I've never known? And the world seems so mysterious with so many hidden rules. I don't know if it's safe enough. It doesn't seem very safe to me. Seems like anything could happen at any time. The whole thing could just pop out of existence like a balloon bursting. The Somalians could all die without food. Maybe we could too if the Bank of England broke its' promises..."

He was starting to get worked up again.

"Sshh..." She stroked his hair.

"Just because we don't know where your genes came from doesn't mean they aren't there. You are a healthy, walking, talking normal boy and you will have children Anselm. You will meet a girl one day and marry her just like Peter and me. You will have children in the normal way. Peter and I couldn't because there was something wrong with my womb...I couldn't make an egg and keep it...but that is very unusual. You will find a girl who doesn't have that problem, I'm sure."

He wondered how Martha could know these things but for perhaps the first time in his short life decided simply to believe what she said, without questioning.

The stone continued to dissolve.

"And I know you can't remember the experience of being a baby, then a toddler and learning all those basic skills but very few of us adults can remember much of that stuff either. It's a funny thing about memory :we remember very few things from those early days. It's like the camera wasn't working properly or we only had a few shots left on the film; not enough to make a proper record of all the things that were going on then.

“I don’t know where people learn to bring up children,” she felt that momentary flush of barrenness....then looked again into Anselm’s eyes this time to draw courage for herself,...“ but somehow we know. We learn from others. It’s trial and error, and we share the job with the person we marry.”

She searched for as many assurances as she could find. Anselm no longer heard the words, just the soothing tone of Martha’s voice. He felt waves of tiredness. Carrying the stone had been such an effort and now even his eyelids felt heavy. Gravity would have its way.

Martha sat still until the regular, slow, rise and fall of Anselm’s chest confirmed his sleep. She carefully peeled her lap away from underneath him holding his head cupped in her hands and laying it onto a cushion.

She stood and looked down on him. He pulled his knees up into the foetal position as if searching for the birth he had missed.

***

V11 HOW DO I FEEL?

When Peter arrived home, Anselm was still sleeping on the couch in the TV room. “Early for him to be asleep .Is he OK?” asked Peter .

“He was upset this afternoon. Poor child, I think he’s exhausted,” replied Martha. She recounted Anselm’s anxious outburst , and her attempts to reassure him.

“Poor kid, he’s having a mid-life existential crisis at fifteen,” joked Peter feebly.

“After a fashion he is. I think the avalanche of new experiences....everything .....has finally caught up with him. He was really disturbed this afternoon, railing against rules and God but most of all against his own differentness ."

"I guess growing up in a few months is going to create more than the usual dose of teenage growing pains," said Peter.

"Maybe, but I think we've been beguiled by his quick command of language, his physical size, his intelligence. We've been treating him like an adult with a few things to learn. He's not. He's not an adult. He's a tiny child inside, one who's overwhelmed by things we take for granted and one who's missed out on lots of steps. When I held him this afternoon I realised this boy hasn't been cuddled, he hasn't had the reassurance of being held by someone who loves him."

Peter looked at Martha. He couldn't voice his own longing.

"All this intellectual debate about reality, money, laws, time, is all very well, but the rest of us had time to learn about this stuff through interacting with the world and other people. It's like Anselm is having to cram for an exam. Worse still he doesn't have the anchor of a personal history, memories and relationships outside this house which help us to know who we are. The world must seem a pretty arbitrary, disconnected , hostile place to him."

Peter was feeling about five years of age himself at this point. Yes, Anselm's energy and inquisitiveness was childlike but his questions and glint of mischief, his impishness had made him seem in command of the world. He, Peter, should have known better.

"He can't express his feelings. He doesn't know how to name them. Can you remember him saying he was happy, sad, angry, fearful ? I can't. He was crying this afternoon and that seemed to be as much a surprise to him as it was to me. He was ambushed by his own anger and frustration and not even able to give them a name. Imagine how frightening that must be."

Martha had the bit between her teeth. Peter felt accused, unaware that Martha's reproach was for herself.

"We have to be more conscious of his emotional development. Fifteen years of old; his hormones will be running riot; any normal teenager gets pretty screwed up but think of the cocktail inside Anselm. I'm amazed he hasn't blown a fuse before now. We have to help him become more aware of his feelings, give him the language and space to express them."

"Express his feelings, like we do? Do you think we're qualified?" Peter blurted. "When's the last time we gave each other space to express how we're feeling. I don't know about you but I'm not sure what I'm feeling most of the time. Ask me to put a name to members of this elusive category called 'feelings' and I'll struggle to get past three…sad, lonely and angry."

Martha stopped, stock-still. The truth lay on the floor between them.

At that moment Anselm wandered into the room, rubbing his eyes. "What are you shouting about?" he asked.

***

Time froze. Martha was stuck in the moment before and the echoes of what Peter had said. Stuck with the discomfort of truth.

Peter felt a mixture of relief that the genie was out of the bottle, and fear of what the consequences could be.

Anselm bought them time to gather themselves as he went to the cookie jar.

"Not too many of those Anselm. I'm going to make dinner soon," Martha tried to anchor herself back into familiar routine .

"Why don't you two go for a walk along the river bank before it gets dark .It's a lovely evening." She needed them to go.

Peter took the opportunity, "yes, let's go Anselm...put a jacket on the weather's getting cooler."

Minutes later they were pushing through the gate at the bottom of the garden and onto the path along the brook.

"What were you two talking about when I came in?" asked Anselm after a few minutes.

“Oh ,nothing much”, replied Peter immediately aware of how implausible he sounded.” We were talking about feelings actually,” replied Peter, not sure how much more to offer.

Anselm remembered the last walk along the riverbank when they had talked about ‘I’ and the self. Peter had talked then about feelings...feeling pain for example.

Peter thought of a game they could play...a variant on ‘I spy’. It was as much to divert himself as Anselm.

“Suppose we each start a sentence with I’m feeling or I feel....and then name a feeling. Then maybe....the other says a colour or a thing that’s like that feeling or reminds us of that feeling.”

Anselm thought for a moment. He wasn’t sure he could do this; it seemed a bit too much like French vocabulary. He decided to have a go anyway. “I’ll go first,” he said. Somewhere at the back of his mind he was worried he might run out of feelings so he had better get in first.

“I feel...the breeze,” announced Anselm.

“Ah!” exclaimed Peter. Not quite what he had in mind but he’d play along. “Makes me think of...clouds...clouds moving with the breeze .”

Anselm thought this a rather weak connection and hoped the game would get more interesting .“ Your turn,” he said .

“I feel...hungry,” responded Peter.

“Roast potatoes,” said Anselm, imagining Martha busy at home cooking dinner. “Ok. But what colour is hungry or can you tell me where you feel hungry?” Anselm paused. Colour? He closed his eyes. “Brown.”

“Why brown?”

“Because that’s the colour of those lovely roast potatoes Martha makes.”

“Ok” said Peter. “***Wher***e do you feel hunger?”

Anselm now looked for the hunger .

“It’s in my stomach, here,” he pointed.

“Good,” said Peter.

Anselm disagreed.

“Now you,” said Peter.

“I feee ... eel...cold,” offered Anselm.

“I did tell you to put your jacket on,” admonished Peter.

“It’s just a game you know” said Anselm.

“So, what does ‘cold’ make you think of Peter?”

"It makes me think of...a shiver, a shiver through my body."

"And what colour is it?"

"It's like ice."

Anselm mimed approval .He had had ice cubes in his coca-cola. "Your turn again," he said .

"I feel happy," said Peter.

Anselm paused again. He knew the word. He knew it was good; but he wasn't very sure what would count as happy.

"Somalians with food" he guessed after a few moments.

'Very altruistic,' thought Peter. "That's a good image Anselm. But can you think of another thing that has made you happy?"

Anselm searched.

"How about Gull Cove ?Do you remember when at the end of the day Martha, you and me stood arms linked at the water's edge? You were happy then?" asked Peter.

Anselm nodded. He remembered and felt his body relax. This was 'happy'.

"I feel afraid," said Anselm.

“Yes. My ‘afraid’ is...spiders, big, hairy with long legs....in my bed,” confessed Peter.

Anselm blinked . “Really?”

“Well, yes a little bit. I don’t care for spiders much. Never have done since I was tiny,” explained Peter trying to water down his confession.

“And where is this fear....and what colour?” quizzed Anselm..

“It’s in my stomach and in my throat,” replied Peter.

“Are you sure you’re not just hungry?” asked Anselm.

“No, it’s different. It’s sharper. It makes me hold my breath and sometimes my hair seems to tingle. It’s black and deep, without a bottom,” said Peter.

“That sounds pretty horrible,” said Anselm sympathetically.

“Have you been afraid Anselm?” asked Peter.

Anselm imagined the blackness and remembered a nightmare he had had weeks before when Martha had come into his room hearing his shouting and woke him .He no longer remembered what the dream was about but Martha had said then he had been ‘afraid’. Maybe he had seen spiders in his dream or something even more horrible. He didn’t think spiders would do the trick to be honest and was a bit surprised Peter seemed to have such a strong reaction to them.

Peters tried a different word ."I feel....sad," he said.

Anselm drew a blank. "What's sad?" he asked.

"It's the opposite of happy. The opposite of Gull Cove. It's maybe how those people in Somalia feel as well as being hungry. Perhaps a bit like you feel when you want to see Martha and she comes home late; or when bedtime arrives in the middle of an interesting TV programme. I think you might have felt sad when you said goodbye to the shepherd."

Anselm tried to remember these events. They were different....but yes there was something they had in common. But it was all mixed in with other things like 'afraid ' and .... 'angry' .

"I'm angry." exclaimed Anselm.

"Whoops. Sounds like we've finished with sad." said Peter. "Well, angry is fire, red, boiling water, lips tightly closed, a stare, arms waving and shouting...."

"So, you and Martha were angry when I came into the kitchen just now?"

"Yes, I guess we were. But I don't think either of us really knew it," replied Peter.

Given the way Peter had described ‘angry’. Anselm couldn’t see how either of them could not have noticed it.

“I was angry this afternoon. All this stuff about God and rules started it.”

“And what was it like?” asked Peter.

“Like...like I wanted to hit something or someone, but there was no-one...like the cartoon cat and mouse...like I wanted to shout and make them change things.....like I couldn’t stop thinking this isn’t fair! Is it like that for you?”

“Yes. Yes it is Anselm,” said Peter quietly.

“But you don’t want to hit Martha do you?” Anselm’s voice got smaller.

“No, no, I don’t...I wouldn’t do that,” replied Peter, but with only ninety percent of him signed up.

“I wonder what it’s like for Martha....I mean, being angry. Why are you angry with each other?”

“You know Anselm opposite feelings can sometimes be very close to each other. Love, anger...even hate can be separated just by a few moments, a few words said... or left unsaid. The more you love someone, the more angry you can get with them if you don’t get what you need from them.”

"I remember how happy we were at Gull Cove...but that changed; must have been 'sad' that I was feeling when we had to leave," Anselm continued. "So , I see how quick you can go from one thing to the opposite. What is it that you need from Martha?"

Now Peter had to pause. He needed to wait a little until the flood inside subsided; until he could get the words out without breaking in front of Anselm.

"I guess I want more of her....but I don't know how to get that," said Peter.

This was strange. All of Martha lived in their house as far as Anselm could see. There she was and Peter could see her any time he wanted....well except when the two of them were at work. But there were the evenings, weekends...and every night they went to the same bed. On a rough calculation Anselm figured they could be with each other at least twelve hours a day and twenty-four at weekends. Surely that was enough.

"You go to your study quite a lot, and Martha doesn't go in there. If you want to see more of her then maybe you could go there less," suggested Anselm.

Peter smiled. "Yes, maybe. Being with someone isn't just about being in the same room. It's about talking, sharing one's feelings...being connected....We don't do that anymore. Sometimes people drift away from each other; they lose each other's hands in the fog and can't find their way back. I think Martha and I need to start looking for each other."

This wasn't making much sense to Anselm but he knew he didn't like it. He was beginning to feel something like a small fear – not as big as the nightmare, but a feeling like there could be something nasty around the corner. The world felt a bit less safe again. He resolved that he would help Peter and Martha find each other, if he could. He just wasn't sure how that would work.

"So how many feelings have we 'I spied' so far?" asked Anselm, changing the subject.

"We've got the breeze, we've got happy, sad and cold."
"....and hungry, afraid and angry," Peter completed the list.

"Is that the lot then? No, there's warm, hot, love..." said Anselm answering his own question. "How many feelings are there, I wonder. Do you know Peter?"

"Many more than we've mentioned. More than most men can put their finger on. Women tend to be more fluent in this language. Some would say there are as many feelings as there are different people and moments in the world because each of us feels in different ways, in different colours or shades at different times."

"But we don't know. It's like the 'I' problem. We can't see exactly what each other sees; we can't be each other and so I suppose we can't feel each other's feelings. Maybe your version of angry is reallydifferent to my angry, although they seem similar. Maybe your angry is different to Martha's....and maybe your love is too," Anselm speculated.

"And maybe dinner's ready, so we can each put paid to our hungers with those roast potatoes. Shall we turn back?" asked Peter.

***

It had taken Martha half and hour to get back to some sort of equilibrium after Peter's "sad, lonely and angry" accusation....for that's how she saw it. The words she hadn't said "and what about me; how do you think I feel?" had kept ringing in her ears. She had salted the potatoes with her tears and gone into a cold place.

She asked how the walk had been and that was Anselm's cue.

"Full of feelings", was his summary. He told her about the game they had played. "We came up with breeze...though I'm not sure now that really counts...cold, warm, hot, happy, sad, afraid, angry, love and...most of all hungry " he said launching into the brown skinned potatoes.

"An interesting list," said Martha. "And what about their colours and where these feelings are to be found."

"Well, let me see, we had black, ice-coloured, red, brown and… I think the strongest feelings were in our tummies, some in our throats."

"Sounds like the kind of list I might expect a couple of men to come up with," said Martha "though I wonder what happened to ‘lonely’,” She shot a glance at Peter who averted his eyes.

“What do you mean?” Anselm asked.

“Well, it seems most of them are in your body and are fairly basic...sort of cave man standard.”

Both Peter and Anselm frowned in irritation at this comment. Since when were they being judged on the standard of their feelings? Martha would be handing out marks out of ten soon.

“I did tell you Anselm,” said Peter. “Women are a different species with a much wider range of feelings to play with.”

“What feelings do you have Martha...wait, I’m going to write them down,” responded Anselm.

“Well let me see....there’s....

•Love,Hate•Lust •Excitement •Hope Fear •Longing •Envy •Greed •Depression •Tiredness •Impatience, Desir,Passion •Affection •Worry •Embarrassment •Joy Compassion •Pity Jealousy •Irritation ,Regret •Hurt ,Stress •Boredom •Despair •Loneliness •Interest •Pride•Disgust •Guilt•Anxiety…

“Shall I go on?”

“Wow, that’s quite a list. I don’t know most of those. How long did it take to collect them?” asked Anselm .

"Oh, I can get through most of those in one day," replied Martha, warming to the subject. "It depends who I'm with." Another glance towards Peter. She wanted to make eye contact; any kind of contact. He looked up and began to smile cautiously until he got confirmation from her that it was OK.

"Well, it does seem that you have a lot longer list than us. I wonder why God decided women should have so many more."

"To reflect the subtlety of the fairer sex and so that we can beguile men," replied Martha.

"Hmm." Anselm didn't have a clue what she was talking about.

"How do I know when something is a feeling and when it's not? How do I know all the things you've just listed are feelings or when I'm feeling one of the things on your list...or maybe I can't because it's a woman's list? "

"It's not easy. It takes practice, like building up your muscles," said Martha. "It might help to think of colours and where the feelings are in your body just like you were doing in the game with Peter," she tried to lasso Peter back into the discussion.

"Let's think about colours. Just like an artist, we all have a palette of different feelings and if we mix a couple of feelings together we can get a third one, different to the other two but sharing something in common. Lots of the feelings I have are mixtures. We talk sometimes of having “mixed feelings” about something. Let’s see if I can find some examples:

Anger + Tiredness = Depression ;

Fear + Excitement = Anxiety ;

Hope + Impatience = Longing

Anselm got the idea but was finding the maths of feelings a bit difficult. He wasn’t familiar with some of the X's and Y's in these equations .“Tell me about hope, impatience and longing, what are they like when you feel them?”

“It’s difficult to describe them. Hope is like looking over the horizon, around the corner; something good is on its’ way; I feel like I’m leaning forward, being pulled forward into the warmth; I feel positive, optimistic...”

“More feelings,” said Anselm. “You describe one feeling by talking about another one. I don’t know; how am I to break into the circle?”

“Let me try again. Hope is the future tense of happiness .It’s a wish and a maybe of roast potatoes for dinner.”

“Now I get it”, said Anselm ,as if he’d finally spied a ship out at sea through one of those seaside telescopes – just before the coin ran out and the shutter fell.

And 'impatience' is a 'can't wait' feeling; wanting the French lesson to end and the cartoons to start", Martha continued

"Now you're talking my language," said Anselm.

"So longing is the sum of the two. It's like that roast potato in the oven that never seems to arrive on your plate," said Martha.

"Can you mix any feeling with another to get a third?" asked Anselm.

"I'm not sure; I don't think so. Sometimes feelings don't mix ...like opposites; or when they are just too different....like oil and water," explained Martha. "But they are like colours in a different way; there are shades of feelings. For example, we have light blue, sky blue, navy blue, dark blue. Well feelings like worried, anxious, dread, fear are a bit like that. They have different strengths and are used to describe one's feelings in different situations. Like you dread an event, fear a person and worry about the future."

" Most people know the names of the primary colours red, blue, yellow. But what about ultramarine, sienna, umber, vermilion .We don't use them so often; in fact, some people might find it difficult to identify those colours," said Martha.

Peter had been half listening and half trying to invent some equations or colour mixes of his own...

“Love + Anger = Hate”..... he said out of the blue.Martha looked at him, this time with compassion .

“Love + Guilt = Shame”.....she said, as if to apologise for something. Anselm watched.

“Love + absence = Loneliness” returned Peter.

“Longing + Lonely = Regret” replied Martha.

“Love + Trust = Hope” said Peter.

Martha paused, then said “I hope so. “

‘Well,’ thought Anselm, ‘this is some kind of clever maths.’ Martha and Peter were looking at each other. Anselm recognised the look. He had seen it a few weeks ago and also in the early pages of the memory book.

***

Dinner eaten, dishes washed, Anselm had retired to the TV room.

Peter hung on at the kitchen table, for once not bolting for his study, hoping he might get Martha’s attention. She was finishing putting the plates and cutlery away. She always insisted on doing this herself on the pretext that

Peter inevitably put things in the wrong places. She was in control in the kitchen and the simple physical chores that took place there were hers and not to be shared.

“That was clever of you to think of mixing the feelings like colours,” said Peter.

“It just came into my head. Anselm not only doesn’t have the labels for his feelings, he’s not sure when he’s having one. It must be like being taken over by something nameless and you’re not sure where it’s going to take you, or if and when it will end.”

“How is he going to learn?” wondered Peter aloud.

Martha finished wiping her hands on the tea-towel, placed it over the rail on the Aga and came over to the kitchen table sitting a measured distance at three o’clock to Peter’s twelve.

“We have to talk about feelings. When something is happening with Anselm we need to be ready to give it a name and to compare it to how he or we felt on other occasions. He has to build up his scrapbook .That must be how we all learn, isn’t it?”

“I guess so” said Peter, thinking that ,at some level , he was being blamed.

“Anselm’s got a good grasp of the language of things. We need to put more focus on his feelings... on ....our feelings too,” said Martha.

Peter felt a bubble of anxiety. The safety of the study called. But he yanked himself back into the kitchen and took another step.

“Is that how it is for you...I mean....longing and lonely equals regret?”

There, he’d got the words out. The words sat on the table; Martha’s eyes fell to look at them; her lips trembled and then slowly a pearl tear-drop formed, hung on her eyelash, waited for a tick of the clock and splashed to the tablecloth.

Peter’s anxiety turned to tenderness. His hand made its’ way to hers. As he folded his fingers round hers she squeezed, hard, and the act of squeezing seemed to burst the dam. Tears streamed down her cheeks accompanied first by a child’s whimper, then a sob.

Peter got up, went around to three o’clock and pulled at her arm. She seemed to pop out of the chair like a rag doll into his arms. The sobbing grew as she hung on to him. Peter smoothed her hair...woodenly. It was an effort to remember how to hold her...how to be.

Even now, with Martha at her most vulnerable, he was hesitant to make a false move and hit up against that glass wall. What would he say? He said nothing, Some part of him edited out any words of comfort he might have spoken; any vulnerability he might have shown.

She gulped for air and then.....started a nervous, girlish giggle. She pulled away from him. “I must look a mess,” she said looking for a handkerchief.

“No. Not at all,” said Peter realising he’d missed a Sir Walter Raleigh moment. Where was his cape or at least a handkerchief?

“I’m sorry”, she said.” All that talk of feelings seems to have stirred a few up.”

“There’s nothing.....nothing to apologise for”. Too little, too late The moment was gone .

Martha felt the withdrawal. “I...I’m going to run a bath”, she said and hurried from the kitchen.

Peter stood there, stranded. He’d opened a door but hadn’t been able to walk through. For a few moments he felt cowardly, ashamed. But these then passed into anger and resentment. How was he to know what was the right thing to do, the right thing to say? Things always seemed so fragile , so precarious. One wrong step and Martha would turn back into that hard-faced critic. How was he supposed to know?

***_

Martha made a calendar with columns for days of the week and the horizontal lines each having the name of a feeling. At the end of each day she or Peter would talk to Anselm about what had happened that day and how it made them feel. Anselm would place a gold star on the chart against the feelings he could claim each day; a blue one for Martha and a green for Peter.

At first, Martha seemed to have so much more to report that Anselm started to feel jealous. He got a gold star for that one...for several days, until the stars moved to pride as he accumulated a wider variety of feelings to which he could give a name .

Some patterns emerged. On days when Emily taught him French (or tried to) he would get a star for irritation and boredom. Saturdays and Sundays would always bring happy stars, except those when he got a ticking off for an untidy bedroom .

Martha's pattern seemed to change over the weeks. Tired made a regular appearance on the calendar in the first few weeks as she was still busy at work. Late nights usually meant stars for stress and impatience. But her score on stars for longing and lonely fluctuated up and down ,as did Peter's. Anselm was sure the two must be connected. The law of causew eand effect were surely at work

'Hopeful' appeared now and then for Peter and Martha together with some new ones.... like. 'belonging', 'accepted' interspersed with old ones....'empty', 'blamed'.

As time went by, however, Anselm's pattern seemed to get stuck. Few new lines appeared on his chart.

"He is cotton-woolled here, just seeing us and being taught by Emily. We take the rough edges off life for him," said Martha one evening. "I don't think he is going to develop a full emotional 'palette' unless he gets the company of others; others of his own age. It's time for him to go to school. He needs the socialising influence of other teenagers; to have some of their hang-ups, hopes, fears, desires rub off on him and to learn to make his way."

Peter agreed but cautioned "He'll find it hard you know. Children- teenagers- are an unforgiving lot and what they like least is someone who's different. Anselm is different."

"I know, but we can't protect him forever. What happens when he's full grown? He'll have to find a job. And I don't want him hiding away in a study writing academic papers"

There were still these echoes of reproach. Long lived habits die hard.

"No need for that," Peter said softly.

"I'm sorry. I don't know where it comes from."

"You're right," said Peter moving on. "We just have to be there for him at end of day and equip him as well as we can to survive in the playground."

"You make it sound like a jungle or a desert."

"It was. When I was at school.....it was," replied Peter wistfully.

They decided they would both visit the local High School to check it out and see if Anselm could be enrolled to start after the October half-term. He would have missed the beginning of the academic year but Emily said he was already very advanced in core subjects. He was a very gifted boy and would surely catch up in those where they had spent less time.

It was after dinner one evening that they spoke to Anselm about the idea of him going to school.

“So, what do you think?” asked Peter.

Anselm had listened carefully to what Martha and Peter had to say. They seemed to be trying to persuade him that he should go. He couldn’t immediately see why they would think he needed persuading. Emily had told him about her teaching days. Yes, it would mean he had to study and do homework but he had to do that now...and most of the time it was interesting. Doing it with lots of other teenagers his own age sounded pretty good.

He thought for a few moments before he answered Peter. A few moments were enough for the voice of doubt to come into his head. Of course, he wouldn’t know anyone there.....so that was a bit of a worry. Would they like him? How would he get there and back? What about lunch?

“Yes, I’d like to go...but...”

”But what?” asked Martha gently.

“What if I don’t like it....or they don’t like me?”

Martha and Peter exchanged glances. Martha thought she had better answer given Peter’s ‘playground jungle’ comment.

“I’m sure they will like you Anselm. What’s not to like after all?” she laughed.

“And I’m sure you will make lots of friends; it’s time for you to have the company of others your age. They’re a lot more fun than forty-somethings like us two,” Peter chipped in.

Anselm had observed on a number of occasions that when adults say they are ‘sure’ about something, especially that something will be good for you, what they really meant was that they hoped it would but had absolutely no way of controlling what would happen.

‘I’m sure it’ll stop raining soon; I’m sure the time will go quickly; I’m sure the traffic will start moving soon; I’m sure you didn’t mean that’, all came into this category of an adults triumph of hope over probability.

Martha and Peter’s ‘sureness’ was fuelling the doubt in Anselm’s mind. “Will there be room for me? Won’t they all have picked their chairs in class? And how will I know where to go....Emily said there were ‘school rules’. How will I know what they are...?”

“Sshh...don’t worry. Peter or I will take you to school each day and pick you up to come home. The teachers will show you the ropes and I'm sure the other pupils will help you find out how things work," soothed Martha.

'Ropes?' thought Anselm, 'what are they used for? There was that word 'sure' again.

"Listen it's not all work and no play," said Peter. "The boys will play football. You'll get a much better game with them than with a geriatric Professor. And you'll meet some girls..."

That pressed the right button. Girls.

He hadn't thought of that. Things were looking up. Why had he assumed they would all be boys?

"How many girls?" enquired Anselm.

"How many do you want?" beamed Peter.

"Peter." admonished Martha.

"Well he's a growing boy. Bound to be interested . Nothing wrong with that is there?"

"Just keep it platonic," advised Martha.

Anselm had heard of Plato from Peter but couldn't quite see how a long dead Greek could be relevant to his interest in girls. He made a mental note to check this with Peter later in case there was something he needed to know.

The introduction of girls into the equation changed the image he had of school. The girls on TV seemed very nice with soft edges....and he liked Martha and Emily very much. They seemed to make the world safer.

Later that evening he put three stars on the calendar chart. One for Excitement, one for Hope and one for Anxiety.

***

The next day Martha had to travel to Edinburgh for an industry conference at which she was a guest speaker. It meant an overnight stay as she was first on the following morning. She decided to travel by train rather than fly; easier to stay in touch with the office and she could work on her e-mails. It was to be a late arrival so she called Peter from somewhere around the frayed boundary between England and Scotland.

“Hi....should be there in...hour. How was....day?” “Okay. The usual......marking........”

The signal was poor. She only caught every other word from Peter. Then a beep and the line went dead as they went through a cutting. She pressed the recall button.

“Might lose you again ....signal ..weak.....Did you hear.....paper....?”

Peter had submitted a paper to the Philosophical Journal entitled ‘Of Mysteries’. He was waiting to hear whether it was to be published.

"...next week…"

Martha wasn't sure whether he was saying he would hear next week or that' when it would be published.

"Say again..."

The line went dead again. She pressed recall.

The phone rang several times without answer.

"Come on. I know you are there. Pick up."

"Hello"

"It's me. You cut out again."

"I didn't cut out....your.....phone did..."

"Okay, okay, I'm not blaming....How's Anselm...

Peter thought 'What about my paper being published......no comment'.

"Seems to have ....school..."

"What; say again, I missed that."

"I said, he seems to be getting ....excited about...school..."

"Oh good ; any other feelings?"

"None that he's reported ."

“And what about you? ”

“What?”

“What about your feelings?”

“...irritated…”

“Why?”

“I only get every other word....can’t ....”

“So what’s new ?” Martha said under her breath, losing her patience.

“What?”

“Nothing what are you doing this evening....”

You’re fading again.....you tomorrow....”

They hit a tunnel and lost each other again.

Across the aisle ,a few seats up a woman was watching her intently and smiled when their eyes caught. Probably a fellow sufferer thought Martha.

She left it a few minutes after they emerged again into the late afternoon sun. Peter didn’t re-dial. She was damned if she was going to again...she had been doing all the work

***

VIII STARTING SCHOOL

It was six weeks later when the car crunched on the gravel drive of St Thomas Aquinas High School.

Anselm had been taken earlier to meet the Head of the Upper School, Mr Smart. The man wore a black cape and sat behind a large oak desk. The cape reminded Anselm of the Batman cartoons and it was all he could do at first to keep a serious face.

After the first few moments that wasn't a problem, because Mr Smart was a very serious man.

He had asked Anselm about sports and what interested him. When Anselm announced that he was chiefly interested in football, girls and the laws of the universe, Mr Smart was slightly taken aback, but then said "Well, you are coming to the right place because we have all three of those here at St. Thomas Aquinas."

As the car now came to a halt in a 'visitor's' parking space, Anselm could hear the sound of young voices........shouting. He got out of the car and stood looking at the blackened sandstone walls of St. Thomas Aquinas rising before him. It must have been twenty times the size of Peter and Martha's house. He felt small.

Anselm's form teacher was to be a Mr Dowty and it was to his office they were supposed to go that first morning. As the three of them climbed the steps to the front entrance Anselm thought that life would never be quite the same again.

"Welcome Anselm," said Mr Dowty as they entered his office.

Mr Dowty was a rather portly, red-faced man wearing spectacles. Anselm had met him briefly when he had been to see Mr Smart and had formed the view that

Dowty was the friendlier of the two. And, so he was this morning.

“Now, you will come with me to registration and I’ll introduce you to some of the other boys and girls. I think your Mum and Dad can get on their way now; you’re in good hands.” Dowty winked at the two of them.

“Anselm, Peter will pick you up after school at four o’clock. Where will we find him Mr Dowty? asked Martha as if a five foot six, fifteen-year old might be easily mislaid.

“Oh, the boys and girls usually mill around in the quad at home time....it’s just beyond the car park.”

“Well...have a....good day, darling and if there is anything you need just speak to Mr Dowty here, I’m sure he will help you settle in.” Martha gave Dowty the look she usually reserved for Peter if he tried to put their best bone china in the dishwasher.

Anselm felt a bud of panic in this throat. He hadn’t got a star for panic yet but was quite clear that he didn’t feel great right at that moment. He edged towards Martha. He was feeling very different....far too different for this place. Martha put her hands on each of his shoulders and pulled his chin up.

“I know. It’s all very strange. Everyone feels like this starting in a new place. Remember when you came to us from the shepherd? That was strange too, wasn’t it. Took a bit of getting used to. It’s the same here. A few days to settle in and it'll seem like a second home, I'm *sure*," said Martha, unaware that all her words of comfort had been undermined by the last word.

Anselm nodded; more a bowing to the inevitable than any assent.

Martha turned to hide the tears. "See you later," she called over her shoulder. "See you later, mate," Peter parroted, unable to think of anything more profound.

"Come Anselm, it's time for registration. I have asked another boy in your class, Freddie Johnson, to help you get your bearings. He can show you around the school and help you navigate between the different lessons and classrooms. He's a good sort, a popular lad. I'm sure you'll like him," said Dowty keen to reassure.

As they entered Form IV B's classroom the hubbub that had been echoing up the corridor subsided and clumps of boys and girls separated, each moving to stand at their desk.

"Morning Class," boomed Dowty.

"Morning sir," came the usual muffle of adolescent voices ,with some abstainers.

"Now then, I want to introduce you to a new boy, Anselm Swinbourne. Anselm is joining our class and I'm sure you will make him most welcome.

'New boy', thought Anselm. Little did they know how 'new'. He looked at what seemed a blur of faces and forced a pained smile. Two of the boys at the back were digging each other in the ribs with their elbows and muttering something Anselm couldn't quite catch.

"Now Anselm, you can sit down over there. Dowty pointed to a desk a third of the way back on the opposite side of the classroom from the window. The window desks were all taken. Anselm walked over to the desk every step scrutinised by what seemed a thousand eyes. His brand-new school uniform and perfect knot in the school tie (the result of several attempts by Peter to do a mirror image of tying his own tie.) contrasted with the half-mast, off-centre, dinner stained appendages and grubby collars of many of the boys.

Anselm became very conscious that his shiny, brown leather satchel seemed to scream out his newness....his differentness. He sat down, locked his eyes on Mr Dowty, not daring to look to either side.

Mr Dowty called out the names from the Register ".James Abbott....Nathalie Cooke........Susan Fenwick.......David Gaunt......."

Anselm practised in his head saying 'yes sir' as his name approached. "Jennifer Hollioake....Freddie Johnson....Stephen Jones...."

Anselm rehearsed again. No two words had ever seemed so important to get right. And they should be said casually, matter of fact-ly so as to tone in with the others.

“Mark Lambert....Philip Norris....Kim Nichols.....Jane Pennock....” “Anselm Swinbourne”, it came suddenly.

Anselm opened his mouth and ....nothing but a croak came out. The class burst out laughing.

“Doesn’t have a lot to say for himself sir,” called out some wag at the back. “That’s enough,” said Dowty. “Anselm?”

“Yes...sir,” Anselm almost shouted the words as if to claim his space....and then went beetroot red.

“Look he’s blushing,” whispered one of the girls behind him.

Anselm was to collect a few stars for embarrassment in the weeks ahead. It seemed to him to be possibly the most unbearable of the feelings that came his way. One to be avoided at all costs .

“....Margaret Walsh,” finished Dowty.

“Right, everyone off to Assembly and then on to your first lessons .”

Chairs squealed on the floor and the hubbub started again as the other ‘students’ (Mr Smart didn’t like the word pupils; pupils were things in your eyes whereas students were people who studied) made their way to the door – in twos like Noah's Ark.

For a moment Anselm felt adrift...until one of the boys came up to him.

“Hi, I’m Freddie Johnson. Mr Dowty told me, er...asked me to act as a guide for you...just for today like...to show you where things are; sort of teach you the ropes, like....bit of a gaff that wasn’t it, not getting your words out, like...eh?”

“Yes,” said Anselm. ’Thanks for rubbing it in,’ he thought...but didn’t say anything. At least if he was with Freddie maybe he wouldn’t stand out too much. But what’s this ‘like’ business...every other word. Like what for goodness sake?

Assembly was a strange affair. Mr Smart appeared in his Batman cape and proceeded to give a lecture on the evils of smoking. He then handed onto Ms Bentham.(Anselm later found out that Ms stood for neither Miss nor Mrs. It was a kind of undisclosed in-between state that everybody knew meant Miss really. But the wearer didn’t want to acknowledge she was rather too old to be still a Miss and rather too single to be a Mrs.)

Ms Bentham wore tweed .Brown tweed. She made a number of announcements in a shrill voice about sports days, parent’s evenings, a charity walk and graffiti both in the girls and boys toilets.

“She shouldn’t be going in the boys loo....serves her right if she found some extensions to her vocabulary in there,” whispered one of the taller boys behind him.

Then Mr Dowty led the Lord's prayer. Heads bowed around him so Anselm followed suit, and all of the boys and girls proceeded to mutter indistinctly, each getting perhaps one word in three and with varying time lapses between Mr Dowty's lead and their repetition. The result was a sort of undulating hum around the room with the odd word bobbing to the surface.

"MmmmMhmmmm...shepherd...I'lll...mmm....temtayshun...mm..trespassus... mmm...daily bread...mmm ah men."

When the prayer was finished they all filed out again into the corridor, which became a melee of adolescents in random motion.

"Follow me," said Freddie," we've got Maths in room 21 first. Double Maths..... yuck. Mr Chambers. He's a right misery. You any good at Maths Swinbourne?"

"Not bad. Algebra's a bit tricky sometimes."

"Algebra? Wow stick with me kid. We'll sit next to each other and if sir asks you a question try to answer this time will you. It's not good for my rep to be seen hanging around with a dumb boy yer know."

Class IVB wasn't the brightest in its year. It was what Mr Smart had called 'mixed ability'. He'd explained to Martha and Peter that fourth year was the beginning of the GCSE course and given that Anselm had not had any formal schooling up to this point, it would be better if he started in a class where he would "not be too stretched."

“There will no doubt be some catching up to do. If he shines then we can move him up a set.”

Martha and Peter were not convinced. Emily had set out the syllabus Anselm had covered together with a written note on her views as to his level of attainment. Nevertheless ,they were relieved he hadn’t been badged remedial. He would have enough to cope with coming to terms with the school routine and society of other teenagers. So, they went along with Mr Smart’s proposal. It didn’t seem to be up for negotiation anyway.

Anselm and Freddie sat together on the window side as the other members of class IVB wandered into the room. Mr Chambers was sat behind a desk near the blackboard with a large pile of books stacked next to him, head down pouring over an open exercise book, occasionally making sudden movements with his right hand in which he held a red biro.

He was known by the class as a fierce disciplinarian.. You didn’t cross Mr Chambers or he would cut you to pieces with sharp sarcasm.

“Right,” said Chambers rising from his chair. He was a tall man, bearded with wiry hair and a dusting of grey. On his left cheek was a scar, which gave him a touch of pirate. The boys had asked him once before where he had got it but only got the enigmatic answer ”sometimes reason and logic are not enough to make your way in this world.” This only added to the speculation and the general aura of someone you needed to stay on the right side of.

"Where is Anselm Swinbourne?" asked Chambers.

Anselm cleared his throat. He didn't want a repeat of registration. "Here, sir."

"Ah, there you are. Welcome to St Thomas Aquinas and form IVB Anselm."
He laid an exercise book and textbook on Anselm's desk.

"Take good care of these , young man , taxpayers money." With that he wheeled round and went to the blackboard.

"Okay. Trigonometry," he announced.

A few boys at the back groaned then came to a dead stop as Chambers cocked his head and looked over the top of his spectacles in their direction.

"Right, what's the sum of the angles in a triangle?"

One of the girls' hands shot up in the air.

"Yes, Jennifer."

"One hundred and eighty degrees, sir," proclaimed Jennifer.

"Good," said Chambers, drawing a right-angled triangle on the blackboard. "And how do we calculate the 'sine' of this angle A?"

The class went quiet.

"No-one? We did this last week. Come on," said Chambers, a hint of irritation in his voice.

The class stayed quiet. No-one moved in case any motion might be taken as a bid to give the answer...like an auction when the bid price has gone through the roof.

"Opposite over Hypotenuse...sir," said Anselm breaking the silence.

"Quite right, Swinbourne. Well Class IVB; wherever our new addition was before coming to Aquinas it seems he was listening...perhaps you can take a leaf out of his book."

There was a murmur at the back of the room which Chambers immediately extinguished with... "Abbott and Lambert...you listen with the flaps at the side of your head not with the one in the middle of your face."

Anselm turned cautiously to look over his shoulder to the back of the class. Two boys sitting together were giving him an icy stare.

"So, Swinbourne, if I were to tell you that the hypotenuse was six centimetres long and this angle thirty degrees, do you know how to find the length of the opposite side?" Chambers took the opportunity to test the boundaries of Anselm's understanding of the subject.

"You, er...look up the sine of thirty degrees and multiply by six centimetres, sir,"replied Anselm. He decided not to turn around again.

“Right again. Now can you each do just that using either the trig tables at the back of your text book or using your calculator if you have one with Trig functions.”

Freddie was looking at Anselm with a mixture of surprise and faint disapproval. “Don’t push your luck,” he whispered. Anselm wasn’t sure what Freddie meant. There was no luck about it. Emily had taught him trigonometry when they were learning about light reflecting and refracting. The maths of angles was not a matter of ‘luck’, it was about laws of the universe, and these were not left to chance.

Having reminded Class IVB of the rules regarding cosines and tangents, Mr Chambers then handed out a sheet of questions for them to practice. After half an hour they were to swap papers then mark each other’s answers by reference to the correct answers which Mr Chambers put up on the blackboard.

Freddie said to Anselm at the end “Wow you got them all right.”

“So did you,” said Anselm.

Freddie grinned. “Course I did....I copied your answers, idiot.”

Anselm wondered ‘who was the idiot here’ .

When the bell rang for break Freddie suggested they went to the tuck shop. Freddie was a round boy who was clearly a frequent visitor to the shop.

“The jam do-nuts are ace,” said Freddie.

Martha had given Anselm two pounds “in case he needed it.” And though he hadn’t much practice with money he felt this sudden wealth made him more a sort of ...man of the world, with independent means. Freddie was right about the do-nuts.

As they stood around licking the raspberry from the centre, some of the other pupils from Class IVB gathered round.

“So ,where did you get so good at Trig?” asked Jennifer, a blonde, blue-eyed girl who looked to Anselm like one of the gazelles he’d seen on the wildlife programmes on TV.

“My teacher taught me.... Emily,” replied Anselm.

“What school were you at before you came here?” she continued.

Anselm felt the catch of anxiety in his throat. If they were going to ask him about his history it was going to be a short conversation.

“Have you just moved into the area?” pressed Jennifer.

“No,” replied Anselm.

“Talkative aren’t you?” teased Jennifer.

Anselm felt backed into a corner. "I didn't go to school before. I had a private tutor...and I live with Martha and Peter. Peter's a professor at the University...." Anselm blurted. 'There that ought to be enough,' he thought.

"No wonder he's so good at Trig, his Dad's a professor," called one of the boys from the back of the group.

"Actually, he's a professor of Philosophy...not Maths," explained Anselm.

"Phil who?" exclaimed the boy at the back of the group again. Anselm turned to see who it was. James Abbott....one of the boys who had been giving him that stare in class.

"Philosophy," said Anselm. How could this boy not know what Philosophy was. "It's the study of ....er....reality and mind and....self....pretty important things really. It's really about asking questions. There aren't many answers."

"Like our maths classes then," Freddie chirped up, drawing laughter which seemed to take a bit of tension out of the scene.

But James Abbott wasn't about to be deflected.

"Sounds pretty weird to me. Your old man must be a bit weird. Come to think of it you seem a bit weird to me. Whaddyou think Dave?" He turned to the other boy with the icy stare on his left, David Gaunt.

“Yeah...a bit weird I’d say,” said Gaunt.

“Leave him alone you two,” said Jennifer. “He’s new here; give him a chance. So, what if his Dad studies that stuff. Your Dad’s a second hand car salesman James Abbott....nothing to crow about,” Jennifer returned with interest.

“So how come you didn’t go to school?”Wouldn’t mind hearing how you pulled that trick off,” asked one of the other boys in the group.

“Peter and Martha didn’t think I was ready for it until now...I had...er...some catching up to do.” Anselm stammered. He didn’t know how to avoid the. questions without telling an outright lie.

“There he goes again....I tell you he’s weird. Wot's he bin doin’ for the last fifteen years whilst we’ve ‘ad to suffer the Chambers of this world? “ Abbott was enjoying himself.

The bell rang to end break. The next lesson was English. “Follow me,” ordered Freddie, tersely.

Freddie bolted off down the corridor with Anselm trailing in his wake. Afraid to be left behind, Anselm put on a spurt to catch up and get abreast of Freddie.

“I don’t know what the big secret is,” said Freddie in a tone of accusation. Why don’t you tell us how come you haven’t been to school before? You made me look a right jerk back there. I’m supposed to be showing you round the school but I don't know a thing about you. What are you, some kind of alien who landed here last week and recruited a couple of parents. Or maybe they are aliens too. Your Dad certainly sounds out of this world...."

"Sorry," was all the response Anselm could muster. Amongst this teeming mass of adolescence, he felt totally alone.

***

Anselm sat next to Freddie again in English, even though Freddie still seemed pretty steamed up and rather distant. The English teacher was a lady. Miss Jolliffe. She was much younger than Martha. She introduced herself to Anselm and welcomed him in that reassuring way which seemed to be reserved for women.

They were studying Shakespeare...Macbeth. Miss Jolliffe told Anselm he would have a chance to catch up on the reading over the next week but asked one of the class to give a summary of the story so far.

Unusually, James Abbott volunteered. Miss Jolliffe cautiously accepted. She was new to the school that term having graduated from teaching college the previous year. She had been told on teaching practice that the James Abbotts of this world existed and had been sent so that teachers might learn the virtue of patience.

James Abbott stood up.....and began his oratory.

"Well there's this Scottish geezer, Macbeth ,who lives up in some great castle, surrounded by woods. His wife, Lady Macbeth isn't much of a lady...she's a real schemer and puts her old man up to no good. Ambitious she is. Anyway ,one day the King visits the Macbeths, taking a bit of time off from affairs of state or some other affairs." Abbott winked and got a ripple of giggles.

"So, Mrs Macbeth has the idea that they should bump 'im off....the King that is... .and her hubby take over the throne of Scotland....for wot it's worth. So, she puts 'im up to it and gets him to stab the King in his bedroom. Don't ask me what the two boys were doing in the bedroom togevver. .."

"You can leave the embellishments out James," said Miss Jolliffe.

"Old man Macbeth, he knifes the King and gets blood on his 'ands and then he starts to go nuts...and that's as far as we've got." Abbott sat down, beaming.

"Well, James' summary may lack the poetic expression of Shakespeare but he's given you the headlines," said Miss Jolliffe. "Now let's pick up where we left off. Act Two, Scene 1...turn to page 20 in your books. What about two volunteers, one to take the part of Lady Macbeth and one to be Macbeth. We'll read two passages from the parts I set for homework. A few hands went into the air. Class IVB had its fair ration of extroverts.

"Yes, Jane and ...Philip."

"Which one of them's going to be the lady?" quipped Abbott.

"That's enough," said Miss Jolliffe, trying to be firm. Start from the line.... "Is this a dagger......." Act Two, Scene 1...Philip."

Philip Norris scanned the page. He was a good reader.

"Is this a dagger which I see before me ,the handle toward my hand ? Come let me clutch thee. I have thee not, and yet I see thee still. Art thou not, fatal vision, sensible, to feeling as to sight ?Or art thou but a dagger of the mind, a false creation…"

Abbott flicked an ink pellet at Fredddie, who swallowed the pain.

"Thank you Philip....let's pause there and ...now go to Scene IV line 49...again Macbeth...

"Thou canst not say I did it, never shake thy gory looks at me er…

Miss Jolliffe filled in : "Gentlemen, rise his highness is not well – Now Jane....you are **Lady Macbeth**:

"Sit worthy friends. My Lord is often thus, and hath been from his youth. `Pray you keep seat; the fit is momentary; upon a thought he will again be well: If much you note him
you shall offend him and extend his passion:feed and

regard him not.Are you a man?"

Macbeth: "Ay, and a bold one that dare not look on that which might appal the devil."

Lady Macbeth:

"O proper stuff.This is the very painting of your fear. This is the air drawn dagger which, you said, led you to Duncan. O, these flaws and starts –impostors to true fear, would well become a woman's story at a winter's fire,authorized by her grandma. Shame itself! Why do you make such faces? When all's done you look but on a stool!"

Macbeth:

Prithee see there! Behold! Look! Lo! How say you? Why, what care I? If thou canst nod, speak too.If charnel-houses and our graves must send those that we bury back, our monuments shall be the maws of kites ."

Lady Macbeth: "What, quite unmann'd in folly?"

Macbeth: "If I stand here I saw him."

Lady Macbeth: "Fie, for shame! "

"Thank you Philip and Jane," interrupted Miss Jolliffe. "Well Class IVB what do you make of that. We know

Macbeth killed Duncan and he had Banquo killed too. What do you think was happening in the first reading from Scene 1?"

"He's seeing things Miss, "said Freddie.

"Why?"

"Because he's scared about what he's going to do....kill Duncan."

"Yes....It is the bloody business which informs thus to mine eyes" read Miss Jolliffe. "How does he know it's not real?"

"Because he sees it but when he tries to grab it...it's not there," answsred Jennifer.

"Yes, so he is so disturbed by what he is about to do that he has a kind of hallucination," summarised Miss Jolliffe.

Anselm was listening to all this....but had a different theory. Shakespeare was writing at about the era Bishop Berkeley, Descartes and others were around. They too were doubting their senses. Must have been a strange kind of society then; everybody wandering around viewing everybody else as most likely a figment of their imagination, or of God's.

.

"Now what about the second reading, what's happening there?" asked Miss Jolliffe.

“Banquo had come back from the dead Miss,” shouted Abbott, “like a zombie.”

“Had he?”

“No,” said Jennifer. “No one else could see him. It was Macbeth hallucinating. He was feeling so guilty, he started seeing things again. “This is the very painting of your fear”, says Lady Macbeth.

Anselm decided he should at least put Berkeley’s case if only because he felt Peter would expect that of him.

“Alternatively,” said Anselm, “the dagger and Banquo were as real as anything else in this play. Just because the others didn’t see them doesn’t make them unreal .They were real enough to Macbeth. I see lots of things you guys don’t see and vice-versa. For example, I can see the back of Philip Norris’ head right now, but he can’t and nor can you, Miss. As Einstein said it all depends on the relative position of the observer; and Bishop Berkeley said that everything we see and sense is really just an idea or picture in the mind of God, including us. Well, given that God is pretty clever He might be kind of ‘in two minds,’ running two or more different videos at the same time...” he was conscious of the flaws in his argument as he spoke but continued manfully to dig the hole... “or rather, since all the people only exist in Gods mind he had some of them see Banquo and some not. The knife and Banquo were in Macbeth’s mind, who was in Shakespeare’s mind, who in turn was in God’s mind... ike those Russian dolls you see in the shops...” Anselm tailed off.

“I told you he was weird,” muttered Abbott.

***

The bell for the lunch break rang. Not a moment too early for Anselm.

Freddie said, reluctantly, “Come with me; Mr Dowty said I should show you how things work in the refectory. Once you’ve got your lunch you’re on your own. I’ve got trumpet practice.”

The ‘dinner lady’ was a big bosomed woman in her fifties. She could have been Freddie’s Mum thought Anselm...she clearly enjoyed her food. She slapped a wedge of lumpy mashed potatoes on his plate to join the stew ladled by the equally large lady next to her. “There you are dear...stick to your ribs.”

Freddie went over to one of the large trestle tables in the middle of the great room, sat next to some boys Anselm hadn’t seen before, and immediately started to chat. Anselm was a few yards behind him and hesitated. Should he sit there or was he ‘on his own’ now. He looked around; groups of boys and separate groups of girls seemed to occupy all the benches, each in animated conversation. He couldn’t see another space except the one across from Freddie. He bolted for the gap....better unwelcome than stuck out like a sore thumb with nowhere to sit.

Freddie kept talking to the other boys, not acknowledging Anselm as he slid in beside one of them.

"....so Ziggy said to Ms Bentham 'what's graffiti Miss...how would I know it if I saw it?' And she says :"writing with marker pens, and anyone found doing it will have a week's detention and a warning letter sent to their parents." So ,he says ..."can't blame someone for expressing their creativity...what else are you supposed to do while you're sitting there Miss...?"

"He didn't?" questioned one of the boys in amazement.

"He sure did. I was there," said one of the others.

"Awesome!" exclaimed Freddie. "And what did she say"

"She lost it....totally. Gave Ziggy a week's detention there and then and he's to write an essay titled something like...er....'Creativity is not a four -etter word,'" said the first boy. "But the best is yet to come....waddya think Ziggy said?"

"Should 'ave thought he'd said, or written enough already." said Freddie.

"He said: "Well perhaps I can do the detention in the lavatory Ms....I do my most creative work there."

"No!," the second boy and Freddie chimed in unison.

"Yup," said the first.

“God, he’s going to be out on his ear,” opined Freddie.

“He’s going to be hauled up in front of the Head at the end of the afternoon,” continued the first boy.

Anselm had been listening to the boy’s conversation as he toyed with the lumpy potatoes and stew. He kept his eyes dipped on his lunch. All he wanted right now was to disappear. He felt naked sitting there. A naked alien from another world; frightened that any moment one of the groups around him would run out of conversation and point at him. “Look at the new boy, the extraterrestrial .Never been to school but a mathematical whiz; guess you’ve got to be if you’re going to find your way here from another planet. Hey weirdo.” His imagination knew how best to taunt and hurt him.

The other boys continued talking, ignoring Anselm. He hoped they would keep doing so. He could pretend to be invisible. He kept his movements to the minimum lest he draw their attention.

“...Man United will stuff Spurs on Saturday....she’s going out with John Richards in the sixth form...getting an iPod for Christmas....he’s a real rude boy...”

Anselm only caught sound bites of what they were saying. He was buried deep inside himself.

He wandered back to the heath and the shepherd; heard the bleating of the lambs and the chatter of the stream that fell down the valley side...and he longed for the aloneness ....he place where there was no-one else to explain himself to... justify himself to....the place where there were no questions just the green waves of grass and restless shadows for him to watch. He understood Martha's longing.

"Hey, Swinbourne, wake-up." It was Freddie's voice.

"Listen, I'll catch up with you outside room 20. It's next door to room 21...so you should be able to find that yourself," grinned Freddie. "I've got to go and take my anger out on that drum skin. Two o'clock...Geography...it's whistling Baker."

All three boys stood up and took their trays. Anselm looked at the clock on the wall of the refectory. One-fifteen. What was he going to do till two o'clock? He picked up his tray and took it over to the racks along the side wall and slid it in as the others had done. When he turned around they were gone....and he was naked again.

He decided to walk purposefully to the door and outside...as if he had somewhere important to go. The next forty-five minutes he kept walking...down the corridor, out into the quad, past the sports block, around the corner ...out of sight. Behind the sports block was a long line of trees bordering a path that went straight for several hundred metres to the end of the playing fields and the boundary of the school. He walked slowly now for fear he would run out of path before two o'clock. Even in his French lessons time had never stood so still. Each time he looked at the watch Martha had given him "so you're not late for lessons," it seemed hardly to have moved. No fear of being late with such a watch, in such a place.

***

He arrived outside room 20 at a few minutes to two. Some of the others from Class IVB were already milling around the entrance. He saw Jennifer Hollioake with one of the other girls and for a moment thought of turning around...he slowed his pace.

“Anselm, hi. We didn’t see you at lunchtime. Where did you go?” Jennifer spotted him.

Another question. Martha and Peter had sent him to this place to ‘get to know other teenagers’...but so far he wasn’t sure he wanted to ‘get to know’ anybody here.

“Never mind,” said Jennifer seeing the spacey look in Anselm’s eyes. “This is my friend Susan. Come and say hello. Anselm’s just started today. He’s a bit mysterious but that’s okay...we like that don’t we Susan?” she dug her friend in the ribs. Susan nodded and smiled at Anselm.

“Must be a bit scary, starting at a new place where you don’t know anybody. But I think you’re in well with Mr Chambers and Miss Jolliffe. Class IV B's not the brightest bunch so you’ll probably come top of the class, no problem,” said Susan.

Anselm felt his muscles relax a little. Even if he was an alien, these natives at least seemed friendly .

At that moment Freddie appeared as if from a trapdoor in the floor. Anselm had shut down his peripheral vision during that naked lunch. Freddie seemed back to the friendly mood he'd started the day in.

"You're going to love Mr Baker," he said and the girls laughed at some in-joke.

They filed in. Mr Baker said the usual welcoming words to Anselm...but this time with a difference.

Mr Baker had a slight speech defect, which resulted in him making a whistling noise every time he pronounced the letter's'. Class IVB found this enormously entertaining and would go out of their way to ask Mr Baker questions where they knew the answer would be packed with the letter 's'. Anselm's joining the class was a godsend. Anselm Swinbourne was doubly so. Mr Baker got through six whistles when he welcomed Anselm Swinbourne to St Thomas Aquinas School. They loved it!

Mr Baker had one other foible. He was hard of hearing and wore a hearing aid. He didn't like noisy classes so when he was doing the talking, or had set the class an exercise to get on with quietly, he would just turn his hearing aid down and relax in a solipsist silence. He was aware of his whistle and the quiet smiles and grins it put on the faces of Class IVB...he wasn't aware of the uproar of laughter he occasioned on introducing Anselm.

"See, I told you," said Freddie. "Isn't he a riot?" Freddie no longer seemed to be treating him as an embarrassment. Poking fun at Mr Baker seemed to be the game now. He was the alien amongst them, not Anselm.

He looked round to see Abbott and Gaunt. They were sniggering with two of the girls completely oblivious of Anselm. Gradually he felt less naked.

They were studying the Geography of North America. Anselm had already worked on this with Emily. Mr Baker asked them each to name a city and a state in the United States.

"New York, New York," said Abbott.

"Pittsburgh, Pennsylvania," said Jane Pennock.

"San Francisco California..."

Anselm was feeling more confident....and the mischief that Peter had so often seen started to waken.

"Houston Texas..."said Jennifer.

"Washington ...er...

"DC", said another voice from the back.

Anselm plucked up his courage. "Mississippi...Missouri," he whistled.

For what seemed an interminable moment his whistles hung in the air.

Then Class IVB fell apart at the seams. Snorts of laughter from the boys mixed with giggles from the girls and howls from Abbott and Gaunt at the back.

Mr Baker froze. His hearing aid was not turned off. He looked at Anselm with a grim face. Anselm stopped breathing, the class fell silent...then...the grim face dissolved into a broad grin. Mr Baker was a sport. Class IVB knew that, and now so did Anselm.

"God, I wish I'd thought of that," said Abbott when afternoon break came around. "Way to go Swinbourne," said Gaunt.

"Didn't think you had it in you," said Freddie, "what an ace move". Freddie seemed to be taking proprietorial pride in Anselm's little joke.

Anselm was amazed at how six whistles had changed his status from alien to 'cool' earthling...but he wasn't complaining. Maybe he didn't have to be a stranger here after all.

At four pm, he was standing in the quad. Peter appeared around the corner of the hedges from the car park. He saw Anselm stood alone watching some of the other boys playing football. His heart sank...remembering another boy thirty -five years ago.

Suddenly a boy came bouncing up to Anselm, engaging him in some apparently top- secret conversation, one hand held up to his mouth conspiratorially. Anselm spotted Peter. “Hi Dad,” he said with the emphasis on Dad for Freddie’s benefit.Freddie turned around to see Peter.

“Hello, Mr Swinbourne, I presume,” he said, whistling his s’s. Freddie and Anselm creased up laughing again.

***

That evening Peter and Martha were eager to hear news of Anselm's first day at school. Anselm started with Mr Bakers speech defect demonstrating a growing talent for mimicry.

“And what about the other children...was there anyone you particularly liked ? What about that boy Freddie...do you think you will become friends?” asked Peter.

“Maybe...dunno yet.” Anselm's answer was short on words and long on uncertainty .

He jumped to Macbeth and explained, mostly for Peters benefit, that Shakespeare clearly had some of the existential doubts that beset Berkeley. Macbeth represented more comfortable ground than having to describe the personae dramatis of Class IVB and in particular Abbots hostile welcome.

“What did you do at lunchtime; were there things to do ...football maybe,” Martha enquired.

Anselm felt a sudden bolt of shame. “Not much; just walked”

“Well, it can take time to get to know people...every thing's new and unfamiliar. I’m sure you’ll make some friends... even if it may seem hard at first because they all know each other and you are the new boy on the block.” Peter tried to spread a blanket of reassurance, knowing, however, that a thousand words of his were worth less than one smile, grunt or word from a member of Class IVB.

After Anselm had been despatched to bed, Martha and Peter stayed in the kitchen. “He wasn’t exactly bubbling with the events of the day was he?” said Martha.

“Do you remember your first day at school?” asked Peter.

“Too long ago I’m afraid”

“Well, I still remember vividly my first days at Grammar school. Or at least the feeling .

“And...?”

“The isolation and loneliness... they were hard enough...but I could bear them if I were in the world alone. The real pain comes from being amongst other people who seemed connected to each other whilst I was separate, different ,apart... the contrast created a sense of shame… as if I was somehow faulty, defective. It took ages for me to get over that...not sure I have to this day.”

“You think that’s what’s happening to Anselm?” asked Martha, her compassion split between past and present.

“I don’t know . I hope not. He seemed happy when I picked him up. We just need to watch out for him.

“Nobody watched out for you did they?”

Peter was silent.

“Well look at you now. A professor at the top of your profession; giving lectures to audiences of academics; teaching the brightest students in the land...always in demand...”said Martha

Peter looked at her unconvinced.

Martha wasn’t sure what to say, what to ask. Peter seemed so young at that moment, as if time had bent back upon itself.

She remembered Peters outburst when they were doing ‘feelings maths’.... “Love + Absence = Loneliness”...and felt a stab of sadness and recognition.

“I’ve got some marking to do...essays from second year tutorial group...they’ll expect them back before Fridays Session.” Peter made his excuses before Martha could find a next step.

After Peter had gone, Martha wondered what she could have done differently. So far but no further; both of them seemed stuck; neither able to trust that the other could hold their vulnerability. Maybe it was the embarrassment of strangers; too unsure of each other to stay in the moment.

***

IX IMPROBABLE UNIVERSE, IMPOSSIBLE GOD

As the days and weeks went by Anselm became more integrated into Class IVB society and the school at large. The'Man from Mars' comments died away. Abbott and Gaunt directed their bullying instincts towards one of the boys in the lower school. Freddie stuck with Anselm. The whistling incident had put Anselm into the 'supercool', premier league....associating with him was good for Freddie's 'rep'.Good for his class marks too.

Anselm was getting a growing reputation for being slightly oddball but a 'real diamond geezer'(which words according to Jennifer, meant a nice guy) with a wicked sense of humour. At least they thought he was joking. Class IVB particularly liked Anselm's cross-examination of the teachers. Demonstrating the limits of the teachers' knowledge seemed to legitimise Class IV B's own state of ignorance on a subject.

He was at his most mischievous in the Physics class.

"Sir, if large bodies attract smaller ones to them under the law of gravity, how come the earth doesn't fall into the sun?"

"Well, because the earth orbits the sun, Swinbourne. It's travelling through space at a speed which prevents it falling," said Mr Roberts, the Physics teacher. He demonstrated as Emily had done with a length of string tied to the board rubber, whirling round.

"Must be an awful long piece of string connecting the earth to the sun," said Anselm. "What is it fixed to and why doesn't it burn, sir?"

"Of course, there isn't really a piece of string, that's just a way of demonstrating the principle," replied Mr Roberts. "It's just that the speed of the earth through space creates an equal and opposite force to that of the suns gravitational pull...so the earth stays at the same distance from the sun."

"But you did say that the orbit of Mercury is an ellipse. Sometimes closer to the sun when it gets very hot, sometimes further away when it gets very cold. How come? It's not in balance is it?"

"No, but as it approaches nearer to the sun then the suns gravitational field exerts more pull on the planet which results in Mercury accelerates, increasing the 'centripetal' force to balance the greater pull of gravitation as the planet gets closer to the sun," explained Roberts feeling on somewhat shaky ground.

"So, what you are saying, sir, is that gravity speeds things up and that creates a kind of 'anti-gravity' and the two keep cancelling each other out....so Mercury doesn't fall into the sun?"

"That's about it," said Roberts.

"Isn't that just a way of saying 'We don't really know why the earth goes round the sun and not off in a straight line...so we'll invent an invisible force called gravity to keep the earth in place. But, then the consequence of inventing gravity is that it could get pretty hot around here. So, we invent another force to cancel gravity out or at least so that 1-1=0. Now we've got two mysterious forces needed to explain one thing. Two things we don't really understand instead of one," challenged Anselm.

"I see your point," conceded Roberts. "Actually, scientists now believe that gravity is a sort of distortion in space-time .It bends space and, as a result, objects like the earth follow the curvature of space....ust like a ball bearing might run round the inside of a cylinder."

Class IVB were unanimous in their view at break time that Roberts had been clutching at straws. As soon as Anselm had de-bunked one law of nature as meaningless, Roberts came up with an entirely different explanation...and a pretty lame one at that. Curved space indeed! Some of the boys suggested that space might be curved around Freddie given the effects of his frequent visits to the tuck shop.

"Explains why we are so attracted to you Freddie!" remarked Jennifer.

Anselm was at his most provocative when they got onto the subject of atoms and the structure of matter. Mr Roberts explained the atom as being comprised of negative particles, called electrons, orbiting around positive particles, protons, with a few neutrons thrown in for good measure.

“A bit like the earth orbiting the sun,” said Mr Roberts immediately regretting the analogy.

“So, this desk I’m leaning on, sir, is made up of things too small for me to see, right?” Anselm started his interrogation. “And with lots of space between those things....
in fact it’s mostly space, sir?” Anselm took his elbow off the desk in a precautionary move.

“That’s right,” said Roberts, waiting for the coup de grace. Class IVB were all ears. Physics lessons were starting to be fun.

“And all these electrons are going round in circles, because the space they are in is curved. But when you add all these very small curved spaces together we get a flat thing called a desk, sir.” Anselm wasn’t sure himself where he was going with all this.

“Well, that may be but we talk of the positive and negative charges of the electron and proton attracting each other... a bit like magnetism...” said Roberts.

“A bit like gravity and anti-gravity then sir!” piped up Abbott at the back, keen to get in on the act.

“Well...yes...but it’s more complex than that. Scientists have discovered different forces at play in atoms. The nuclear force, weak and strong gravitational forces and more. But all of that’s outside the scope of our GCSE syllabus. When some of you go to University and do Physics, you will study such things.”

This wasn't the last time Anselm would hear this get out clause 'outside the scope of GCSE' from a number of teachers.

Class IVB were intrigued to hear that gravitation might have variable strengths. This was one thing that fitted with their own experience, having noticed it was particularly strong in the mornings when they were told to get out of bed.

"And these protons and electrons, sir, what are they made of?" asked Anselm.

"Scientists have discovered literally hundreds of sub-atomic particles each with a different direction of spin or other properties. There are positrons, muons, quarks and many more. They find more particles each year as they sub-divide the atom," said Roberts.

Mr Roberts decided that instead of having himself cast as the defender and explainer of a bizarre world he'd be better off joining Class IVB in its' incredulity at the oddness of it all.

"Worse than that, he said, "scientists now think of these particles not as if they were miniature billiard balls but as 'probabilities' of energy being in a given place at a given time."

Now the desk had been relegated from being made up of mostly space with particles too small to see dotted around in it (a bit like the stew they served at lunch time) to being merely a bunch of probabilities, a bunch of maybes...and maybe nots.

"This is all explained in quantum theory and 'string theory'", continued Mr Roberts.

"There's that string again, holding things together," announced Abbott.

"So, really sir, you're telling us that the Universe is kind of made up of string and ceiling wax which may, or may not, be there at any point in time...depending on the laws of chance," said Freddie, finishing off the job Anselm had started.

Anselm looked at Freddie with surprise. 'Not a bad summary for a copycat,' he thought.

"Sir, have you cross-checked any of this stuff with Mr Thomas in R.E? My Dad says that some old philosophers had a different explanation. Bishop Berkeley said that this desk...or his desk...or rather, everything, was just an idea in God's mind and didn't really exist physically in any sense. And we are ideas in Gods mind too. Like God's having a dream...a very long one and we are all just part of his dream. I guess a bit like Macbeth seeing Banquo....only we never existed separately from God's dream. If we believe that then doesn't it simplify things big time? We don't need to worry about gravity or atoms or strings. Things just happen because God dreams them to happen and as long as he's on the case I can lean on this desk without any fear of it disappearing."

Class IVB fell silent, somewhat stunned by this notion. Anselm was a being a bit wacky again...but he had a point.

"Well...you could say that's the difference between Metaphysics and Physics. It's worth discussing with Mr Thomas. All I can say is that in your GCSE Physics paper it would be wise to keep God out of your answers. The examiners are not really looking for a religious explanation... keep that for the R.E. paper.

Class IVB had observed before that what amounted to 'truth' and 'reality' seemed to differ between teachers. The art teachers' version of reality seemed miles away from Mr Roberts. Miles away from anything recognisable, come to think of it. And Mr Chambers seemed to think the Universe was one big set of simultaneous equations... if only he could solve them. Anselm decided God needed a bit more investigation. He remembered his conversation with Emily about the creation of the Universe. Much seemed to depend on God. 'Time to get a better understanding of 'Him'thought Anselm. 'I wonder if Mr Thomas could shed some light."'

***

Anselm was playing football most lunch times now. The Class IVB boys had teamed up against Class IVC. IVA were not invited. They were considered a bunch of swats and everybody knew swats were crap at football. Anselm wasn't the best, nor was he the worst. The relative anonymity of being 'average' on the football field appealed to him in a way. He was just one of the lads. And although his 'oddball' performances in class drew attention they didn't seem to draw rejection. He'd even taken to sprinkling in a few wrong answers in his homework so he didn't get labelled a swat. The first morning at school had taught him that: Different+ Clever=Lonely.

He played Left Back which gave him a perfect view of the game as IVB usually trounced IVC. As he watched the ball ping around in random motion like a ball- bearing in a pin-ball machine he thought Mr Roberts might have a point about atoms and probability. The football seemed to be behaving in much this way. If all of this was simply a kind of video God was playing in his mind, he couldn't see what possible entertainment God could be getting out of it.

Jennifer Hollioake and Susan were watching on the sidelines most days.

Anselm jumped up and down to get the blood moving. It was November, and the air was getting chilly.

Abbott tackled one of the opposition in the centre circle and the ball fizzed out of the tackle bouncing down field in Anselm's direction. The pitch was on a slope and IVB were playing uphill this half. The ball seemed to gather momentum as it bounced down field. Like Mercury, thought Anselm. He shaped to give it a whack, swung his leg but the ball hit a muddy patch, skidded off to the right ,past the belated dive of Freddie (anchored by his lunch) and into the net. Anselm got a panoramic view of the sky as gravity took over and dumped him on the turf.

Abbott and Gaunt had eased off on Anselm as he had become more popular with the rest of the class. Nobody enjoyed it more when Anselm was giving the teachers a good grilling. They judged they had a common enemy then and Anselm's wit was a useful weapon. But there was still an edge. In fact, Anselm's popularity just drove their resentment underground. So, Anselm's agricultural attempt to clear the ball, costing a goal, gave them a much prized opportunity to vent their spleen.

"Hey, Swinbourne, try kicking the real ball not the imaginary one. Or was the bit of space you were standing in unusually curved," shouted Abbott.

"For someone who's so good at 'Trig', you seem to have a bit of a problem with angles," shouted Gaunt following Abbott's lead.

Freddie trudged over to the corner of the net, shoulders drooped, to recover the ball. He was used to keeping 'clean sheets'. Not particularly because of his goal keeping prowess but because IVB were usually so much in the ascendant that the ball hardly ever got near Freddie. But today IVC were playing out of their skins, aided and abetted by a ball that seemed to have a mind of its own. Anselm's slip put the match at 1-0.

Anselm collected another star for embarrassment.

“Come on Anselm. Chin up!” shouted Jennifer from the sideline. Well at least he seemed to have one fan. He looked at her, thinking fleetingly that if he stuck his chin up he would have even more trouble seeing the ball. She was jumping up and down waving her school scarf. Her breasts wobbled. For a moment Anselm was mesmerised. He was inching up the pitch attracted by another universal force that seemed to have more to do with Biology than Physics. Eyes still locked on Jennifer’s differentiators , he entered the centre circle miles out of position.

“Get the ball Swinbourne, for Christ sake! Get it! Abbott’s strident voice again. Anselm looked around. The ball was squirting towards his feet. What happened next was a blur.

He kicked the ball forward and again past a lunging tackle. And again, to the right.
He looked only at the ball. Every few yards another pair of legs slid into view. He just kept going. Time held its breath. There was a sort of eerie silence as if Anselm had slipped into some parallel universe; one where there was only him and the ball and a random assortment of legs. He kept going. Then, thinking “this can’t last,” he took an almighty swipe at the ball aiming to the right where he thought the goals must be, sliced his kick and looked up to see the ball scudding past a motionless IVC keeper into the left -hand corner of the net.

Suddenly he was smothered by IVB boys, shouting with glee. Face in the mud he was thinking of the softness of Jennifer Hollioake. For that moment he could believe that his goal and Jennifer's breasts were the definitive proof of the existence of a God who was both a great scriptwriter and an imaginative designer.

***

Anselm replayed the goal several times that evening for Martha and Peter. With each telling his football skills grew in brilliance; he dribbled past yet more opponents; his placing of the ball into the net was more accurate and the crowd more awestruck.

He went to bed early to dream in slow motion.

"Well today seems to have been a bit of a breakthrough", said a relieved Peter . "Maybe he's not headed down the hard road you feared after all," said Martha

"I hope not. A boy his age needs the acceptance of his peers. That's something you and I can't give him."

They fell silent. The ticking of the clock on the wall seemed to fill the room.

"And what do you need....Peter?" Martha asked finally.

The clock was insistent ; more metronomic moments passed.

"I think I need more of you. You seem to disappear in your work....or I do. I don't know which comes first...... We let each other drift away, didn't we.

She nodded

"You just seemed to go away into that abstract world of yours. And I felt I'd let you down....when the doctor said no babies. I wanted to call you back but I guess I was grieving . It all just seemed so final....and I felt a fraud, not whole..."

" I hadn't realised how much I wanted kids," said Peter. It always seemed to be you who was pushing ... and then when you couldn't..."

"***I*** couldn't". That was part of the problem; it seemed to be all my fault. Even now you talk about me not 'we'.

"***We*** couldn't," said Peter, "we couldn't" as if repeating it would repair the situation "Maybe I couldn't bear your pain and what I was feeling at the same time. It was like there was nothing else we could talk about; nothing else worth talking about by comparison. Neither of us had any skin left."

Martha was watching him carefully.

"Then I got lost in my books. You became very busy at work. Each of us found our own anaesthetic...apart."

"So, you ***are*** saying it's my fault. If I'd been able to have a baby everything would have been alright. It's because I couldn't cope that you buggered off to your study?" Martha flared up. "Maybe you could just take a little bit of responsibility for things...for once."

The ‘for once’ was a step too far.

“I didn’t say that,” Peter retorted. You’ve got the cart before the horse. You became self-obsessed. I didn’t get a look in. What was I supposed to do? Hang about waiting for you to notice I was still there, hurting too? The only thing that mattered was conceiving. Otherwise there wasn’t a minute in your day for me.”

“And why do you think that it was so important to me, then? Why? Because it was clear to me how important it was to you. You wouldn’t admit it but you wanted a son every bit as much as me. And if I didn’t deliver, what use was I?”

Peter was numb. It hadn’t been like that. Not for him. He hadn’t known what to do other than just get on with life. They hadn’t really talked about it ;not really talked; just turned their separate ways to cope. And all this time she thought he had blamed her?

Martha continued “The further you retreated, the more angry I became…and the more you seemed to go away. Sometimes it seems we sabotage ourselves. I think that Mum did the same with Dad...God what an awful thought,” Martha gasped.

“You always seem so critical. My work’s a waste of time; my ideas are wrong; I don’t perform to specification at dinner parties. It’s not much fun living with your worst critic you know,” groaned Peter. He was conscious he was over the top but couldn’t stop the flow.

“Is that how it feels to you?”

“Well yes; often it does. When we first met , you thought I was the best thing since sliced bread. You would always take my side in any argument. Maybe you were blind to my faults, my limitations; but it was a wonderful blindness. The blindness of romantic love; of being ‘in love’.

“So being alone seemed safer...a familiar place. You can’t disappoint anyone if you are alone and don’t have to take the risk of being less than expectations. Maybe the loneliest place is to be around someone you love and feel the distancing of their anger.”.

Peter felt the glass barrier starting to reassert itself....but pushed through.

“I don’t mean to say it’s down to you. I can see my part in where we have gotten to. It’s just that I...well , guess I took the easy way out.

“Anselm said to me the other day that he liked the way we looked at each other in the photograph album...and...where had those looks gone,” Martha whispered.

“Do you think we could get back there?” Peter asked.

The clock on the wall stopped.

“I hope so.”.

Later that night they lay in bed, her head on his chest and arm across his waist; each of them waiting for time to wear in this unfamiliar feeling of being close.

His hand fell to her breast. She squeezed his chest. "One step at a time....," she whispered.

***

Class IVB had been studying comparative religions in R.E. It had become clear that there were different versions of God, depending on whether you were a Muslim, Taoist, Christian, Jew, Buddhist or one of several other, minority , religious faiths.

And these different versions of God also seemed to have different sets of rules and a different game plan for human beings. Depending on which one you subscribed to then you might meet a different bunch of people in heaven as and when you died. And what you would find there seemed to be radically different too, ranging from becoming one with the universe through to a rather luxurious, everlasting, holiday camp where everybody was on his or her best behaviour.

Class IVB were not greatly interested in the subject. It seemed rather remote

although there was now a growing minority who thought that if R.E. could make Physics obsolete , the world and St Thomas Aquinas school in particular, might be a rather better simpler place. Anselm wanted to go back to first principles. Mr Thomas seemed to be taking it for granted that God, of whichever variety, existed and his job was simply to talk about the belief set around that basic assumption, and about the rituals and the rules.

It seemed that adults were fixated with rules although they had some problem agreeing amongst themselves what the rules were. This was, of course, with the exception of St Thomas Aquinas School were everyone was clear what the rules were and that Mr Smart, the Headmaster, was the undisputed author of those rules. Mr Smart's favourite rule, which served on any occasion where the rest of the rules seemed not to cater adequately for a particular circumstance, was:

'Any offence against common sense is an offence against school rules.'

Mr Smart would, if stumped, pronounce this rule with absolute conviction of its clarity and indisputably. One fifth former was reputed to have challenged this once, enquiring "who decided what common sense is, sir?" Smart had bellowed "Young man, common sense is a rare commodity these days particularly in the young. So , if I were you I would simply follow the example of your teachers. Can't go far wrong there, eh!?"

The fifth former, who had been caught smoking behind the bike shed left Smarts study rather puzzled having seen the fug in the teacher's common room. But he decided not to press his case.

R.E. lessons were on Friday afternoons; last lesson of the day. Mr Thomas had protested that this timetabling was not helpful given the reluctance that the average teenager demonstrated towards the subject. Mr Smart had replied that this was driven by the requirements of the Maths and Science teaching timetables and the 'sets' the pupils were in. "No doubt the good Lord will find a way of keeping the pupil's interest or perhaps He might like to change the number of hours in the day or permit Mr Roberts, Mr Chambers and others to be in two, or preferably more, places at once!" said Mr Smart. That was the end of the discussion.

So, one Friday afternoon in late November as dusk fell and the weekend beckoned, Anselm asked his question: "Sir, how do we know God exists?"

Mr Thomas had studied Theology at college so had not ignored the question but the R.E. syllabus rather assumed God as a given and spent most of its energy on his various manifestations in different religious faiths. His answer therefore reminded Anselm of the one Emily had given.

"It's a question of faith ; a question of belief, Anselm. There is no 'scientific' or logical proof that He exists. But believers know Him as a result of religious experience, of His presence in their life and through the medium of prayer."

"So, if you believe in Him, He exists and if you don't He doesn't," replied Anselm.

“No. I believe he exists. Others may not because they haven’t had that enlightenment. They haven’t ‘found’ God.”

“So, where does he hang out then, given he’s not easy to find?” asked a sceptical Abbott.

“We don’t think of God as a physical being, not some white bearded man up in the clouds but rather an eternal spirit who is everywhere and, most important, ...in our hearts,” replied Mr Thomas.

“Wot, like Banquo then,?” sniggered Abbott. “A Holy Ghost.”

“That’s not an appropriate comparison Abbott. You are sailing close to the wind,” snapped Mr Thomas.

Class IVB were finding this a little unsatisfactory. Freddie was thinking that, given that atoms were a matter of chance, maybe Anselm’s theory that everything was just an idea in the mind of God had some legs to it. But then that would make God just an idea in Gods mind... talk about self-delusion. Freddie’s head was starting to ache! And why would God imagine all these doubters?

Anselm continued. “My tutor said God was the ‘maker of the Universe’; He started everything and He didn’t need anything to start Him off because He’d existed forever.”

“That’s the view of Christians,” agreed Mr Thomas.

“So, He’s responsible for everything, including the things that don’t work very well in this world,” said Anselm.

“Yeah, like the school bus this morning,” Abbott quipped.

“Well, I guess He set the ball rolling and created the laws of the Universe but, within those constraints, physics, evolution and man took over. We should, perhaps, blame Volvo for the bus breaking down,” replied Mr Thomas.

“Sounds a bit of a cop-out for a ‘perfect’ being,” said Freddie. Being perfect ‘n all, surely He could have produced some physics and people who could put a bus together properly?”

“Yeah, but don’t forget He only had seven days to do it all and not surprisingly He needed a rest on the seventh, so it was really six days working flat out. Even the best is going to make a few mistakes, leave a few rough edges, when creating something as big and complicated as the Universe in six days....don’t yer think?”

Gaunt was coming to God’s rescue .

“Don’t be stupid! He didn’t make all this. All He had to do was create an infinitely small, infinitely dense bunch of ....stuff, matter...and then stand well back. We did that in Physics, dummy,” said Abbott.

This was turning into the liveliest lesson Mr Turner had ever had with Class IVB... though he had no idea where it was going to end.

"Actually, when you think about it ,God took a hell of a risk. Creating the big bang and then letting the Universe get on with it for billions of years. Then there's the hit and miss of evolution... and eventually we arrived. I mean man He had no guarantee any of us would make it here and end up believing in Him. And if nobody believed in Him, He wouldn't have existed , would He... or at least there'd have been nobody to build His churches and put money in the box on a Sunday. Then where would He have been?" Freddie was confused again.

"Listen just 'cos nobody believed in Him wouldn't mean He didn't exist . Nobody believes in you Freddie Jones but you, unfortunately, exist...you great lump of lard!" sneered Abbott.

"That's enough!" said Mr Thomas.

Freddie went red. Anselm diagnosed it as anger.

"Sir, David Hume said that there were only three kinds of statements....ones you can test through experience, through your senses; ones that can be logically proven ...like 2+2=4 and thirdly nonsense statements that aren't meaningful. In other words, he said there were only two kinds : the ones like you get in Science and can test and ones like in Maths or logic," said Anselm. "When you say God exists but that it can't be proved scientifically or logically then aren't you really saying...well...that you're talking nonsense?"

A murmur of approval went around Class IVB like a Mexican wave.

“It depends on what we mean by ‘experience’. Christians experience God in their lives in a way that doesn’t use the five senses. It is a spiritual experience.”

“If I said I had had a spiritual experience of a man from Mars, would you believe me, sir?”

“Probably not Anselm .”

“I would,” said Abbott, “Swinbourne has friends there, sir.”

“You see, Anselm, the man from Mars doesn’t really help...doesn’t help me make sense of the world. Whereas , God does. He gives meaning and purpose. I can conceive that the Universe started without a man from Mars and that there are consistent physical laws; I can conceive that there is love in the world without needing to assume a man from Mars and that there are moral rules that most of us agree on. But I can’t imagine why all these things would be so without a God who is interested in the world of men and women.”

Anselm paused. He was reminded of what Emily told him about the time when men could only understand gravity and light as working through the ‘ether’, an invisible medium that connected things and through which gravitational force and light waves moved. Now the Universe is proved to be mostly vacuum...and bent.

Maybe one day men would set aside the God theory in favour of a new way of understanding the world.

He was getting Freddie's headache and decided to stop there...for now.

The bell rang to start the weekend. Class IVB all tried to get out through the door at the same time.

***

That evening Anselm told Peter about the discussion with Mr Thomas and the unsatisfactory 'existential' status of God.

"Philosophers have attempted several arguments to prove the existence of God....but all of the arguments have sort of 'sprung leaks' over time. The argument that there must be a prime mover who started everything else just defers the problem. The ontological argument boiled down to a sort of play on words. The teleological argument, though, had more resonance with ordinary people", explained Peter.

"What's the teleological argument?" asked Anselm.

"Well...just imagine this. You are walking on a deserted heath and you see an object shining by a stone. As you approach it you see that it is a watch gleaming in the sunlight. You may not know what a watch is but picking it up you are struck by the intricacy of its designs; you open the back, see the escapement and all of the mechanisms that make it work; you see the evenness with which the hands move, and so. What would you conclude?"

"That someone had been careless", Anselm suggested.

"Would you conclude that the watch was just a random aggregation of material with no purpose...come together by chance. Or would you rather assume from its design that there was a watch maker who had made this timepiece; who had designed and made it for the very purpose it fulfilled?"

"I think I would expect such a thing to have been designed and made by someone... a watchmaker," replied Anselm.

"So, look around you. Look at the world. Look at the orbiting of the planets around the sun, the spinning of the earth...so regular...such a complex system working as if by clockwork. Look at Mother Nature, the plants, animals, man...complex organisms...more complex by far than the watch and no less elegantly designed. Wouldn't you for the same reasons deduce that all of this showed the hand of a maker...a chief architect...an intelligent and powerful force with purpose in mind...? " asked Peter.

"God?" replied Anselm.

"Just so...that is the argument from design," said Peter.

Anselm thought for a few moments. Peter waited for the next chess move.

"It's a good argument," offered Anselm. Better than simply "He exists and I just know it" which was what Mr Thomas seemed to say.

"You think so?"

"Well yes...but...if I look at your car I believe in a maker...Volvo...the badge says so. And I know roast potatoes show the hand of Martha...and so on. But you know when I was on the heath and saw that cottage with smoke coming from its chimney, I didn't know what it was. It was only when the shepherd found me and took me inside and I saw the fire, the place he slept and how he cut the wood, that I saw its purpose. And he told me he made it. I would never have guessed that a shepherd...or any person made the cottage when I first saw it. I didn't really know what a person was. And I never thought of a person making the heath either. It just was...there."

"So ,I think, today I might imagine a watch maker... but maybe that's just because I've got used to the idea of people making things .If you think about it, everything we see is either made by people or it's just nature. Just because a lot of things which work are made by people, why do we extend that assumption to nature? It's not clear what the purpose of nature is...not like a watch. And if there's no clear purpose then why assume someone designed it?"

"Well," said Peter "not everyone buys the argument from design...just for the kinds of reasons you are coming up with. But here's a puzzle. Scientists have shown that the

Universe is a very marginal thing. By that I mean they have discovered that many of the physical laws of the Universe are very finely tuned and if there was a small change in them the Universe would be a very different place or could not exist at all.

"For example, they have found that the balance between gravity and electromagnetism...two opposing forces in a star is so delicate that were either one to get the upper hand the stars, and our sun, could not exist. Tie this to the very narrow range of conditions in which life, and still more so, human life, could arise then it's little short of a miracle that we are here asking these questions. So, you might argue some force, let's call it 'God', must have been involved in designing and making such laws which determine a whole string of events...which, well... if they were pure chance, pure coincidence...would be so unlikely to happen."

"So, the Universe is a kind of a million to one against bet?" added Anselm.

"Even a billion, billion to one against," replied Peter. "It is an exceedingly improbable thing."

"But I don't really see that it's made a whole lot more probable by inventing an invisible, disembodied, eternal, all powerful being called God....himself a very improbable thing as I see it," replied Anselm.

"And actually,....if the Universe wasn't precisely right we wouldn't be here, asking these questions...yes that's true; but who's to say there aren't or haven't been, billions of

Universes during eternity. And this, the one in which we are standing, is one that, at last, came out right...everything fell into place just so...to make stars, life and you and me possible...by chance. But after billions of Universes that didn't turn out right?

So, I think this Universe may be rare...but there could have been a billion, billion Universes before this one. It might be very long odds to get a Universe that produces you, me and this question but it seems just as long odds that someone, or thing should exist fitting the description of God that Mr Thomas and Emily gave me."

"And why do you think God is improbable Anselm?"

"Well, I just don't think the things claimed about him make sense. For example, Emily described him as eternal; he has always been and will always be...no beginning... no end. Like for him the past stretches back forever and the future stretches forward forever. That's two forevers by my reckoning! And as time ticks by he still has forever in front of him...I just can't see it."

"Maybe that's more of a problem with infinite time than with the idea of God. Suppose someone said that 'eternal' means outside of time or in a kind of forever now...with no past or future but sort of 'omnipresent'; God just kind of stretches across all the 'nows' of time but doesn't live in a sequence of steps, events like we appear to. All of eternity is present for Him – He sees every now at once."

"That seems so difficult. He's supposed to be watching the world So, He's seeing everything that ever happened or ever will happen all at once. Kind of like looking down on time?"

"You could put it that way," replied Peter.

"I can't see how he could take it all in. And if he answers people's prayers when they ask what they should do about a problem...doesn't he already know the answer...already know what in fact they decide to do?"

"That's another difficulty with God. He's said to be omniscient; so, He knows everything."

"Maybe He knows who drew all the graffiti on the toilet walls that Ms Bentham was complaining about the other day?"

"I guess He does," said Peter.

"Wonder if He would 'split' on whoever it was," mused Anselm.

"If He knows everything then presumably He knows what you or I are going to do tomorrow. In which case we don't seem to have much choice in the matter. If God already knows what's going to happen then it's inevitable and we can't change it. This is the dilemma about freedom of will. It seems that God's existence means you and I have no say over our future actions even if we think we have some choice, between alternatives, some ability to act freely," Peter continued.

“I hadn’t thought of that. Then what’s the point in God picking out who goes to heaven and who doesn’t when people had no choice about what they did? He lays down the laws, sets things off like clockwork, we get no say in it and yet some of us get to heaven and other go to a less pleasant place...by far. How fair is that? And what’s the point of the game?” asked Anselm.

Just at that moment, Martha called from the kitchen. Dinner was ready.

***

“What have you two been up to?” she asked as they settled around the kitchen table.

“God and freedom”, Anselm announced.

“Big subjects. And what have you concluded?”

“Seems like you can’t have both. If one exists then the other can’t.”

“That seems a bit of a shame,” Martha responded. “I’m not sure one is much use without the other. Seems to me that they go together rather well.”

“Logically it’s difficult to see how you can have both,” said Peter.

“Well then, I think I would come to the conclusion that you have to abandon logic. Human beings need both God and freedom and if logic is getting in the way then out the window with logic is what I say-clearly it's too heavy for this balloon."

"You see, Anselm, this is one of the many differences between men and women. We experience the world in completely different ways and draw completely different conclusions from the same data. In fact, the extent to which we need any data to reach conclusions also differs profoundly.

"Like Wittgenstein's picture of the old witch, or is it a young woman. Different people see different things in the same picture. And there are no more different people than a man and a woman. We all have our own interpretation, our own lens through which we see the world around us and make sense of it."

"A bit like Einstein's relativity theory where things depend upon the position and speed of the observe," Anselm chimed in precociously.

"Or, beauty's in the eye of the beholder," added Martha.

"So, I guess you two may look at the same thing and see it in two very different ways. Like when Peter sees a politician he sees a liar; whereas Martha sees a realist, a pragmatist."

Martha blushed, unsure about being the defender of politicians.

"And when Martha sees a kitchen table she lays it for dinner whereas Peter sees a bunch of sense data which he is not sure are substantial enough to bear the weight of plates. Which maybe explains why Peter doesn't set the table and leaves it to Martha, eh?"

"When Peter sees the universe around him he sees a question. When I see it I see an answer," said Martha.

"I guess it's true of feelings too. We often feel quite differently in the same situation. The same event, sight, sound impacts each of us in different ways dependent upon how we are at that moment;" Peter changed tack.

"So, one day when you see Martha you are happy but she is angry; and the next day it's the other way around. Maybe if you are lucky you can both be happy on the same day. I've noticed sometimes you are angry at the same time; in fact, one of you can start off happy and catch angriness from the other."

Martha and Peter looked at each other in embarrassment.

"Ah! It looks to me like you might be feeling the same things at the same time right now"

"Enough of that now I think; my head is spinning," said Martha. "You two can continue after dinner if you must."

***

"There is a kind of way out of the problem," said Peter. "If we say the future is not yet settled for men; we have a choice and are free to act. It's just that from God's perspective, standing outside of time He sees the outcome of that choice.It's not that He has looked into the future whilst stood alongside us in the now, with us trying to decide which way to go and Him knowing all along. It's more that me make free choices as we go along and the eternal He 'sees' all of our actions in His forever now. If we had made different choices He would see those instead. It's our choices that decide what lies on the field of time in front of His eternal gaze."

"I need to think a bit about that. I'm not even sure whether I want to be free...I'd have no-one else to blame if things go wrong," Anselm responded. "It seems to me if you were to ask God now 'what will I be doing next week,' He knows and by telling you would show that you have no choice. He doesn't have to wait to see what happens."

"Yes, that's a problem if you have an eternal being in communication with one who lives in time with a past, present and future. As long as God is sat in eternity, you can be said to be free. Once you get into dialogue with Him, you drag Him into time and suddenly He knows the future. Then life could be said to be pre- determined," replied Peter.

That's not really very helpful is it...a God who as soon as you get the benefit of His wisdom you're handcuffed to a particular future," said Anselm.

"Maybe that's why even people of strong religious faith make no claims that God predicts the future and...sort of...tips us off as to what's going to happen. In fact, Christians would say that would defeat the whole purpose of God's creation. It would deny the purpose of mankind which they believe is for men to make a free choice to take the path of righteousness, and to do good in the world," said Peter.

"So, God sees everything that happens across eternity but he doesn't let on...he doesn't tell man...he kind of leaves men with the illusion that they are free to make choices," summarised Anselm.

"The believer in free-will believes that those choices truly are free. They argue that just because God has perfect knowledge, he *knows* what we choose but he doesn't determine what we choose. He leaves that to us," replied Peter.

Anselm looked unconvinced.

"Look at it this way. The statement 'you will go to school tomorrow' is not a fact that can be known in advance. It's more of a prediction...and whether it turns out to be so depends on what you actually choose to do. God doesn't 'know' that you go to school come what may .He just knows that you go to school because He knows what free choice you actually decide to make. I suppose in that sense looking at the world from the vantage point of eternity,..looking down on the field of time is a bit like looking at history for God even though some parts of the story are in what we call the past and some are in what we. call the future."

"I didn't know I had any choice about going to school," said Anselm.

“A bad example, maybe . But you take my point?”

Anselm decided to move on.

“Whether God is all-knowing or not, I can see another problem of freedom. If He created the world so it obeys the laws of physics and these never change then surely what happens in the world is determined right from the beginning. He set things up, wound up the mechanism, then let it go and everything that happened after that had to follow a set path dictated by the laws of the Universe.”

“That’s the principle of ‘determinism’ and some philosophers have argued just that,” said Peter.

“Well my Biology teacher says that the brain is really just a biological computer; it works with electronic signals and, just like a computer, it works to the laws of physics. So, whatever happens in my brain is...kind of ...inevitable, decided by the laws of chemistry or electricity. In fact, you can go right back to the beginning and everything that happened after that was decided by the laws of the Universe acting on each state of the Universe as it developed. So where is the free-will to make choices between alternatives...to have the sense that I could have done something different if I’d chosen to?” asked Anselm. “I’m a slave, a machine really!”

“Yes, that is another argument against free-will...but somehow it doesn’t seem satisfactory does it? It doesn’t really fit to how we experience life and ourselves,” said Peter.

Anselm reflected for a moment. Actually, quite a lot of his life did seem to be determined...by other people like teachers, and Martha. But he did believe he could make choices...even if they were only rather small choices like which roast potato to eat first or which side of the bed to get out of in the morning.

Peter continued, "Some philosophers have taken the line that acts of will, or choices, are actions of the mind and do not have to follow the physical laws of the Universe. Even though science indicates that your brain has much to do with your mental processes, the brain might be viewed as a kind of environment in which thinking, deciding and 'willing' take place. Those events are totally different to physical events,; they don't have to follow the same laws or any laws, and aren't therefore determined by anyone or anything other than the 'self'."

Anselm remembered his walk with Peter weeks ago by the brook trying to catch his elusive self. It had seemed like trying to catch the breeze. He wondered if something that seemed so slight, so insubstantial could really do things like lift his arm, turn his head. He lifted his arm, as he had done on the walk. He was aware of a fleeting moment perhaps, when he decided to lift his arm but nothing in between.

His arm just came up. He didn't detect a self or a moment that might have held 'an act of will' before his arm moved. It seemed spontaneous. He didn't detect any clockwork mechanism either. He was stuck. Yes, he would agree that it didn't seem that the lifting of his arm was just the inevitable outcome of a mechanical brain state, but equally he couldn't really detect this event called 'willing' something to happen ...things were too fast. It was like the only way he could really tell that he had 'willed' something, was when it happened. Couldn't those happenings just as easily be the result of internal mechanisms behind the scenes that he was not aware of but nevertheless were just that...mechanisms. Maybe all of this was just in the 'too difficult' box.

"Hmmm," said Peter seemingly having exhausted any comfort he could give on the question of human freedom. "Whilst we are on the subject; the all-powerful, 'omnipotent' claim made for God is a problem too."

"How come?" asked Anselm.

"Well can God make a square without corners? Can He make 2+2 =5? Can He make a stone that is so heavy that he, himself cannot lift it?"

"No one can make a square with no corners or a triangle with four sides," replied Anselm. They can't do it because it doesn't make sense...they are contradictions. The definition of a square is a shape with four sides and right angles at the corners... that's what we mean by a square."

"You're right," Peter granted.

"I think it's the same with numbers and arithmetic, although I'm not so sure 2 and 2 means four...it just *is* four," said Anselm.

“Yes. We can prove it mathematically and it’s pretty much impossible to see how it could be otherwise.

“But what about the stone ? If He can make such a stone He wouldn’t be able to lift it...and so that would be a limit to his power wouldn’t it? Equally, if He couldn’t make such a stone that too would be something He couldn’t do. Either way it turns out there is something He can’t do,” explained Peter.

This argument beguiled Anselm for a while. His mind wandered a little. “Seems God has gone down in the world somewhat since the beginning of this debate,” he thought. “He started off as a supreme being, the only plausible explanation of the world as it is with all its richness of design .He was all-knowing, all-seeing and all- powerful. Now He seems to have been relegated to the side-lines; not really needed to explain the world; stranded in eternity with no past or future, supposedly knowing what’s around the corner but, because of His omniscience or of His granting free will to humans, unable to do anything about it; and now losing His powers...”

A light bulb went on inside Anselm’s head.

“But God, if He exists, can make a stone of any weight...even infinite weight...there is no limit in weight of stone he could make. Likewise ,He can lift a stone of any weight....there is no limit. So ,God’s power to make and lift stones is limitless no matter what the size and weight of stone,” he said triumphantly.

“Bravo, Anselm,” applauded Peter, “you see the flaw in the argument.” They decided to leave God there, basking in His omnipotence....at least for that evening.

***

X RIGHTS

In those first weeks at school Anselm's star chart progressed rapidly. From a starting point of 'anxiety' and 'excitement', he went through 'lonely', 'embarrassment' and on to 'hope', 'happy' and a feeling the other boys helped him to name ... 'lust'. This seemed to be somewhere between a physical sensation and an emotion. It cropped up particularly whenever Jennifer Hollioake was around...which was most of the time.

Anselm would sit slightly behind Jennifer and to her left in English lessons. It was in English that he got the best view of her breasts, straining the buttons of her white shirt. They seemed to grow each day and Anselm wondered at Mother Nature's ability to keep them perfectly in balance...how one did not get ahead of the other in this growth phase.

But it was towards Miss Jolliffe that Anselm's attention had now turned. She too had large, round breasts with nipples which in the chill late Autumn days seemed to stand to attention as she entered the room from the quad. Miss Jolliffe didn't just have breasts...she had legs, legs which were dressed in black nylon stockings and which disappeared into the mysteries beneath her 'above the knee' skirt.

Most of the boys in Class IVB drooled over her but Anselm had a special relationship with Miss Jolliffe. She often visited his bed at night, or so he imagined. They say that boys think of sex at least three times every five minutes. This average increased considerably during English lessons and after ten o'clock at night.

Anselm was attracted to Jennifer....but he was obsessed by Miss Jolliffe. She was perhaps only six or seven years older, fresh out of teacher training college, but those years added so much more...grown-upness. She was out of Anselm's reach, yet tantalisingly close, standing at the front of the class. Anselm's fantasies about caressing her breasts and legs were more real to him than the table was to his elbows.

If all of this was simply an idea in the mind of God then he could only marvel at God's imagination and creativity in producing Miss Jolliffe.

"So, let's see what you've come up with for your homework Class IVB," Miss Jolliffe called out one morning , disturbing the boys' collective dream.

"I asked you to write a poem, about 'Time'. Who'll volunteer to read out their poem?" she asked.

Anselm's hand shot up...without any detectable act of 'willing'. He assumed this was one of those examples Peter had spoken of...an 'automatic' reaction to some stimulus. Miss Jolliffe was the stimulus.

"Yes Anselm. Perhaps you'd like to come out to the front to read."

Anselm shuffled back his chair and stood. Class IVB was quiet. Somewhere at the back he heard Abbott mutter "teacher's pet...just tryin' to get close to Miss... wouldn't mind getting' close meself...know what I mean..."

Miss Jolliffe gave Abbott her sharpest look.

Anselm loped to the front...trying to look cool, indifferent. Girls seemed to like that…it made them come back for more, trying to get some attention. Maybe it would work with Miss Jolliffe too. But it's not easy looking cool ,and relaxed, when you're turning crimson and your legs feel about to give way. Anselm was five feet eleven inches tall but felt the size of an elephant, trying to navigate the narrow aisle between the desks without giving away his adolescence by colliding with one of them.

Five feet eleven and long limbed. He could get from his desk to the door in three nanoseconds when the bell rang to end any other lesson. But in English the distances were much greater. Minutes seemed to elapse before he reached Miss Jolliffe's side and she kept looking at him with a faint smile on her lips...her lips, as if she knew his deepest secrets, could look inside him and see his fantasies. His cheeks were now beetroot red.

"Just take your time, Anselm. When you're ready," she said. Anselm opened his exercise book and tried to clear his throat.

"What have you called the poem?" she asked.

"In the...beginnn…errr... "he croaked, gravel filling the back of his throat. This happened all too often in the company of girls with large round breasts and always with Miss Jolliffe.

"In the beginning, Miss," he managed to clear away the gravel. He read:

God made the world in seven days Made from nothing but empty space With just imagination in his hands The original maker worked his grace.

Did He first chisel the mountain tops And then nail up the clouds and sky How did He make the rivers run When oceans and seas still were dry

How did He cut out the warming sun From all that dark and endless night Then fix the green of fields and leaves Before He gave the gift of sight

And did He first build the East Before He turned and shaped the West ?

Was it the nightingales song came first Or the eggs which lay within her nest?

What was it that He first did make In the earliest morning of day one ? Before the cockerel began to crow Before that first beam from the sun

He made the long bow of creation And strung it tight with golden twine Then stretched it to its fullest length And shot the arrow of endless time.

There was a hush across Class IVB.

“That is...absolutely beautiful, Anselm. Beautiful . Where did you get the idea from?” asked a delighted Miss Jolliffe...feeling a rush of pride in one of her protégés.

“Er...I don’t know, it just sort of came to me. I was talking to my Dad about God and how He made the Universe and all its’ laws a few days ago...”

“A few days ago? I think you’ve got your timing wrong Swinbourne... The world’s been around a lot longer than that....least ours has....not sure about yours!” Abbott interrupted.

The class stayed quiet. Abbott looked around furtively wondering why he had not got the usual snigger. He elbowed Gaunt next to him who let out an involuntary “hah!”

“Did you have something to say David Gaunt?” asked Miss Jolliffe.

"Er... no Miss, no." Gaunt replied feeling Abbott's stare.

"So class, what do you make of that?"

Abbott tried again. "Swinbourne has found God, Miss," he quipped. Still no snigger. Abbott retreated into sullen silence.

"It's about the mystery of how God made the world Miss, "Jennifer Hollioake piped up. Maybe by commenting on his poem she could claim Anselm...be part of his poetry, "...and ...like...well, where would you start? How can you make East first without ,at the same time ,making West?... and...how could anyone make everything? There would just be too much to do,and in what order, even for God. So, I think Anselm is saying that God started from nothing but his own imagination and just kind of kicked off time...and everything followed after that..."

"Is that what your poem is saying, Anselm?" asked Miss Jolliffe.

"Well...yes Miss, something like that." He looked at Jennifer. "Yes, that's right. I think God didn't build the world as it is but He gave it a start and some laws to live by...like a big experiment; and then watched as things evolved," replied Anselm.

"Well thank you Anselm for sharing your poem with us," said a sugary Miss Jolliffe. Anselm went back to his desk; elegantly.

That evening he, Martha and Peter all awarded themselves stars for 'proud.'

***

Martha was late home the following evening. She had been working longer hours for some weeks. The deal she was working on was always just about to close; then something happened to delay things.

She was often irritable. But ,tonight, there was something else in the air. Something more negative Something without energy.

"The deals off," she announced in a tone that seemed to say :"there you are; I told you so ."

"What do you mean?"

"The bankers have pulled out; won't provide the finance." "Why?" asked Peter.

"They say the market conditions aren't right. Too much market risk; people pulling their horns in; interest rate rises....bookings for summer season low.. not .hittting forecast cash flows..."

"So.,one dodgy Summer isn't the end of the world is it?"

"Don't you start ...I've been trying to explain to the staff most of the afternoon"

"So, what's it mean?"

“The bankers see negative cash flow this year and next, an increasing interest burden, no asset backing and the equations don’t stack up.”

“What’s it mean for you?”

“Oh, we’ll keep going , but.....”

Martha drifted off.

“I’m sure things will work out.” He knew it was trite as soon as the sentence left his lips but, as usual, couldn’t summon an apology quickly enough.

“Oh, you’re sure are you. Well that’s fine then .I needn’t worry.”

“No need to snap. Just trying to look on the bright side....”

Peter fell back on the defensive. The undelivered apology receded rapidly giving the high ground to his own need to be in the right.

“Well there isn’t one far as I can see. I’ve been working on this for nearly twelve months. Without it we can’t expand the business and penetrate the European market. I really wonder whether it’s all worth the effort.”

Peter was silent. Part of him felt the need to say something to comfort her but, as he rehearsed in his head ,couldn’t find anything that didn’t run a high risk of provoking a similar response.

He began to feel angry. Typical of women, of Martha, to tie you in knots; damned if you do and damned if you don't. Whatever you say isn't right.

Eventually he found another question; a practical one; no opinion, no attempt to give false comfort: "So what happens next?"

" Nothing. I don't know .We just stay as we are...I don't know what we'll do; how should I know?" Martha ,usually so certain, was all at sea.

"Can the business carry on without the new money?" he asked.

"Yes, for a while. But the competition will overtake us; they will have access to funds from their parent company..."

"Maybe you could try some other banks," offered Peter, still trying to find a fix.

"If it were that simple don't you think we would have done so. All of the banks have the same attitude. The problem is the numbers don't add up. We can't offer any collateral and the cash flows are too uncertain."

"What about re-mortgaging the house to raise the finance?"

Peter wasn't sure where the idea came from; it was out before his editor could check it for sense.

Martha looked at him.

“We’re looking for ten million pounds. How much do you think this house is worth Peter? You really don’t understand what I’ve been doing do you?”

“Okay, you’re so clever ,you fix it.” Peter stomped out of the kitchen in the direction of his study. A loud slam announced his isolation.

Martha slumped in the kitchen chair.

Anselm had been listening intently through a crack in the garden door. A few minutes after Peter’s exit he pushed the door fully open, entered and greeted Martha.

“Hi Mum.” The words Mum, Mother were still on trial but he was becoming more attached to them.

“Hello, son,” Martha replied in kind.“ I didn’t know you were out there,” she said gathering herself.

“ You and Peter had a row, right?”

Martha blinked and thought for a moment. Was that what it was.“Yes, I suppose you could call it that. How could you tell?”

“Well I heard Peter slam the door. But before that I heard your voice go from sad to angry. And as your voice changed so did Peters; like they had decided to keep each other company or, like, one voice pushed the other. It was weird really because it’s not like either of you had done anything wrong and you didn't shout, like they do at school when they are mad; you both just kind of went cold and quiet. Is that how grown-ups do 'angry'?"

"Sometimes, Anselm. Sometimes we aren't very good at letting our anger out in a noisy way."

"Why not?"

"I'm not sure .Maybe we think it's too dangerous. Maybe we feel we have to be careful.... so we use cold and quiet instead of hot and loud."

"What was it about?"

Martha hesitated for a moment.

"A problem I have at work. Not enough bank promises to expand our business. A bit complicated but it's very disappointing ."

"Did Peter steal the promises?"

"Oh no, no, nothing like that. Peter isn't involved."

Anselm wore his puzzled look.

So why are you angry with each other?"

Martha hesitated once more.

"I don't know Anselm...Well...perhaps I do; but it's complicated. Have you got some homework to do tonight?"

'Homework?' What's that got to do with anything? It'd s not me who needs to do their homework,' thought Anselm. He decided not to push any further; Martha didn't really look up to answering any more 'complicated' questions.

***

Ms Bentham taught Geography and Social Studies. She was a stark contrast to Miss Jolliffe. Anselm didn't have to rely purely on his eyes to conclude that; he could listen to his body.

"Imagine waking up next to that in the morning," Abbott had asked. "Bet she wears tweed pyjamas."

"No need," said Gaunt...."if the rest of her body is covered with as much hair per square inch as her top lip!"

They had studied weather systems. Ms Bentham had said the weather was possibly the most complex of things in the Universe. Especially the English weather. So many things influenced it, including random sun spots, that, really, it was beyond the science of man to predict with any accuracy and even more beyond the science of man to control or influence it in any way.

Anselm had wondered why the man on the television had pretended to forecast what the weather would be the following day. He had noticed the man's tendency to wave his arm broadly at the weather map on the wall and to talk in vague terms like "we might expect some rain, later in the day in Westerly areas; temperatures will fall to below average for this time of year; a few sunny spells should appear."..and so on.

Ms Bentham had explained that the art of Meteorology had much in common with Astrology....both were to do with heavenly bodies and application of spurious logic in trying to predict the future. If God really did make the laws of the Universe He seemed to have sprinkled them with a fair dose of randomness or chance. Nevertheless, Ms Bentham insisted they learn some of the principles of weather formation and patterns.

"It's on your GCSE syllabus and though I wouldn't put much store by it...it might just stop you getting wet one of these days!"

Class IVB were unanimously of the opinion that they would rather take their chances than have to listen to Ms Bentham's interminable soliloquies on occluded fronts. After all, you didn't actually see big wavy lines with bumps and triangles on in the sky to warn you showers were on their way. Had God thought to do that, it would have been rather more useful than the BBC weatherman's arm waving.

Class IVB had also studied climate, population distribution and economic development across the various continents of the world. It was here that Anselm found out where Somalia was. It became clear that

Somalia wasn't the only poor country in the world. Quite the reverse. Ms Bentham told them 80% of the wealth is in the hands of only 10% of the world's population.

Ms Bentham had done her best to explain the wealth of nations . She explained the principles of division of labour and specialisation; natural resources; industrialisation; international trade; the virtuous circle of jobs where people made things to sell to others in turn using the money they received to buy...which in turn created more jobs....until most everyone was so busy making things they had little spare time to enjoy the things they made. And others were busy inventing things and persuading people they needed them so more factories could be built, more jobs created and more money available for people to buy these things they never knew they needed and so on....and so on.

But in Somalia and Ethiopia this virtuous circle didn't get squared. These countries were largely desert and barren with little rain. It was difficult to grow things and "agriculture is the basis of an economy", explained Ms Bentham. "Agriculture puts food in the local population's mouths and provides a commodity, which can be traded with other nations in exchange for other goods the country needs."

Anselm had asked about the country just across the Red Sea from Ethiopia...Saudi Arabia. It turned out that Saudi Arabia was desert, hot, with little water too...and was one of the richest nations on earth measured in GDP per capita! Ms Bentham explained that oil was the basis of this economic miracle...rotted vegetation and animals from millions of years ago, when the county was more lush and green, and had a very different climate.

Anselm was struck by the unfairness of all this. All that separated luxury and poverty ,or life and death ,today was swamps and prehistoric animals which disappeared several million years ago.

It turned out also that Britain didn't make much of anything anymore and yet was classed as a developed economy with a 'well-off' population. All the British do is have the Bank of England issue promises and trade these promises...in different forms....called equities, bonds, gilts. The rest of the time people in Britain did things like cooking for each other; serving at supermarkets; doing each other's hair; building houses for each other and transporting, mostly British, people around so they could get to the places where they did these rather incestuous things.

Anselm felt a sense of outrage on behalf of the Somalians and wondered why they didn't start issuing promises of their own to get a similar 'virtuous cycle' going. They could print a whole lot of promises and exchange them with the U.S.A. and Saudi Arabia to get the things they needed.

Ms Bentham snookered this idea by saying that the promises wouldn't be accepted as they were not worth anything unless there were some resources backing them up... something you could trade them in for.

Abbott had suggested sand but this didn't seem to do the trick with Ms Bentham; so, the Somalians were back to square one. Starving.

It occurred to Anselm that Britain could easily find itself in the same position as the Somalians. The Bank of England was a bit of an emperor without clothes! Maybe he needed to take some precautions against this. He stored the thought away.

He learnt that the Americans had rights, laid down in the American 'Constitution'. Each person there had the right to: "Life, Liberty and the pursuit of happiness." Mr Dowty ,who taught them History, had explained this. Surely if American people had rights then so did the people in Somalia and in Britain; and so did he, Anselm Swinbourne.

Ms Bentham showed them a formula, which was a bit like Martha's emotional Maths:

Happiness = Material Consumption divided by Desire

"So," said Ms Bentham "if the material resources you consume are large and your desire for such things is low then one divided by the other produces a large amount of happiness. On the other hand ,if you don't consume many resources...or don't have them in the first place....and really want them then you have a low level of happiness. The Somalians have very little...and their desire is high...many of them have too little food. So, they are suffering in a big way."

"And Freddie goes to the tuck shop at least twice a day so he should be happy," said Abbott. "Trouble is....his desire is enormous so he's a miserable git! The more he eats the more he wants so he can never catch up with himself...that's why he's so fat."

"Shut your gob," Freddie snapped.

"That's enough!" said Ms Bentham.

"The formula also says that if you don't feel you need a lot of things then you can be happy even if you're poor," added Jennifer.

"That's true; but I guess it depends on the kinds of things that are missing in your life and your aspirations. For the Somalians it's very extreme. They need food to live and so their desire is very high. But these things are relative. You can find unhappy people in rich societies, usually because the desire is high...because they see others enjoying a better standard of living than they do or because advertising stimulates people's interest in a product or makes them want to have some outward sign of wealth like a big house."

"So, these people who advertise things are going to make us unhappy, all other things being equal," Anselm piped up, "particularly if we can't afford to buy the things they are advertising. Best thing is not to get used to the good life or look at what other people have. That way, although your consumption goes down, so does your desire."

“ In fact, the Buddhist monks have got it right. They have got themselves into a state of mind where they want very little to eat or wear and so they have enough. They don’t watch TV and they live only with other monks.”

“That’s true,” replied Ms Bentham. “But you could argue that would mean there’d be no progress. Man would stand still and not invent new things...new things for people to consume. We would be stuck in a kind of equilibrium...everybody would have just enough to meet their needs and be moderately happy.”

“So, what’s so bad about that Ms?” asked Abbott.

“Well...it’s one way...but some would argue that man needs a purpose...and discovery of the Universe and continual improvement in people’s standard of living are an important part of having such a sense of purpose,” Ms Bentham replied.

“Not if it just gets people craving for things they can’t get their hands on. And even if they can...doubling their desire and then doubling their consumption just leaves them with the same happiness ratio....whilst someone else might be really devastated seeing others with things which are beyond their reach.” Anselm challenged.

“Does the formula only work for material consumption Miss?” asked Jennifer. “I don’t think so...it can work for love, too,” she said answering her own question. If you replaced ‘Material Consumption’ with...say, ... ‘Love Received ,’ then I can see it works with feelings too. If I love someone but they don’t love me back as much, or at all, then I'm going to be unhappy aren't I?" she looked over her shoulder to Anselm for a second.

"Hah! Don't worry Jenn...I'll love yer...lots," Abbott called out.

"It's got to be from someone you desire," said Jennifer.

Abbott muttered something to Gaunt about sex...rampant desire and no opportunity.

"OK. Let's move on," said Ms Bentham. So, the Somalians are very unhappy, suffering badly as they need food, clothes, medicine...the basic necessities of life to keep them alive and healthy and they do not have the resources to exchange for such things. So, what are we going to do about it?"

We? Class IVB fell silent. How come we are suddenly responsible for the Somalians? How come we are supposed to do something about it? We've only just learnt where Somalia is! The collective consciousness of Class IVB was feeling this was a rather unfair, and unrealistic, expectation. The sum total of their pocket monies annually would hardly buy the Somalians a jelly bean each.

Then a few ideas started to surface. "Get the Bank of England to print some more money and send it." "Export sand." "Dig for oil". "Build a bridge over to Saudi Arabia." "Tow icebergs from the Arctic...melt them in the desert so they can grow stuff." "Get our Mums and Dads to take out a second mortgage...lend them the money to build egg-timer factories." "Make sand an international currency." "Start a dot-com business offering virtual reality camel rides to people in the U.S."

The bell rang. Ms Bentham set homework...to research and write an essay on one idea to solve the problem of starvation in Somalia.

***

When he got home that evening, Anselm was still fussed that the Somalians seemed to have got such a raw deal. He'd never met a Somalian but, as far as he knew, they were just like anybody else; they were part of the world that an 'omnipotent' God had created. Was He running out of ideas and interest when He got around to making Somalia...so just filled it with desert and rocks? How come there was no oil....at least He'd made sure there was some oil for the Saudi Arabians; although Ms Bentham had said that had been the cause of some trouble at times.

He decided to ask Martha and Peter what they knew about all this and to start from the American Constitution.

"Don't the Somalian's have a right to Life, Liberty and the Pursuit of Happiness?" he asked.

"Well...yes, Anselm...just like we all do," replied Martha.

"Oh. I was told it was just the Americans...it's in their law, their Constitution," said Anselm.

“Well...they may be one of the few nations that have it actually written down as such. Americans like to have things written down. But I think most people would agree that those things are the right of every person...all over the world. It’s kind of ‘natural justice’, explained Peter.

“What do you mean ‘natural justice...is it a kind of law?”

“Not quite. It’s not the kind of law that governments pass...it’s more a statement of what we generally believe is right, fair...er...just,” replied Peter.

“It’s more like...God’s law. Whatever Governments come up with...and they do some pretty awful things and pass some oppressive laws sometimes, natural justice is a kind of universal set of rights we believe all people have, from the moment they are born...or maybe even beforehand. They are rights no-one can take away from you... and if a Government tried to pass laws to take away these rights we’d say they had no right to do so,” explained Martha.

“So, God made up these laws of natural justice,” Anselm replayed.

“If you believe in God then, yes, that’s likely what you’d believe. But even people who don’t believe in God would still subscribe to the idea that there is such a thing as natural justice and fundamental human rights,” Peter continued.

Anselm couldn’t really see how there could be rights without laws and if there were laws surely someone had to make those laws.

“I understand God made the laws of the Universe and those laws rule over whatever happens in the physical Universe. Without exceptions. In fact, ‘no exceptions’ is a big part of how you tell what is a law of the universe ,and what isn’t. So, a law saying :‘everyone has the right to Life, Liberty and the pursuit of happiness’ isn’t one of those types of law because...look at the Somalians; they seem to be an exception to the rule.”

“Just because they are suffering doesn’t mean they don’t have a natural rights. We would say they do, but the lack of resources in their country in practice results in a poor quality of life and the suffering we see on our TV screens,” Martha replied.

“That’s a weird sort of law then,” said Anselm. “Natural law says they have the right to life, liberty and happiness but the laws of the Universe seem to have made sure they didn’t get those things...by dumping them in a country full of sand and rocks and too little water. Seems like God can’t make up his mind about the Somalians. He gives with one hand and takes back with the other...after all , He made both sets of laws.”

”Yes; and that’s one of the most difficult things to understand when you believe in a God who is good, loving and concerned for the welfare of men,” Martha admitted.

“You told me that if someone breaks the law they are usually punished. That’s why the police, judges and prisons are there. People vote for members of Parliament who pass laws and if we break them, like stealing something, then we, the people who did the voting, get punished. But it seems to me God didn't get voted into power. He just took power and there's no one in a position to punish God if He breaks His own laws by letting people starve.

" We seem to have plenty of rules...natural laws, laws of the Universe, school rules, house rules at home, the Government's laws...plenty of things that say what we can't do or what we must do and God seems to be behind all of them ultimately. But it's not clear that there's really much freedom...much liberty around." Anselm was in one of his 'I'm not impressed with all this' moods.

"You know...I believe we are essentially free. Yes, God made certain laws if only to give the Universe some order and pattern to enable man to evolve and survive. And ,yes ,he planted some idea of natural law...of morals...in us as a touchstone against which we could test and judge our actions. But He also gave us free will...the freedom to choose how we live our lives, to choose what actions to take. The freedom to live in accordance with 'natural law' to choose between good and evil. In fact, I think that was the very reason he started the whole thing off. He wants each of us as individuals to make these moral choices between good and evil and, by so doing, to earn our place with Him in the everlasting."

Martha had not before expressed her beliefs in this way to Anselm. He saw her go to church each Sunday morning but she said little about what happened there. Now she was using similar words to the ones Emily had used.

Peter had been silent for a while. “Martha has her faith. It gives her a strength and purpose that many of us might envy. Though there is suffering in the world a Christian’s faith in God and His essential goodness is not shaken. That’s something I admire...even if my logic rebels against it,” he said finally, looking at Martha with a smile.

“But you don’t believe in God, do you Peter?” said Anselm

.

“I wouldn’t go that far. It’s more that...for me...the jury’s out; the evidence for isn’t strong enough and there’s quite a lot of evidence against.”

“What do you mean...evidence against?” asked Anselm.

“Just the points you have been making Anselm. How can a God who is supposed to be good, to love man and to be all powerful...how can He allow evil and suffering in the world? How can a good, a perfect, all-powerful creator allow the Somalians to suffer so?”

“And what is your answer?” asked Anselm.

“I don’t have a clear one. And I don’t have Martha’s faith. For me faith isn’t a leap I can make. I need the stepping stones of logic. Martha and I are different in this. But there are arguments that people have used to reconcile God’s goodness and omnipotence with the existence of evil in the world. Enough arguments to fill a long walk by the brook Anselm .”

***

The gate creaked as they opened it as if it too wanted to join the debate. "Must put a spot of oil on it," said Peter.

The brook babbled. The trees whispered. And the gravel path crunched. It seemed to Anselm that God had sent all His messengers out that evening.

"So, last time we spoke we had a bit of a problem fitting God and free-will into the same Universe," said Peter, reminding himself.

"And now we have the problems of evil and of suffering."

Peter hadn't wanted to continue the discussion at home with Martha there. He felt fettered by Martha's faith. His logic couldn't accept pure, unverifiable faith and her faith wouldn't accommodate his logician's dilemmas. They had long ago agreed to differ.

"I just don't see how the God Martha believes in could make a world where some countries have no water, no food and people starve. When we say someone is good it's because they do good things," said Anselm.

"Some have made the argument that you can't have good without at least the possibility of evil. Like night and day. They are relative terms which depend upon each other for meaning. But I don't think God allowed evil because the symmetry of the English language needed it.

“ I think it is true to say, though, that the virtues of courage, unselfishness, bravery, compassion do need some adversity, some problems in the world that people have to overcome. Much of art comes out of suffering. There is a sense in which the finest of the human spirit only comes through in adversity...and if it is part of God’s purpose that men show those greater qualities then maybe a touch of evil or suffering in the world is needed and is not too high a price to pay.”

“We don’t seem to know what to do about Somalia; where is the unselfishness and compassion. If that’s God’s plan then it’s not working. I don’t see why millions of people have to suffer so much just to give others the chance to be heroes. It is too high a price to pay,” replied Anselm.

“Well, you could say that Somalia is suffering because of the drought (and civil war). It is the climate and lack of physical resources which are the root causes.”

“And who made the Universe?” challenged Anselm.

“We discussed that. I think we concluded God started things with the big-bang and a bunch of physical laws but He didn’t produce the Universe we see today, fully developed. The dice were rolled and when they finally landed Somalia got a certain destiny. God didn’t write the script for every country and every human being.”

“But he could have if He’d wanted to. He didn’t have to leave it to nuclear physics and evolution,” Anselm rejected the apologetic.

“Maybe. I don’t know why He chose the hard way and billions of years. But I can see that there needed to be some physical laws to give order to the Universe. If He wanted a stage for man to act out His plan then the stage props needed to be reasonably stable. And you could say that evolution was needed to make sure the

actors were fitted to work on that stage, to interact with the stage scenery and furniture.

“ Once he had decided on some physical laws, even He had to stick to them consistently. Interfering to adjust things that didn’t fall out right....like Somalia... isn’t really a workable approach. Where do you draw the line? Everything's relative. As soon as He interfered to get rid of one bad feature, there’d be another that didn’t quite measure up to perfection...and so on. He’d be fine-tuning every hour of every day... to the point where man couldn’t rely on any consistency in physical laws.”

“The world would become a place which behaved very randomly, unpredictably. Continually changing the rules would likely have created even more suffering. Imagine, God realises a race of carnivores has evolved so He decides to make animals inedible to avoid them becoming some hominids next meal. What then happens to the hominids?”

“And earthquakes...why do we need them?”

“Just a natural by-product of how the earth was formed...how things developed in line with the laws of the Universe,” replied Peter.

Anselm thought that if God was all He was made out to be then it should have been within His power to come up with a bunch of laws that didn't result in such a dangerous world. Still, he was just about willing to believe that there was some hidden logic within the laws that meant God had to make a few compromises. Like if you needed gravity to keep planets in orbit so they could sprout life ,maybe you just had to accept that there would be a few accidents and some unlucky people would break their necks falling off ladders!

He decided to turn his fire on another kind of bad or evil in the world...the evil from the misdeeds of men rather than things.

"People are killing each other in bloody wars. Some guys flew air planes into the twin towers in New York. Abbott is horrible to Freddie Jones. How come people do bad things . There's no laws of the Universe forcing them to ...not as far as my Physics teacher's been able to find. I suppose you are going to tell me that God gave us free-will, so we could make choices about what we do...and some of us choose to do bad things," said Anselm.

"Well, yes, I guess I am. Remember what Martha said. He gave us free-will and an idea of what's right and wrong . Maybe the whole point of the exercise is for us to develop, to achieve our soul's purpose through doing good, resisting evil."

"Do not lead us into temptation....deliver us from evil", replied Anselm. "We pray in assembly asking God to fix it. That doesn't make much sense on your theory."

"I don't know about that "'said Peter, "but I can see that there would be little point or interest in God making a bunch of puppets. It's only when Pinnochio came to life and started being a bit naughty that the story got interesting. So, if God's purpose, is more than his own entertainment, and is to do with the moral development of human beings then we need to be free; no strings, no hidden puppeteers hands. Free to do good and that means free to do bad also."

"Maybe we could have been free but, just by our natures, made such that we always choose to do good, never choosing evil," replied Anselm, unwilling to let the point go.

"Maybe, we could. But then wouldn't 'we' ,in some sense, be pre-programmed? If no- one ever committed evil acts, I wonder really what idea we would have of evil. Would the notion have any meaning for us? Would we ever encounter temptation and resist it? Would there be a real sense that we were making a free choice between alternatives if our DNA just totally predisposed us to good? I'm not clear there would," replied Peter.

Anselm went quiet.

"So, what do you think of all this Anselm?"

"I'm not sure really. I understand the arguments you've raised...but...I don't think you are convinced by them either. I really wonder whether God created the world and us, or whether we invented God. Maybe we invented Him as a way of explaining things. People made him a person because much of what they see around them gets made by people...houses, cars, tables, schools and so on. People can't think of things which are not made by someone or something...they think the Universe is just like a very big house. As babies, people, get used to their parents shaping, moving things...maybe they just extend that model to the Universe."

Peter was struck by Anselm's use of the word 'they'.

"...and, once they had invented God , He had to be perfect because nothing less will do. Being merely superhuman just wouldn't measure up, really. Being very bright but not 'omniscient' would be a bit second rate in the God stakes. And being indifferent or mostly good with some mean streaks wouldn't be very comforting.

So ,they give him all these characteristics...all-powerful, all-knowing, perfect, eternal and then... they stop and realise they've just invented the most unexplainable thing of all; and they find all sorts of problems with the idea of such a God. And, finally, they split in two...like you and Martha. One logically doubting the whole story; the other saying it's all a matter of faith and that the mystery itself is the reason to have faith."

"And do you have such a need of God, Anselm?"

"I was found on a heath at the age of fifteen and came from...nowhere, it seems. My mystery seems even bigger than other people's; so, I suppose I would need even more faith. I don't know why Martha's God would make such a sudden exception to the normal rules of getting born. Why one isolated example... why start taking short cuts... why me?"

Peter didn't answer. Anselm always seemed to come back to that question. Peter felt a sense of loss for Anselm. Peter's academic viewpoint on life had always served as insulation for him. At the age of fifty he had had his chances to choose a different way, to enjoy the revelation that Martha found...if he had been open to it. He counted it as his choice to wrap himself in logic and the insurmountable doubt that was logic's shadow...and he accepted the responsibility to live with that.

But Anselm, still so young, seemed already to be using intellect to rob himself of joy.

It was much too soon for that .

They turned back home. Martha's roast potatoes beckoned.

***

In bed that night Peter told Martha of the conversation with Anselm by the brook, and of Anselm's summary.

"He seems to have an issue with God. I guess there is so much that doesn't make sense to him," said Martha. "But he's trying to access God through logic; he'll never connect on that level. God looks for faith and logic leaves no room for faith."

“I’m not the one to show him that way... Twenty- five years in academic philosophy has made me a dissector of language, of concepts...a rationalist...a walking syllogism.” Peter sounded lost.

“Is that how you see yourself?”

“I’m not sure. I thought there was more once upon a time. Just feel like a dried up river bed sometimes. You know I often feel that I would trade all the elegant dilemmas of my work for one leap of faith; one irrational moment. One moment free from all binding logic.”

“So, what's stopping you letting go?”

“Habit, I guess or fear.”

“What are you afraid of?”

“Are you psychoanalysing me?” “

I’m not qualified,” Martha smiled.

“It’s as though a structured world based on logic is a safer one. Predictable, under my control in some way or at least I can fool myself that it is. Hah! I’ve led a sheltered life. Never left University; never really went out into the big, bad world. Not like you, starting that business of yours and taking risks even if it was mostly with other people’s money.” Peter laughed nervously worried that Martha would be offended.

“Do you wish you had done something else?”

“Yes , but I don’t know what. Or rather, maybe , depending on what the something else was. Oh, I don’t know. Isn’t this what supposed to happen in mid-life; men start to get haunted by ‘what ifs’ and maybes’. I seem to have caught a big dose of the ‘might have been's’. If I look back and add it all up, what’s it worth; what footprint will I leave. Who will be better for all those words?

Martha moved over to his side of the bed, held his head and looked into his eyes.

“You are a brilliant man, hugely respected in the academic world . A man who has taught countless bright young things to reflect, to examine the world and to think beyond the commonplace. I’m proud of you...I haven’t said or shown that enough.”

Peter’s eyes glistened. Part of him couldn’t, wouldn’t believe what Martha was saying. There seemed to be a silent, insistent voice within that either didn’t want the validation or daren’t trust it...maybe both. He remembered his father...the cold logic of their arguments...and the scornfulness...

“I’m proud of you...do you hear?” repeated Martha seeing she had to say it again and again if she was going to drown the doubt in Peter’s eyes.

“Too much time in that study chasing shadows,” he said, continuing the self-critique.

“Maybe. But that can change. “I wasn’t available either; so , where else would you go but to your study? Things can grow cold if you don’t keep putting fuel on the fire.”

“You seemed to disappear into your business. I don’t know who left first, you or me. What’s it matter now? But every time I popped my head above the parapet I felt criticised; there was something I wasn’t doing right whether in the kitchen or around the house.. You always seemed to a have a downer on my work, saw it as irrelevant. Maybe you were right after all.”

“Oh, come on, you’re sounding like a victim.”

“So, I was imagining it was I?”

Martha froze for a few moments.

“Well, perhaps not. I mean...I do remember sniping at you sometimes; but...I guess I was jealous.”

“Jealous of what?”

“Jealous of your study, your books...maybe now even of Anselm, I’m not getting any attention...don’t you see...I’m not getting enough of you.”

“Funny way of showing it.”

“What was that about Venus and Mars? Look...if I’m irritable or cold then the first thing you need to say to yourself is ‘Martha isn’t getting what she needs’ and the second thing you need to say to yourself is "I, Peter, am what she needs!" replied Martha, this time giggling.

"Anselm thinks God's a mystery... wait till he starts to encounter the female of the species," grinned Peter.

"That's better," said Martha.

"What is?"

"A bit of light-heartedness. Less of the earnest professor. That's what I want. I want more of the you that you: the charmer, the idealist, the jester, the romancer...the lover."

"I'll try..." Peter hesitated. "Those people seem like lost friends from younger days. When I remember back, it's like...they were someone else; someone related maybe but not the guy here today. I'm afraid...that they died somewhere along the way."

Martha pulled herself up and took him in her arms...rocking, as he let the fear and loneliness out . She kissed his salty cheeks and kept rocking him for minutes...until the sobbing subsided. She thought for a moment of Anselm.

"I want to find those guys again...but I wonder if I can," he said as he calmed.

"You will. I'll help you. I'm going to keep this particular page open... always on...so I can reach you. You...I...we, have been out of reach for too long. We are going to work on that. And the second thing you can do to keep connected is to take me out for a romantic dinner tomorrow night."

"You're on...what's the first thing?"

She brought his lips to join hers. Her tongue flicked like a butterfly on his; her lips warm, wet and sweet .

***

It was a few days later when Martha found some folded pages under the cookie jar. They were marked-'For Martha and Peter'

The handwriting was Anselm's. She read:

"Dear Martha and Peter ,

I have been thinking about our discussions about the law and human rights. It seems to me that I must have some rights too. When I listen to the other boys and girls at school I think they have been given more rights...or are using more of them than I. So, I thought it would be helpful for you if I wrote down some of these in the hope that we could discuss how we go about making sure I have my full share of them. It seems to me that the rights that teenagers have depend quite a lot on their parents and so I am bringing these to your attention.

1 **Pocket Money**

I've asked around and most of the children it turns out seem to get money from their parents on a regular basis which they call pocket money- though I don't think the money stays in their pockets for long. Not just money for the tuck-shop but money enough to buy other things like clothes, skateboards, earrings. I could make a longer list. I don't really feel in need of any of these things but then again it doesn't really seem fair if other children are able to buy them from their own money and I'm not. One or two of them have said it's weird that I don't get any pocket money. I must say I still feel odd enough at times without this additional difference. How much they get seems to differ. Some as little as a £1 coin a week, some £5. Freddie Jones suggested I 'negotiate'. Can we do that please?

2 Mobile Phone

Nearly all the children have one of these, Tough I 'm not sure it is one of the most fundamental rights; but as far as I can tell those few that don't have one want one and those that do are keen not to lose them. So, they seem pretty important. I've asked the others who they speak to on these phones and the answer is their friends and parents. Given that they see their friends all day at school and their parents every evening and weekends I'm not sure what they have to say on the phone that they can't say in person. Anyway. I think I'd feel more complete if I had one.

3 **Nike Trainers**

I have shoes, I know. It hadn't crossed my mind that the ones you gave me are not really what a teenager needs. Well, not until Freddie pointed out that mine didn't have a label. He said 'Nike' are 'cool' and mine aren't. I think I'd like to have cool shoes. And while I'm talking labels I think I need at least two or three chosen from Tommy Hillfiger, Puma, Adidas, Kappa.

4 **A Brother or Sister**

Most everyone at school has one or both of these. Some have several of each. As far as I know, I don't. I think I would probably know if I did have one because they don't seem to be the sort of thing one can easily forget or ignore. Most of the people I know at school seem to hate theirs or at least have some problem with them. But they do talk about them quite a lot...almost as if they were another part of themselves. It's 'my sister' this 'my brother' that. I've been asked why I don't have a sister or a brother. From what Peter told me about marriage, I guess it's really up to you two to make one. Could you consider this as I think it's maybe the most important thing missing right now.

Well that's all I can think of at the moment. Can we discuss these at your earliest convenience? (I learnt that writing a business letter in English).

Martha waited a few moments for the mixture of old sadness and new joy to wash through her, then folded the piece of paper and tucked it in her handbag.

***

XI FANTASY AND FAITH

English lessons had become Anselm's favourite. Miss Jolliffe was always full of praise for Anselm's essays and his poems. Her approval was worth Abbots sneers.

“Always thought –provoking and sensitive,” she had said... on six occasions. Anselm was counting.

Anyway, the sneers from Abbot had subsided quite a bit since the whistling and football incidents had given Anselm ‘street cred’ .But there was still the odd nudge and wink when Miss Jolliffe picked him out in class to do a reading.

Miss Jolliffe was centrefold in Anselm's fantasies... he worried that Abbot and others in class IVB might be able to read his mind.

Anselm wondered if Miss Jolliffe was married. “She’s called Miss, right . Not Mrs or even Ms...so that means she’s not married”, said a reassuring voice in his head.The voice seemed to belong to the same person that brought him such vivid pictures of Miss Jolliffe at night.

Then another voice would push its way in.

“Even if she’s not married she’ll have a boyfriend; someone a bit older than her because women like older men. They don’t go for young boys, wet behind the ears who don't know how to order a bottle of wine in a restaurant."

He didn't like the second voice but feared it might be right.

At end of school he'd loiter near the car park before Peter or Martha arrived to pick him up. He'd watch some of the teachers leaving promptly and look out for Miss Jolliness car. She always seemed to leave alone and no-one picked her up. "If she had a boyfriend surely he'd pick her up some days..." He ,Anselm, would.

How old was she? One of the other boys had said twenty -three "cos she's straight out of teachers college." So, he was fifteen...probably nearer sixteen although they hadn't fixed on a birthday for him yet.

"Eight years difference is nothing said the encouraging voice. Peter is five years older than Martha....different ages is not a problem".

The the cynic would retort. "Yeah, Peter is older....the man is older. Miss Jolliffe will be looking for an older man. She is nearly half as many years again as you, loser."

Whoever it was , the argument in his head was getting confusing.

Anselm wondered if he couldn't settle matters by asking Miss Jolliffe if she would go out with him. But go out where? He would have to look up restaurants and get some money; not sure the tuck money would run to that.

But was he allowed to do that anyway? The teachers seemed to be different to the pupils...not just because they talked and the class listened; not just because of the age thing. It was more like they were kind of 'day parents'. Like they told you what to do and you weren't really on the same level as them. After all you wouldn't dream of asking Mr Smart to play football at break time ,would you?

"Teachers are different," the cynic confirmed ." We're not supposed to be over friendly with them. It's against school rules; against home rules as well. It's like trying to pass the ball to the referee...he's not part of the game, not a player...he just enforces the rules. Try asking her out and you'll be in deep trouble...and a laughing stock."

The cynic had a powerful voice but as soon as he paused for breath...hopeful fantasy took over again.

"She's always very nice to me... more than to the other boys. And she seems to look at me in a different way, at least it feels different... I think. Ms Bentham doesn't look at me ...at anyone...like that."

And Miss Jolliffe was being very nice to him today. It was end of class, break time, but Miss Jolliffe had asked Anselm to stay behind for a few moments.

'What was this about? What did she want?' He questioned himself as the other pupils flocked out the door. Had he done something wrong? Did she know about his fantasies, his imaginings....? He couldn't bear that. What would he say?

He slowly walked to the front of the class where she was seated at her desk.

"Anselm , your imagination..."

'Oh no. She does know. How?'

"....is absolutely wonderful. This latest poem is the best yet I wonder where you get your ideas from...the imagery is beautiful.

"This really is some of the best work...no, the best work I have seen in the school. I would like you to read it out at assembly one of these mornings if you would please. Would you mind? I'll have a word with Ms Bentham to arrange it. Is that OK?"

"Well ..er...yes Miss...of course." Anselm could hardly catch up. He was still recovering from her non-discovery of his guilt.

"...and everyday things are made of dreams...; beautiful Anselm." "Yes... Miss"

"Well I'll let you go off to your break now. But well done."

He walked out of the classroom in a trance. The words 'Beautiful Anselm' rang in his ears.

"Hey! Swinbourne. You look like you've seen a ghost. What did Miss say to you? Have you got a date? I've seen how you've been looking at her. Like a starving man in the tuck shop."

It was Abbot's voice shattering Anselm's daydream.

Across the landing, in his bedroom, Anselm heard Peter's voice and later the moans. He knew what was happening...the boys at school had given him a graphic description based on their (alleged) experience.

He hadn't thought of Martha or Peter doing that. They hadn't seemed to touch each other much...but maybe they saved that for the bedroom. He didn't want to think of them doing it. He was jealous.

Jealous felt a bit like...longing + resentment.

He thought of Miss Jolliffe and wondered how her moans would sound...he closed his eyes and brought her face into the room. He tried to imagine how it might be to feel those breasts. But the more his imagination worked the more his body ached. He stroked himself...but the ache grew. He used his hand in the way Freddie had told him and minutes later felt the waves through his body to his scalp and the shooting wetness.

He felt...shame. Freddie and the other boys would talk openly with each other about...'wanking;' but they didn't mention it when the girls were around. It seemed to be a boys secret, not to be talked about other than behind the sports hall where they hung out when not playing football. It was a word to put in graffiti on the toilet walls and to draw Ms Bentham's long censures in assembly.

He felt the afterglow still flushing warmth through his legs and resolved that this source of solitary pleasure should stay his secret...lest someone pass a rule against it. It was not something adults would understand or approve of...especially married ones. Sex seemed to have been designed for a purpose that really should involve two people....a man and a woman.

It was clear from biology what the purpose was and although rather messy and hit and miss, it was clear that the...apparatus...was designed for that prime purpose. So, Anselm's self-pleasure was really just a by- product of God's design for the propagation of the species; a happy coincidence that what was good for two people could, with a little adaptation of approach, also be good for one.

Thoughts started to bob through Anselm's mind like pieces of driftwood.

So, God could hardly have any objection to Anselm...pleasuring himself. Being omniscient, He would have been well aware that this particular part of His design could be used in a slightly different way that didn't result in babies. If He'd thought it wrong (as Ms Bentham clearly did) then He would surely have designed things differently.

For a moment, Anselm wondered what the design difference could have been, but short of leaving out hands or maybe putting the penis out of reach ,he couldn't really see how 'wanking' could have been designed out. Still, He had clearly placed things in convenient positions and that suggested strongly to Anselm that the creator even wanted to encourage the solitary practice of sex.

Yes, practice; perhaps that's what it was. Particularly for boys, young men who needed some form of practice, or testing, to ensure everything was in working order; a well-oiled machine ready to do its part for the future of the species when called upon. Imagine if one hadn't had a dry run...imagine if one day Jennifer took you behind the sports hall and lifted her skirt and...you didn't...you couldn't. Too horrible to think of. The embarrassment...and the regret would be unbearable. No. Better he practised frequently to make sure he was ready. Like going to the gym really to build up one's muscles.

The driftwood was bobbing more slowly now on the oily black sea of sleep.

'Wonder if having sex with a girl is better than doing it alone? Must be...got to be an incentive...otherwise people just do their own thing and the human race dies out...Must be a lot better...to compensate for having to do as you're told by your wife, girlfriend...girls seem to be bossy whereas boys just like to chill out...wonder why they like to have their way so much...Martha tells Peter what to do...they're not as strong as boys...can't just take their chance in the world...need to control what's going on....including sex...the other boys said girls didn't need sex, they could take it or leave it...they just liked talking and presents...the sex thing was something they gave to a boy if the boy was really nice to them and would look after them...whereas boys mainly wanted sex because they wanted...sex...'

No driftwood now; just a dark sea, becalmed and Anselm a hundred fathoms below the surface .

***

Anselm slept deeply. He was standing in a half light behind a high wooden table. Behind him to his right was a presence he dared not look at. To the left in front was a row of sombre looking people; men and women.

Before him was a man with a long gown and wearing a wig. He had an air strangely like the headmaster of St Thomas Aquinas. Anselm felt anxious and awkward in this place. He was the focus of everyone's attention and other people were asking the questions.

The man with the gown approached him,. Anselm could not make out his features; the man's face was indistinct.

"Is your name Anselm Swinbourne?"

"Yes...sir," answered Anselm wondering what he was committing himself to.

"You stand before this court today accused of committing shameful acts."

Anselm didn't like the way things were developing. How did he get here? Who were these people? And what 'shameful acts' was he supposed to have committed?

"You stand accused of three counts. First you are accused of arriving in the world without personal identification.

Secondly, you have expressed existential doubt in relation to the judge in whose court you now stand.

And third, you have practised solitary fantasies of a sexual nature. How do you plead in response to these three counts?

"Guilty or not guilty?" the man persisted.

"Not guilty...I'm not guilty," Anselm responded with rising panic.

The row of sombre people looked even more sombre. This must be the jury. He remembered the courtroom dramas on TV.

"I must remind you that this court will take a dim view of any false statements you make whilst under oath," said the prosecutor. "I ask you again...how do you plead to the three counts?" The prosecutors voice was like thunder.

"Not ...I mean...guilty, sir...but not really. It's not my fault...I couldn't help it," Anselm quivered. He looked towards the jury...their heads were bowed and he couldn't see their faces; couldn't catch their eyes to make any kind of human contact.

"This court will decide the question of intent on the basis of the facts," replied the prosecutor. "Enter into the records a plea of guilty."

"Anselm Swinbourne, can you tell the court where you were born and of what natural parents?"

"No, I cannot sir. I was found by a shepherd on a heath...at the age of fifteen. I do not know where I came from or who my parents were."

"What can you remember of the time before the shepherd found you?" pressed the prosecutor.

"Nothing sir; I have no memory of anything before that time," replied Anselm.

"Are you really asking this court to believe that you came out of nowhere. That you reached the age of fifteen without doing anything, without accumulating any memories? That you just appeared...a physically mature teenager, out of the blue?"

"Well....yes, sir . That's how it was," replied Anselm meekly.

"I put it to you that you are an illegal alien, having entered this world without any immigration papers or indeed any form of personal identification. It is quite clear that you must have existed before being found on the heath. That previous life is something you are anxious others should not know about. That can only mean that you have something to hide and are guilty of goodness knows what shameful acts in your prior life. I suggest you make a clean breast of things and tell this court what it is that you are hiding."

"But I can't. I really don't remember anything. If I did I'd tell you. I wish I could," replied Anselm, his anxiety rising.

"Withholding the truth is as much an abuse of this court as is the telling of outright lies, Anselm Swinbourne. I remind you that you are under oath. Now what is it about your prior life that you have reason to feel guilty about?"

"I don't know...nothing...or something...I just can't remember anything." Anselm was beginning to feel he must be guilty of something. He even felt like making a story up just to stop the prosecutor's questioning.

"Let's move on...to the second count...of existential doubt. Am I right that you have, on a number of occasions ,expressed doubt as to the existence of our omnipotent, omniscient, eternal creator...He whose laws are enforced by this court?"

"I have expressed doubt about God...whether He exists; whether this world with all its faults and suffering is something that would have been created by someone like Him" admitted Anselm.

A big hush went through the jury; faceless heads turned from side to side. Behind, to his right, papers rustled; he still did not dare to look.

“So, you admit to lacking faith in the divine. Worse, you admit to being lawless. Since you do not believe in the existence of He who designed the natural and ethical laws which should govern our lives. You admit to placing yourself above our maker, above the law through your lack of faith.

“I didn’t say that..., “replied Anselm.

“You didn’t need to. Your doubt speaks loudly enough. You have rejected the authority of this court...in fact any authority outside of yourself. An illegal immigrant who has the arrogance to reject the foundation stone of our laws,” the prosecutor attacked.

He moved over to the jury bench. “I put it to members of the jury that Anselm Swinbourne is in breach of the fundamental obligations of any citizen...the requirement to have a traaceable history and memories and to be accountable for them. He also fails to meet the requirement to observe our laws and torecognise the ultimate authority from which those laws are derived.”

Things were going badly. Anselm could see no defence that would be acceptable to this court.

“Finally, let us turn to the third count on which you are being tried here today...that you Anselm Swinbourne indulged in solitary fantasies of a sexual nature...in direct contravention of our laws,” said the prosecutor.

“But I didn’t know it was against the law,” replied Anselm.

“How could you not know?” the prosecutor challenged .

”Well...no-one told me. I can’t help it that I have an imagination. And the Creator you refer to is the one who equipped me...and you...to be able to enjoy our bodies, alone. Why would he do that if to enjoy ourselves in that way was wrong?”

“The Creator equipped you to be able to do many things. You have strong arms...to lift things. You could use them to hurt others, but that was not the Creator’s intent. He equipped you with a mind and imagination so that you could create art. He did not provide the arms and imagination for the purpose you have been putting them to Anselm Swinbourne; those are perversions of the true purpose of the gifts our Creator has bestowed on you...they are temptations to which you...of weak will... have succumbed.

“I put it to the jury that the defendant does not contest the facts...he simply argues that his actions are not contrary to our laws. In that he is clearly wrong; the laws have been clearly communicated by our Creator. We have here an illegal immigrant ; with no identification and unwilling to divulge his origin; a person who rejects our system of laws and even the existence of the chief lawmaker; he abuses the gifts he has received from our Divine lawmaker and Creator. He is guilty on all three counts, and a rampant existentialist,” concluded the prosecutor.

The jury was sent out of the courtroom to determine its verdict. Anselm was left to stand, feeling naked, in the dock and fearing the worst.

After just a few moments the jury returned to the courtroom.

“Does the jury find the defendant, Anselm Swinbourne, guilty or not guilty?” thundered a voice from the brooding presence behind him.

One of the jurors stood. The features on his face resolved into better focus. Anselm recognised the face as that of Abbott from Class IVB.

“We find the defendant guilty on all three counts,” said Abbott, smiling a malicious smile at Anselm.

“Anselm Swinbourne,” said the presence,” you have been found guilty of three crimes against creation. Do you have anything further to say for yourself?”

“I never meant to break the rules...I didn’t know about them...no-one told me. It’s not fair that I should be found guilty...”Anselm blurted.

“Take him down,” said the presence in an unforgiving tone.

Arms pressed on Anselm’s shoulders; he struggled but the arms pressed harder; he couldn’t get away.

"Anselm, Anselm...wake up darling. Wake-up...you're dreaming...it's a nightmare...darling."

Anselm felt the shock of coming back to the surface, lungs bursting and gasping for air. He was in his bedroom, the courtroom had gone, the prosecutor, Abbott and the presence. Martha was sitting on the bed leaning over him with her hands on his shoulders.

***

It was five am.. Martha held the boy until he stopped sobbing. In between gulps of breath he tried to tell her about the courtroom. The details were already fading like footprints in the sand. But the feeling of dread remained.

He managed to get out the words...no history, doubting God and, though he wanted to stop himself saying it,...sexual fantasies...before the dream merged into an undefined feeling of guilt.

Martha did her best to reassure him.

"You know everyone has dreams and, occasionally, bad dreams, in which things go wrong. They say it's just the mind processing bits of what's happened during the day...like a librarian tidying away books. It can be scary at the time, I know, but it's harmless and absolutely normal. You have nothing to be afraid of...and nothing you should feel guilty about." Even the few words he had said were enough to tell her where his distress was coming from.

"I know that you are a child of God just as Peter and I are, and all the boys and girls at school. I also know that God loves you as His own... and the doubts you have are ones that everyone experiences at some time in their lives. He doesn't abandon us, or punish us for such doubt; in fact without doubt there is no such thing as faith..

It is by reaching faith in God and His purpose that we find our true, spiritual lives. But one of the strange quirks of life is that we often don't reach this understanding until much later in our years. I think it takes time and life's ups and downs before God reveals Himself fully to us. And along the way we find many reasons not to believe in Him; reasons to think the world is just a blind machine with no purpose."

Anselm had calmed. Each time Martha said it was okay to doubt, somehow the fear...and the loneliness receded a little further.

Finally, he was able to collect the fragments of his self together and ask her "Doesn't doubting something mean you don't believe in it.. you don't have faith?"

"Well, yes, to a degree," replied Martha. "At least that's how many people understand the words. But I think doubt is essential to faith. It's easy to believe in the obvious; to believe in something everyone agrees on. There's no courage in doing that.

"You can even believe in things which are not absolutely certain but where you believe, on the balance of probability, that it will be so. For example, I believe it will be sunny today. The weather forecast said so and last night there was a red sky. There's no guarantee but on the whole I believe that's the most likely thing to happen...but I don't count that belief as faith. Faith is something more than that. Faith requires us to take a risk, to be courageous...to believe in something in spite of the evidence against it. It isn't a gamble placed with favourable odds and nothing important at stake. 'Faith' implies that there are grounds for serious doubt; it implies, perhaps, that, logically, based on the evidence, we have insufficient basis for believing in something and yet...we do, wholeheartedly."

"So ,faith is a kind of belief against the odds?" asked Anselm.

"Sort of, and yet I think it's more than that too. We believe 'facts' on the balance of evidence. If some strong, new evidence turns up pointing in another direction, then we are usually ready to change what we believe.

"Belief is a kind of 'not quite knowing' because the evidence is incomplete. Whereas faith is a kind of act of will that rises above the evidence. It's a kind of trusting acceptance and surrender. It's not a stubborn belief in the face of contrary evidence like when someone won't back down in an argument. No, faith is more like a direct meeting with the truth , something seen or felt which enables us to trust...to trust that there is a good God even though the world sometimes says otherwise. And we can ask our God to help us to find that faith.”.

”You asked God and He answered?” asked Anselm.
“Yes,” replied Martha. “Yes, He did...more than once.”

“What do you mean when you said ‘our God’? Isn’t there just one God? We don’t have one each do we?” asked Anselm.

“I think maybe in some sense we do. The church I go to teaches that there is only one God...not lots of different ones we can choose from or, worse, lots of different ones we have to keep happy. And I do believe in the ‘one-ness’ of God in that sense. But I also believe that we each have an individual relationship with a higher power and that in some sense, I can’t quite explain, it is that relationship which is the real meaning of the word ‘God’.”

Anselm liked the thought that he might have his own personal God. He felt he might get more attention that way.

“They said I didn’t belong here...in the dream; that I was illegal,” Anselm continued looking for more reassurance.

“Well I think ‘they’ are your fears...the parts of you that worry you don’t fit, worry that ‘different’ is somehow against the rules. We’ve talked about that before, haven’t we?” replied Martha.

Anselm gave a two-year-old's nod.

"You just need to look around you, Anselm. Look at the other boys and girls at school .Look at the teachers...me, Peter. We are all different. And don't imagine we don't feel different...I am sure everyone of us feels different.

"Maybe it's because each of us knows our own inner world but we can never experience each other's, however close we get. We are always separate...we can't know someone else in the same way we know ourselves. And because of that distance between us all, I'm sure that every person on this earth feels different from the rest . Most of us will wonder if we are strangers who are odd shapes that don't quite fit."

Anselm went quiet. He thought about his secret pleasure...and his fantasies about touching Miss Jolliffe's breasts. He knew Freddie did this too...so maybe he, Anselm, wasn't so different after all. But he couldn't name this with Martha. Still something held him back. The subject was a box with the label 'Do not open' on it.

"The last thing I want to say to you before you get up and ready for school is this...it is absolutely normal for a fifteen -year old boy to think of girls. And you, I am quite sure, are no different to any other fifteen -year old boy Anselm," said Martha.

Anselm's eyes were popping...but he found it difficult to look into Martha's.

She continued, regardless of his embarrassment, "and it's normal to have sexual feelings towards girls...you will want to be physically close to them and ...

eventually...make love when you find a girl you really like."

This was too good to be true, thought Anselm. It sounds like Martha's in favour... but then how could she not be ? The noises from down the corridor told him that she and Peter obviously made love.

"But...at your age it is far too early to be taking such a serious step. There will come a time a few years from now when you are more mature, when you can take the necessary precautions Sex between two young adults is natural and something both enjoy inside a loving relationship. So kissing and cuddling are the limit for a while yet Anselm. That doesn't mean it's wrong to let, your imagination wander beyond those limits...that's natural too and doesn't need to involve anyone else."

Might have guessed there'd be a BUT, thought Anselm. Kissing and cuddling only...chance would be a fine thing. He didn't think Miss Jolliffe would be willing. How would he ever dare risk asking her? Maybe this was a job for faith.

Within a few moments he was feeling a sense of relief. By placing limits, forbidding him from attempting what he already saw as impossible anyway, Martha had somehow let him off the hook of his own desires. He didn't have to do anything just because the other boys boasted. Best of all he could let his 'imagination wander!' Martha had said so. It was normal. Nothing to be ashamed of. Just like he'd let his imagination wander last night before falling asleep ... and that was delicious. The nightmare prosecutor was wrong. If Martha, as a woman, thought it was okay then surely it was; she could give his imagination permission in a way that the boys at school with their whispers couldn't.

"Where have you gone, Anselm?" asked Martha.
"Oh...nowhere," replied Anselm, shaking his head. It was six-thirty.

"You might as well get up and get dressed. I'll start breakfast soon," said Martha. She drew the curtains and the first glimmering of sun seeped through the window pane, casting soft dawn shadows in the room.

He got up and headed for the shower, happy that he had some more time for his imagination.

***

Friday came around once more and what Abbott referred to as "the God-slot"; Class IV B's period of R.E. stood between them and the weekend again.

Anselm had been mulling over his conversation with Peter about evil and suffering in the world and man's free will. The more geography lessons they had the more he became aware of the inequalities in the world. Even in individual countries there were rich and poor. Nothing to do with whether the country had sand or oil.

It seemed like the rich did the least important things in society too; in fact ,the richer you were the less you did. Some people just 'inherited' money from their parents; money was a bit like genes, handed down and, sort of, defining who you are and how you lived.

Then there were people who 'earned' millions. These tended to be people who worked in the City, trading different varieties of promises, usually not their own promises but someone else's. Anselm had understood from Martha that bonds and equities were different forms of promises used to raise cash for investment in factories and service industries. He was unclear how this swapping of one form of promise for another was a useful thing and very unclear why the people who did it...'traders' and 'brokers' should be paid so much more than other people.

It seemed to him that people who grew food, drove buses, built houses or took away the rubbish were really doing much more useful things. After all, life would be pretty miserable without a roof over your head, eating berries, unable to get more than a few miles from your cave without sore feet. Isn't that how Neanderthal man lived....he didn't last did he?

No, it was becoming clearer that people who did really useful things were at the bottom of the social and economic ladder and people who lived on promises, played polo or had Corgis were at the top. The world was upside down.

Ms Bentham had explained that one of the roles of Government was to redistribute wealth to ensure that everybody had at least a basic standard of living. This was done by the Chancellor of the Exchequer, who collected taxes, taking more from the rich people and then spending the money on....tanks, teachers and hospitals. Anselm thought one out of three useful things didn't seem a great payback from the tax money. But at least the Chancellor taking money from the rich (apart from Corgi owners) reduced the level of inequality a bit.

A rather uncomfortable thought flitted into his mind during Ms Bentham's lesson. Peter was a philosophy professor and Martha the Managing Director of a dot.com business; how useful was all that? But then Peter and Martha must be paying a lot of tax to keep everyone else in Britain safe, healthy and well- educated. He moved from a negative to a positive self-esteem within the time it took to say 'Robin Hood' – another well-known tax man they had heard about in English lessons.

So, thanks to the Chancellor (who seemed to be doing his best to even things out) people in Britain weren't starving; most had a place to live and could put food in their mouths, clothes on their back. So, what's the problem? The problem is that many of them are miserable, concluded Anselm. Just apply the happiness formula. The poorer people have an adequate 'material consumption' but when they see what the very rich people have and get jealous then their 'desire' shoots up through the roof, dragging them into misery.

If the Chancellor wouldn't put the tax rates up a lot higher for the rich, then at least he should tell them to stay indoors, not driving around in their expensive cars and showing off their Yves St Laurent monogrammed shirts.

As things were , there were plenty of unhappy people in Britain. You didn't have to look as far as Somalia to find a dilemma for God's famed goodness and omnipotence. The argument Peter had left him with-that evil and suffering come about because man misuses the freedom given to him by God- seemed pretty thin, given the facts. How come man had ended up arranging things such that ninety percent of them felt they'd got a raw deal from life? What bunch of people got together and decided to give most of the wealth to the minority? Was jealousy in fashion? No. He wasn't buying the free-will defence of God. This week he was more persuaded that the world worked on mechanical lines; effect followed cause with awful predictability. The laws of the Universe had been so precisely crafted as to be a straight -jacket for the world.

One only had to hear Ms Bentham's routine haranguing of the smokers, the jokers, the players of poker, every Friday morning assembly , or to see that tweed suit of hers. Abbott's predictable wise-cracks were yet another proof point of determinism. Miss Jolliff's nipples erect from the chill; Anselm's penis erect at the sight of Miss Jolliffe's nipples...and so on. The world was heavy with cause and effect mechanisms, tick-tocking away.

So, you see, human free-will could not be the get- out - clause, or refuge of a God trying to avoid the blame for things going off the rails. From where Anselm was standing the Chancellor seemed to be making a better fist of things than the eternal creator. It was in this frame of mind that Anselm walked into the R.E. lesson, wondering if the God of Christianity was the only choice available.

Mr Thomas had decided that he would introduce Class IVB to some of the other religions of the world and encourage some debate about their similarities and differences. He was keen to get back on syllabus after the diversion Anselm had created last week.

"So, who can summarise for me what Christianity is?" asked Mr Thomas.

Stephen Norris put up his hand. "Christianity is the belief in Jesus as the son of God. It's a belief in one God who wants man to lead a good life and join him in heaven...a God who sent his only son to earth to suffer for man's sins so that we all could be ... erm...forgiven.."

"Good Stephen," said Mr Thomas.

"Does anyone know what people of the Jewish faith believe?

A little boy at the back of the class whose name no-one seemed to know and who had even been overlooked by Abbott and Gaunt, piped up saying "Jewish people believe in one God, Jaweh the Creator, who gave to Moses, our prophet, the Torah...which has six hundred and thirteen commandments for how we should live our lives. God is good to those who follow His commandments and He punishes those who don't."

Class IVB could tell the boy knew what he was talking about and passed on.
"And what do we know about the Islamic or Muslim faith?" continued Mr Thomas. Silence. Cambridge had no Middle Eastern minority.

"Well it's similar to Judaism in some respects. Moslems believe in one God...Allah. They believe Allah is the creator and is present everywhere. He is all powerful, all-seeing, all-hearing. The prophet Muhammad, who lived in AD570, received God's revelations through the angel Gabriel. These revelations were God speaking, telling us what relationship he wanted with man, the rules we should live by and how we will be held accountable ,for our actions and for living by His rules ,at the last judgement...when we die. The rules were written down in the holy book called the Qur'an (or Koran -he wrote on the blackboard) a bit like the commandments that Moses received."

"Does anyone know of any other religions...whether today or in the past?"

"Sir," replied Freddie, "we learnt about the Greeks and Romans in History. They had gods...but lots of them. They lived on Mount Olympus and often used to argue amongst themselves. Zeus was top-dog but the others like Poseidon, Athena, all had minds of their own...and they used to show up regularly when things were kicking off down on earth...like big battles; and they would take sides and interfere with things generally...sir."

“That’s a good summary, Freddie. We refer to that as ’Pantheism’ where people believe there are many gods. The Scandinavian or ‘Norse’ gods were similar...Thor the god of thunder, Odin, Tyr the giver of law. The Norse gods engaged in battle. In fact ,there were two camps...the gods of Asgard and the gods of Vanir, another race, who defeated the gods of Asgard...

“Funny bunch of gods, sir,......at each other’s throats, like. I thought gods were supposed to set a good example.Don’t see how we can be criticised for fighting in the playground if the gods are scrapping,” objected Abbott.

“Well these ‘gods’ are a very different bunch to the God we understand in Christianity that’s for sure,” replied Mr Thomas. “There are some other primal religions found in Africa and South America, for example, where people believe in one supreme God who created everything but that God is pretty remote and uninterested in human affairs.

“Not like the Greek gods...couldn’t keep their noses out; nothing better to do I s’pose” Freddie interjected.

....”but those religions also included ‘Divinities,’ kind of powerful spirits, of which there are many with different names, often living objects. These spirits are thought of as the souls of ancestors surviving the death of the body and will interfere in the lives of men for good or ill. Men will make offerings of food to appease these spirits...”

“Wot's apeese sir? “ asked Abbott

"To keep them on their side. So, it's a bit like the sacrifices that the Greeks and Romans would make to their gods to seek favours," Mr Thomas replied.

"Hinduism, which is a religion practised in India, also involves many different gods and goddesses..."

"Hurray," Jennifer Hollioake exclaimed. "I was beginning to think this god thing was something only men had a chance of getting to. Just like a lot of jobs out there, women are discriminated against, you know."

"Hindus ideal of life is the giving up of pleasure and luxury. They believe that a person's soul is continually re-incarnated..."

Mr Thomas saw the frowns. "By that I mean to come back after death in different forms depending on how good the person was in their previous life. So, people are held accountable for their actions in this way," explained Mr Thomas.

"Well, Freddie Jones will come back as a slug, that's all I can say. That'll be his punishment for going to the tuck shop so often he ends up slitherin' around on his belly. Come to think of it...he's a slug already...must have been really greedy in his past life. Just imagine wot you're gonna be next Jonesy...the lowest of the low," shouted Abbott. "Wot's lower than a slug ..?"

"You are!" growled Freddie.

“That’s enough you two,” Mr Thomas interceded with the even-handedness of a ‘drop-ball’ in football when really a red card was needed.

“So, what do you make of all these religions then?” asked Mr Thomas. “Can you see similarities between them?”

Class IVB went quiet for a few moments, hoping some bright spark would shed some light on Mr Thomas’ question. The bright spark’s name was Anselm.

“Seems to me sir there are two types of religion; ones with only one God who lays down lots of laws and expects man to live by these laws, or get into hot water if they don’t...Christianity, Judaism, Islamism are like that. Then there’s the ones where there are lots of gods or deputies for gods and they don’t seem to be big on laws...it’s more that the gods interfere with what men are up to and try to get their own way by getting involved directly, rather than relying on man following a bunch of laws. Greek, Roman, Norse religions sound like that...”

”That’s a good observation, Anselm,” said Mr Thomas.

“I guess if you are on your own as the one and only God then there’s a lot to cover... a lot to watch over. So, you need some rules to keep people in line. Whereas if there are lots of you...er gods,..then you can get stuck into things easier, can’t you? Different gods can cover different angles.” Suggested Freddie.

“Shut up Jones; you don’t know what you’re witterin’ on about,” Abbott reprimanded.

“Shut up yourself!” Freddie pushed back.

“The other thing that gets me,” Anselm continued, “Is that where there are lots of gods they aren’t exactly role models are they? You said they tend to interfere in things to get what they want; they fight with each other. They are neither perfect nor omnipotent...although...they are quite believable. They are...well...human. Then there’s the other kind. The one-and-only Gods. I’m not sure how I feel about a God who sets six hundred and thirteen, or however many rules and then rewards or punishes me according to whether I fall into line with them. It’s a ,kind of bribery don’t you think? And do the Christians, Muslims and Jews have the same laws and same number of laws to follow?”

“Well, no. There are many similarities but the Torah, the Koran, the Bible are not the same,” Mr Thomas replied...almost apologetically.

Abbot woke up: “So ,there we are, one bunch of laws for one set of believers and another bunch of laws for anuvver set. Suppose the whole lot of ‘em meet up at the gates to heaven... yer know...the Christians, the Jews , the Muslims and they swap notes as to where they’ve gone off the straight and narrow. Then the various versions of God show up and send some of their flock to heaven and some to hell. Well there’s going to be no consistency is there? There’ll be folks going to hell for doing stuff that others have done in a different religion and still qualified for heaven. Now where’s the fairness in that the? You’ll have people looking for last minute transfers between religions, queue-jumping and the like. It’ll be chaos!”

Abbott spoke with some passion on the subject as if he had a strong personal stake in the outcome.

“You won’t qualify under any of the rule books so just get used to the idea,” Freddie grinned widely.

“Abbott’s got a point,” said Anselm. “But I guess it’s not a case of all the Gods existing separately: Jehovah, Allah, Jaweh...but that these are different names for the same idea...one supreme creator who ultimately will judge us. The different religions believe in different prophets and different laws or commandments from their God. Problem is when you get to the gates of heaven it’s not just a case of confusion and transfer deadlines. You could just find you’ve been following the wrong rule book all along. Imagine a Muslim turning up and finding Jaweh. He asks: “Where’s Allah?” Jaweh replies “where’s who?” The guy says “Allah....the one and only god; the God who gave us the Qur’an; the one whose laws I have followed faithfully throughout my life...” “No such guy says Jaweh...but my records do seem to show that you pulled an ass out of a well on Sunday 12th March...

” Imagine that!”

“You make it sound like we’ve got to place a bet as to which version of God we are going to believe in, Anselm,” said Jennifer.

“Well it feels a bit like that to me,” replied Anselm, his voice softening as it was Jennifer. “You can’t win...unless you get very lucky. Not believing in any God at all doesn’t seem to be a sensible option. My Dad told me about Pascal's wager which basically says that given the big difference between heaven and hell, if belief in God gets you into one rather than the other, then it's smart to believe. Worst case is it turns out God didn't exist anyhow and there's no heaven or hell."

"But if you don't believe and it turns out God does exist after all, then you are in trouble," Freddie filled in.

"So, you get better odds if you believe in a God...but which one? Get the choice wrong and you could find yourself excluded from paradise on a technicality," Anselm added.

"I don't believe God is so hard, so...black and white. In that situation He'd make allowances," said Jennifer.

"You mean bend the rules," said Abbott "Use a different answer sheet?"

"Okay, okay. It's a mystery," Mr Thomas jumped in, feeling his own exam results might suffer in the final account if he let the debate run on further. "But we haven't quite finished our summary of the major religions of the world. There are two others which are practised by millions of people and which have no concept of God as a person.

Instead these religions talk of a force, or a principle and a way of life rather than a set of rules. The first is Taoism practised mostly in China. Taoists believe in the 'Dao'(he wrote on the blackboard again). The Dao is a mystical power which lies behind all events; it is the flow of events and also the religious path one should follow. Taoism advocates spontaneity, naturalness, abandoning oneself to the current of the Dao...letting oneself go..."

"With the flow," chirped Freddie.

Class IVB though this sounded pretty cool.

"Finally, there is Buddhism...practised in India..."Mr Thomas continued. "Buddhism is, as the name suggests, based on the teachings of Buddha. Buddha said that our goal should be to overcome our worldly attachments and to become liberated, freed from the cycle of birth and death. We do that through meditation. He said we could only be truly happy if we detached from notions of 'me' and 'mine'; if we recognise nothing exists permanently, all is change,....there is no permanent self. He taught that the world we experience is just a product of the mind like a dream and the main task of a Buddhist is to awaken from this dream of existence."

"So, no rules, sir?" asked Anselm.

"Not quite. Buddhists do have certain beliefs about what's right and wrong. They reject violence for example. But the core of their beliefs is not about a set of rules to obey, it's more about a way of life that leads to the ultimate goal."

Class IVB on the whole thought Taoism sounded the coolest...just going with the flow. A few of them tried it out on their parents that weekend as a reason for not doing homework...but without success. Each of their parents simply pointed out that they had misdiagnosed the direction of the flow.

Anselm was more intrigued by Buddhism. It seemed non-judgemental. It didn't suffer from having to invent totally implausible supreme beings who looked on over a grand experiment that was going wrong, but were unwilling to interfere lest the delusion of human freedom be shattered. Most of all it seemed to fit with observation of the world. The idea that the physical world did not exist as such but was 'all in the mind' was not a new one and there was plenty of evidence to support it. Anselm reflected...it sounded like Bishop Berkeley was a kind of Buddhist, in the sense he thought the world was only in the mind. Difference was he thought it was held in God's mind.

Also, Anselm had found the concept of 'self' so elusive, like a dog trying to catch its tail, that he was more than ready to believe it to be a fleeting thing. David Hume had thought there was no such thing, But perhaps, most importantly, the suggestion that the main task of a Buddhist was to awaken .from the dream existence somehow struck a chord with Anselm. It suggested a journey to a higher reality...it seemed to say 'all is not what it seems but a greater truth lies beyond'. He wondered if it was a journey he could make one day.

***

It was Monday morning when the telephone rang. Martha answered it. The three of them were in the kitchen recovering from one of Martha's weekend breakfast specials. Anselm and Peter were talking about the week ahead at school.

“Hello...Sarah...yes of course, how are ...oh, what’s...oh, no...I’m so sorry...,” Martha stopped. Peter and Anselm looked up to see her face drained of colour.

“What is it?” asked Peter.

Martha waved her hand to say ‘quiet’. The person on the other end was still talking. Anselm could hear the sound like someone a long way away, a tinny, distant buzz but with breaks in what was said. Martha filled in the spaces with a soft murmur...mmm .

“Of course, we will...she was so good with Anselm. I’m so sorry Sarah...”

Martha put the receiver down gently, as if made of glass.

“Well?” asked Peter.

“Emily passed away, yesterday...”

“Oh no....what happened...who was that?”

“That was her sister, Sarah. You remember her...she would drop Emily off at the house sometimes...”

”Yes...of course,” replied Peter. “What happened?

“A stroke ...out of the blue...they got her to hospital...but it was followed by a second one...she died during the night,” said Martha.

“My God. So sudden...had there been any warning?”

“Sarah said not. Emily was fit and lively.”

Silence followed. The kind of silence that comes when people are reminded of their own mortality.

Anselm wasn’t sure what was happening but was clear it was bad news. The word ‘hospital’ confirmed that.

“What do you mean, ‘passed away’?” he asked at last.

“ Emily died yesterday, Anselm” Martha replied.

Anselm remembered Martha and Peter’s parents disappearing from the memory book and the explanation Martha had given when he’d asked where they had gone.

“She’s gone to meet God...gone to heaven?”

“Yes , Anselm...she has.”

Again, the mystery struck Anselm. Shouldn’t this be good...Emily going to a happy place. And yet Martha and Peter looked sad; they looked as if something was wrong. They didn’t know Emily as well as they had their parents. Emily only came once a week now and spent her time on Saturday mornings with Anselm...filling in some of the gaps in his learning. So, Peter and Martha couldn't miss her so much really, could they?

Finally, Martha broke the silence.

"Sarah asked if we would like to go to the ceremony. She said Emily had spoken so often about Anselm...was proud of him...so much so that Sarah felt she knew him herself. She thinks Emily will... would welcome our being there."

"Of course,...we should pay our respects. When is it?"
"Next Thursday...at All Saints," replied Martha.

"We should go... we were asked...and Emily was very good with Anselm....least we can do…" Peter's voice tailed off again.

It was three days later that the three of them walked out of the morning light into the hushed shadow of All Saints Church. Anselm had never seen such a huge and silent building. 'If man's time were ever to stand still then it would be inside a building such as this,' he thought. Martha led them to a pew, made the sign of the cross and edged along to sit at the end next to the wall. Peter in his atheism and Anselm in his innocence followed awkwardly.

Anselm smelt something that reminded him of the damp earth in their garden after the rain. More people were coming in, mostly silent, some murmuring words to each other that Anselm couldn't hear. The air seemed heavy. Shoes echoed on the stone floor. It was a bit like morning assembly at St Thomas Aquinas...but then again not at all like that. Anselm looked to the front of the church where shafts of sunlight pierced stained glass windows picturing a man on a cross. He thought of Emily's lessons on 'refraction' of light and the workings of the eye. He wondered where she was right now. Was she with God now or still travelling. How long did it take to get there?

A man dressed in a white and gold...something...a dress...or dressing gown, with a book open in his hands appeared at the front. He waited as the final handful of people found their seats.

The quietness grew. It was like the world was holding its breath. Only the occasional muffled cough and the piping voice of a young girl, swiftly cut off by her mother, punctuated the still air.

The man at the front began to speak.

"Dearly beloved. We are gathered here to say our last goodbyes to our sister Emily...who has left our community to join the Lord..." For a while, Anselm stopped hearing the words and just heard a rising and falling tone , like a comforting song. He didn't know who the man was, but his voice was like music....."she was a much respected, much loved member of our community and of this church. She taught literally hundreds of boys and girls who are now parents themselves. Emily once told me of a family in whom she had taught not just one, not two, but three generations during her career. They shall be nameless but she did say, in her self- deprecating way, that the third generation were more knowledgeable than the first... but only just..."

'Hundreds of boys and girls' thought Anselm. 'I wonder if they are all here.' He looked around. No, not hundreds. Perhaps forty or fifty people dotted around this huge place. But maybe many of them were taught by Emily. He reckoned they would be smarter than average if they had been.

"So, let us rise...and sing hymn fifty-two from the blue books," said the man at the front.

Martha already had her blue book open. Peter groped for one in the back of the pew and then made something of a meal of finding the rght page. He shared his book with Anselm but by the time he found the page they were nearly a verse behind.

Thankfully, Anselm knew the hymn. It was one of his favourites from school assembly 'A Poor Boy's Dream"

He launched into the second verse with gusto until becoming aware of Martha looking at him out of the corner of her eyes with lips pursed in a 'sshhh'. He moderated his voice but thought that Emily would appreciate some energy in the rendition.

The hymn finished, they sat down again and one of the people sitting at the front, went up to the wooden lectern and started to read aloud.

Anselm drifted off again. He thought again of Emily's lesson on 'seeing'. He wondered if she could see and hear what was happening here. But she had told him that when people die their body stopped working. So, if her brain wasn't getting messages any more from her eyes, then probably she wouldn't be able to see. Would she? Then how would she know when she got to heaven? And how could she enjoy it?

"...I see Him with my heart," he remembered Emily's words about how she knew God was there. Maybe that's how she would see heaven. Emily was full of contradictions. All of those Biology and Physics lessons where she explained the workings of the human senses and how light behaved. And yet she could say something like that...and believe it. Anselm became aware his bottom was starting to feel sore sitting on the hard ,wooden bench. He rocked from side to side, then put his palms flat down on the bench underneath each buttock to form a cushion. 'How long is this going on' he wondered. Wherever Emily was he bet she didn't have a numb bum.

She had never married. Anselm had asked her why. "I never found the right man. Never met someone I wanted to spend my life with," she had explained. "And I was always so busy with 'my' children...teaching is a full - ime life you know."

So, Emily's genes would stop there. Just like his seemed to have come from nowhere, hers would go nowhere. That didn't seem right to him; that someone with all that knowledge wouldn't pass on her genes. Maybe that was why she had decided to teach 'hundreds' of children. And at least the fact that she didn't have a husband meant she wasn't leaving someone special behind...someone who would be especially sad.

The people at the front had stopped talking. Loud music started, like a thousand bumble bees from the big organ pipes mounted on the wall. People started to get up and file down the aisle. Martha stood and nodded to Peter. They joined the procession of men and women with handkerchiefs.

Anselm felt sad. It was a kind of borrowed sadness brought on by the sight of the women weeping. He didn't think it was his own but he was glad to have it anyway. Being sad seemed to be the 'normal' thing to do here. And he wanted now to be normal, for Emily's sake.

Ahead of him four large men carried the oak box inside which Emily lay. He remembered how small and slight she was. Do people get heavier when they die?

Martha and Peter had decided not to go to the crematorium. It was for family and close friends. Anselm asked where the long black car was taking Emily. He couldn't think that was the way to get to God. Peter explained as gently as he could what 'cremation' meant. "She has no further use of her body, Anselm."

This seemed to have an awful finality. It didn't leave any room for a mistake; and room for doubt. 'Why did people burn the body as if they wished to be rid of it when their sadness at Emily's leaving was so obvious.'It seemed very strange...removing all trace of the person they would miss so that all that was left were memories...and photographs. There could be no hope that the person would reappear...how could they without their body?

It was only then that Anselm realised he would never see Emily again. She wasn't hiding; she hadn't gone away on holiday for a few weeks. She wouldn't be coming round to their house to give him lessons again on Saturday morning...or any day of the week. However hard anyone searched, they would not be able to find her. She was lost, gone. In a way that was not negotiable, not reversible.

He glimpsed this eerie 'missingness' several times over the following days and weeks. For a moment the strangeness of it would hit him and then it would pass. He knew he wouldn't see her this coming Saturday...but then again he didn't really know it. Her absence was still more of a surprise than would have been her reappearance ,for some weeks after the funeral.

For a while he missed her badly. More than he would have expected had she just gone away. There were other things he could do now on Saturday mornings... pleasant things. No, he didn't miss her because he missed the lessons, or even because he wanted to see her. He missed her because she had left a hole...a hole in the world. One that could never be filled because it was the exact shape of Emily. He missed her because he too would die one day...and so would Martha and Peter.

***

"What are people for?"

It was late Friday afternoon; the three of them sat in the garden watching the shadows gather from the trees like the pointers of sundials. Anselm had been unusually quiet.

"What do you mean Anselm?" asked Peter.

"Well, what are they for; what's the point of people?"

Peter and Martha exchanged quizzical looks . Had Anselm been set a rather challenging homework topic?

"I can see the point of sheep, cows, horses, fish, grass....they are food for something else or they do some kind of work for human beings. But what are people for? Who would miss them if there weren't any people around? They don't seem to be much use for anything really. Nobody eats them .... at least they aren't supposed to . Look at all the fuss that was made when that shark ate the man in Florida last month. People do work, but it's the kind of work that if there were no other people around then there wouldn't be any point in doing it. What's the point of house-builders if there's no-one to live in the house?

"The soil is here for the grass, the grass for the sheep, the sheep for the people ...but what are people here *for*?"

"Do they have to be here *for* something?" asked Martha.

“If they are not here for some reason then why did God bother inventing them? He could have saved himself at least half a day out of the six... had an extra day off maybe or done a better job on the weather. Could have saved himself a lot of sleepless nights watching the goings on in Somalia and other places.

“Look at Emily,” Anselm continued. “What was Emily for.S he’s gone now, no trace of her. Just that tombstone. What’s the point of that?”

“She taught you Anselm. She taught you many things about the world. You could say she has left something very important behind.. in you.”

Anselm thought for a moment. He thought someone like Emily must have been for a reason. But he wasn’t sure he, Anselm, was a big enough reason. Emily couldn’t just have been an accident, an irrelevance... surely not .

“Then what am I for? Why am I here? What am I supposed to ....?”

“You’ll find your way”, said Martha.

“You’ll make your way” said Peter. We all do. There’s no-one to check you are ‘on script’. You just have to make your own choices; decide what you want to be; what you want to do and pursue it.”

Anselm thought Martha and Peters answers were very different. One was about ‘finding’ ones way as if there were some hidden path to be discovered. The other about ‘making' your way. He felt somehow that both were true but couldn’t see how he would do either.

“Life’s about the living of it, I think”, said Peter. “I don’t think it’s about some outcome or some prize at the end. If it were, then think how it would be for those who didn’t succeed, didn’t find the path and didn’t win the prize.”

Anselm had drifted off. He was thinking about the morning; deciding how he would make his way.

XII HOMECOMING

He woke at five-thirty am, from a half sleep, where thought and dream were mixed together to form that other version of reality that only comes to the sleepless. Both fear and excitement had been his bedfellows that night, each voice trying to drown out the other.

He dressed slowly for fear even the noise of his denim jeans would wake Martha and Peter. Then across the landing, walking on eggshells, avoiding the creaky floorboard and gingerly down the stairs, pausing every few treads to listen for any signs of stirring from their room .

. A ghostly light suffused the house. He couldn't tell whether it was the last drops of the full moon or the first glimmer of day. But it was enough to navigate by. Reaching the kitchen, he passed the cookie jar of promises. He wouldn't take any. Amongst the cookery books he had hidden a map of the area...fifty miles around Kirkmoor. He had 'borrowed' it from Peter's study a few days earlier. 'Borrowed' was the word he used to justify the taking of it to the 'no' voice in his head.

He couldn't read the map in this light, but he had planned the route he would take the day before. He knew it was six miles and remembered a wide road leading into town. The faint lines close together on the ordnance survey map told him where the hills lay. Ms Bentham's geography lessons were coming in useful after all.

The kitchen door was the last barrier. He knew it creaked; most painfully when opened slowly. He held his breath and pulled quickly and the door gave a rapid cat's 'miaow.' He froze for a moment, his ears straining for any sound from upstairs, then he plunged into the semi-light of early morning.

The main road at the edge of town was just ten minutes away. He would find it and follow it' route towards the hills. He felt sure he would remember the place when he got there. The air was Spring cool. As he walked along the grass verge, the morning dew ran up the bottoms of his jeans as if on blotting paper. The first feathered soloists were starting up in the trees and sat on the telephone wires 'jammin' to the break of dawn'. A cockerel crowed as if trying to stamp his authority on the proceedings.

He was maybe a mile outside town when he saw headlights compete with the first sun to light up the road ahead of him. A low growling sound became thunder and then a screeching as a large lorry passed him then braked sharply to a halt. Anselm kept walking towards the lorry wondering why it had stopped. The door swung open, attached to a large, hairy arm followed by a man's balding head.

"Need a lift, mate?"

Anselm was level with the cab now, looking up at a giant of a man with a cigarette hanging from his lips.

"I'm heading to the next town...any use to you?" asked the driver.

He saw the early morning in Anselm's eyes.

"Where you goin'?" he asked trying to tease a response out of the boy.

"I just want to go six miles up the road," replied Anselm.

"That's okay. Not much there though...middle of the UpDown hills. You sure?... .Hop in anyway...I'll take you."

The cab smelt of smoke and engine oil.

“What are you doing out here this time of the morning, then?” asked the driver pulling away from the grass verge.

“I’m going to see someone. I have some questions to ask him,” Anselm felt he should volunteer a little information .“He’s a shepherd.”

“Shepherds about al you’re gonna find out there in the hills. Do you live back there in Kirkmoor? How come your parents aren’t taking you to this shepherd?”

Anselm thought for a moment then decided this was one of those times when a lie didn’t do anybody any harm,

“They’re away for a few days...but they know I’m going to meet my friend.” The driver switched off his headlights as the sun got the upper hand.

“So, what questions do you think a shepherd is going to be able to answer for you, young man?” asked the driver.

Anselm hesitated. He thought of Abbott’s mockery.

“I...er...I want to know where I came from and why I am here.”

The driver frowned.“Pretty important questions.You sure he’s going to have the answers?”

“No. I’m not sure. But no-one else seems to know,” said Anselm.

“Well, if the shepherd’s so wise you might ask him a few questions for me too,” said the driver.

“Like what?”

“Well, for starters, how many more miles will I have to drive before I can retire and put my feet up. Or, maybe before he gets to that one, he can tell me when I’ll be able to pay my mortgage off.”

The driver thought for a moment.

“He might want to start with women. Why do women, and my wife in particular, always find something new they need to buy?”

“Oh, I can answer that one, “ said Anselm. “It’s the economy, you see. People have to buy things so as to pay other people wages for making those things, so that those people can buy things...and so on. It’s a virtuous circle.

“What are you carrying in the back of the lorry?”

“Shoes. To be delivered to the shop ,,” replied the driver.

“Well, people are going to buy those shoes...so you can be paid for driving. I bet your wife buys shoes.”

“She’s got enough to keep a centipede shod for the rest of its’ life. But that doesn’t seem to stop her buying more. A new dress always seems to need a new pair of shoes and handbag and the rest."

"Well, that's how my teacher told us the economy works."

"So, let me get this straight. My wife buys shoes so I can be paid for driving the shoes to the store; so , she then has money to buy more shoes...and I have to make another delivery...and so on."

"That's it. Keynesian economics at work," replied Anselm.

"So, the wife is keeping me driving this lorry...and left to her I'll be driving these roads forever. Is that it?"

"Yes, well, until she has enough shoes."

The driver saw his fate stretched out before him....an eternal road. The boy may have a simple view of economics but there was more than enough truth in it to make the driver's heart sink.

The lorry's engine was making a deep throaty growl as they climbed the gradient. "We're at about six miles now, son. Do you know where the place is?"

Anselm looked either side of the road. The grass verge gave way to a line of trees then climbed through rocky outcrops up towards the sun. It had been that way for the last five minutes. He wasn't sure how he was going to tell when he was close to the shepherd. Everything seemed familiar...but it had for miles.

The lorry reached the crest of the hill, it's engine's voice becoming deeper as it slowed as if exhausted by the climb. The road bent to the left starting its downward run. Suddenly the driver braked hard; a sheep stood in the middle of the road staring at the trespassers.

"Damn!" growled the driver. "The thing was nearly dinner."

Just beyond where the sheep stood, Anselm saw a stream cascading off the hillside into a culvert then appearing again on the other side of the road.

"This is the place," said Anselm.

***

The driver went on his way little the wiser about Anselm's quest, but with much to reflect upon about his relationship with his wife.

To the right of the road was a dirt track following the course of the stream down towards the valley bottom. Anselm started walking with a mixture of anticipation and anxiety. It looked like the track he had climbed with the shepherd when they left his cottage that day...but he couldn't be sure.

Martha and Peter would be getting up soon and they would realise he had gone. He had hoped the short note left on the kitchen table "Gone to find some answers; don't worry," would do the job but now he was realising he should have said more.

The morning sun projected shadows of the trees onto the limestone path. The only sounds the babbling syllables of the stream over rocks and fresh birdsong. As the path wound down the hillside he seemed to be descending into a very different time and space. He remembered one of his walks with Peter alongside the brook; he remembered the water-boatman and the meniscus of 'now', the infinitely thin boundary between past and future. He felt he was the water-boatman standing tip-toe on the boundary between two worlds.

The path seemed endless, like curved space. Spring flowers decked the grassy verge between path and stream...bluebells, forget-me-nots and dandelions, their colours the most vivid Anselm had ever seen. The stream chattered faster. It had rained the night before and swelled the stream's voice as it made its way down the valley side. He smelled the rain's sweetness mixed with the pungent decay of last year's leaf fall.

Two, maybe three times, he became aware of some presence just behind him amongst the trees. Each time he stopped, and waited for his eyes to become accustomed to the gloom, stuck like tar between the trees, he could see nothing. He tried walking on for fifty yards then turning quickly to spot whoever, whatever, it was, but to no avail.

By the time his eyes adjusted from the sunlight whatever was there had melted into the shadows.

He wasn't afraid. The feeling was one of being protected, not threatened in any way. He was thirsty. Kneeling by the stream he cupped his hands and filled them with last evening's rain. The water was soft and sweet to the taste. As he knelt a breeze zipped through the branches above his head.

"Anselm.......... A...n...selm."

He was startled and stood quickly to his full height.

"Who's there?"

There was no reply. He wiped his hands on the legs of his jeans and re-joined the path.

The path bent to the right around a large rock sticking out from the hillside. As he rounded it he saw a few hundred yards ahead, a small white walled cottage. As he approached he smelled the wood smoke issuing from the limestone chimney. He recognised the slate roof covered in moss and the oak door blackened by the weather. For a moment he wanted to turn and retrace his steps...back to the things and people who had become so familiar to him. Suddenly he was afraid; afraid of what answers he might find in this cottage and what consequences they might carry with them.

'Nothing to be afraid of,' said a reassuring voice in his head.

No turning back now. ‘Different’ without a reason was worse than afraid. He knocked on the door. A few moments went by and then it creaked open. Standing before him was the shepherd.

“I am Anselm.”

“Of course you are,” said the shepherd “don’t you think I know that? Come in, come in...no need to stand on ceremony here.”

Anselm crossed the threshold.

The shepherd was unsurprised to see him.

“I am making nettle tea. It’s good for the digestion you know. Would you like some?”

“Erm...yes please,” replied Anselm thinking it impolite to refuse.

“No, you wouldn’t. You are just trying to honour my offer. A noble sentiment, but quite unnecessary.”

The shepherd went to the fire, back turned to Anselm, and tended a pot hanging over the glowing logs.

“Sit down near the fire. You must be tired from your journey and there’s still a nip in the air this morning.”

“I got a lift from a lorry driver,” said Anselm.

“Yes,” said the shepherd, knowingly.

Anselm wondered how he would know but let it pass. "You remember me?" asked Anselm.,

"Of course, you have never left my mind since that day going into town," replied the shepherd, settling down into an old armchair opposite Anselm.

Anselm looked around the room. A wooden table with one chair lay at one end and next to it a set of shelves bearing vegetables and some pots. At the other end was the fire and the two armchairs they were sitting in. There was nothing else. No pictures on the wall; on the floor only uneven flagstones. To the right of the fire was a door partially open into a bedroom. Anselm could just make out the corner of a bed, but no other furniture. The windows had no curtains but the glass was thick with dust. Two of the panes in the main room were cracked and let in a whisper of breeze.

"Why do you think you have come back here to the hills?" asked the shepherd.

"I want to find out where I came from and what is my purpose in the world," announced Anselm in his most serious voice.

"Really? And do you think the answers to such questions might lie here."

"I was hoping they would. For me, time started here, with you...and I was hoping you would know what happened before that. Then you took me into town to the adoption agency...I think you must have had some purpose in mind..."

"Yes. There was a purpose in mind for you to live a life you could never experience in this valley. It was no more specific than that," said the shepherd.

Anselm felt the stone in his chest reappear and it seemed to be tied to his heart. If the answers weren't here then how would he ever find them?

"Tell me what you have learnt in the world of men," said the shepherd.

***

Anselm was lost. He couldn't focus on what the shepherd was asking. All this time he had believed that if he found the shepherd again things would become clear. But now the one person he had believed must be able to unlock the mystery just talks vaguely about living a different life. 'How can that be it?'

"Anselm," said the shepherd. "Yes?"

"Tell me what you have learnt."

Anselm thought for a few moments.

"Well, I've learnt that the world is a very uncertain and puzzling place. I've learnt that when we ask the question why, eventually it always seems to lead back to God... and then it stops...as if that is as far as the human mind can go...and yet God is the most uncertain and puzzling of all."

"And why is the world so uncertain?"

"It seems to split into two. Ourselves and the things outside us. But when we look for our 'self' it is a ghost; as soon as you look for it, it is gone. Take away all the things we see, hear, touch, smell, taste and there is nothing. Peter said it was a bit like a football team; take away the eleven players and what's left?"

"Well, you are here now....wondering why you are and what you are for, aren't you?" asked the shepherd.

"If I were to be sure of you I might say yes," said Anselm. But things get worse. It's not at all clear that the things we see or hear are really out there, including you."

The shepherd smiled.

"The philosophers and scientists can't seem to agree....and they have been putting a lot of effort into the problem. The philosophers seem to have emptied the world, saying that what we refer to as 'things' in the outside world are really dependent upon our senses. Without us seeing, touching, hearing, there isn't anything there...or at best it's just a disorganised mess we can never really know or directly experience. You might as well assume that the last man to die just turns the lights out on the world.

“The scientists have done the opposite. They have filled the world to overflowing with a seemingly infinite number of invisible particles which it turns out are not particles but energy, waves, forces, strings. These are claimed to do weird and wonderful things whether there are people around or not but they are very different from the objects ,like tables, that we claim to see. So ,the world isn’t dependent on us...it is something quite different to what we ‘see’ and well beyond our reach. What we see is in our minds...though how it gets there is still a mystery. Having spent hundreds of years, scientists don’t seem to have many explanations for anything. All they seem to have are mathematical formulas which kind of describe ‘laws of the universe’ and can be used to predict things...except when the things are very big or very small when they get rather uncertain again.

So ,the sum of all that seems to be that there is little evidence that either ‘I’ or ‘it’ exists in a form that anyone could understand. Take away sensations of things then the ‘I’ seems to disappear. But as soon as you put the ‘I’ back then sensations are only in the mind and reality disappears. You can’t have one without the other, but as soon as you have both they seem to cancel each other out or at least be totally separated, unable to reach each other.”

“So, you see the problem?” asked Anselm.

“No,” replied the shepherd.

“Why not ? How do you know ‘you’ and ....the sheep exist?”

“’Knowing’ seems to be the problem here...not the me or the sheep,” replied the shepherd. “This search for certainty seems to be the issue. How would life be if you didn’t worry about there being objects quite distinct from each other. How about if there was just consciousness and the contents of that consciousness could come and go and be and not be as they pleased with no need to make an account of their selves’?”

“How would that be?”

“Imagine the shepherd, the hillside, the stream, the lambs to be one...simply faces of the same things...remember Peter talking about eternity as past, present and future all in one? Why not all the ‘I’s and ‘its’ part of one indivisible whole?”

‘How did he know what Peter had said?’ thought Anselm. “Is that how it is for you?” he asked

.The shepherd smiled again and sipped his nettle tea.“ What else did you learn about the world?” he asked after a few minutes of silence.

“That it is full of rules of different types.”

“Explain,” said the shepherd.

***

"Well, there are laws of nature which set how the universe works, supposedly made up by God. Then there are laws of man or society which are made by governments and everyone has to stick to them. Then there are the rules of St Thomas Aquinas school set by the headmaster Mr Smart....and finally there are house rules which Martha sets at home...like for example 'always put your clothes away.'"

"It sounds complicated, Anselm."

"You can say that again. Staying out of trouble can be very tricky."

"So why do you think men need all these rules?" asked the shepherd.

Anselm though for a moment .He didn't suppose a shepherd would have much use for rules, except maybe some of those that God made...and maybe not even them. After all, what kind of rules would you need when there was only you around? Rules for the protection of sheep, maybe. But the shepherd seemed to do that without any need of laws. Even if you could think up a few rules that the shepherd had to stick to ......who was going to know if he broke them and who was going to punish him... No, the idea of rules just didn't make sense out here in the hills.

If the shepherd went to town that would be a different thing . As soon as he stepped beyond the sign at the outskirts of the town , the shepherd would feel the enormous weight of rules descend upon him. 'That's probably why he doesn't go there,' thought Anselm.

"The laws made by men are there to protect people...to stop them doing harm to each other or stealing each other's things," said Anselm, finally.

"Why would they want to do that?" asked the shepherd.

Anselm wasn't used to being on the receiving end of questions. "There sometimes isn't enough to go around. Like the Somalians who are starving whilst people in this country eat as much as they want. Sometimes people get jealous and want what the guy next door has got. If they can't get it easily they might just try to steal it. So, there are lots of laws to stop this...hundreds, even thousands of laws. There are people called lawyers and judges who have to study for years to learn these laws...and new ones are being made all the time. In fact ,one person wouldn't be able to remember them all."

"Wouldn't it be better if there were just a few simple rules or laws as you call them. Maybe just one would do. 'Do good; don't do bad'. Wouldn't that be enough?" asked the shepherd.

"I'm with you," replied Anselm. "Problem is there seems to be plenty of room for disagreement as to what's good and what's bad in any given set of circumstances. So , people have to spend time defining what's good and bad and then writing down the laws to make sure everyone does the right thing."

“Interesting. People can only make laws when they know what’s good and what’s bad...but if they know that then wouldn’t my single law be enough? Surely you wouldn’t need anything else?” said the shepherd.

Anselm paused for a few moments.

“That sounds right, but lots of people seem to have difficulty telling good from bad...so they rely on other people to make laws which make it clear for them what they should and shouldn’t do.”

“So, something is bad because it’s against the law? Or is it that something is against the law because it’s bad?”

“Both, I guess...”

“What happens if no-one has thought up a law against certain things yet? Does that mean those things must be good?”

”I don’t think so. I see what you mean. Good and bad must come first...we have to understand them first before we can make sensible laws,” replied Anselm.

“Seems that way,” said the shepherd.

“So then how do we know what’s good and bad. How did the first men know before any laws were passed?” mused Anselm.

He didn’t expect the shepherd to have an answer to this...after all the shepherd had no need of laws...so maybe he had no need to distinguish good from bad. What could be bad in these hills?

The shepherd got up and put another log on the fire. Sparks flew up the blackened chimney.

"Some people believe that our idea of good and bad is given to us by God and that it is by doing God's 'good' and avoiding 'bad' that we should live our lives. Some even believe that, when we die, God makes a review of what we did in our lives and that determines whether we go to heaven or to hell," said Anselm.

"Do you think it is God who decides what is good and what is bad?" he asked.

"Doesn't that sound like the laws of men, only on a much grander scale? A God who has a list with columns of goods and bads, do's and don'ts and hands out rewards or punishments depending on how many ticks people get in which columns. And such a powerful God, able to reward or punish for all eternity in inconceivably pleasant or horrible ways. That sounds like a pretty powerful stick and carrot," the shepherd said. "Wouldn't you think that someone just following such a God's requirements is just acting out of self-interest? How noble is that?"

Anselm nodded.

"Then how do you think what is good and bad is decided? How do we know what is right and wrong?" he asked.

“Watch the sheep on the hillsides. They are loyal, friendly, grateful; they co-operate with each other and with their shepherd; they are loving and protective of their lambs. They are not living their lives in obedience of someone’s rules. They are concerned for each other and for the welfare of the flock. This is what guides them... .not a rule book but a loving concern...and their lives are the better for it. Do men pass laws to ensure people are loyal, friendly, co-operative, fair, grateful, sympathetic...and loving...?”

“I don’t think so...not really. It’s too difficult to make people be like that. Probably too many people would end up in prison if you tried. So ,men’s laws tend to be about what not to do rather than how to be,” Anselm replied.

“Then perhaps men are missing the point,” said the shepherd. –

***

“Why do you say that God is the most uncertain of all, Anselm,” the shepherd asked.

Anselm studied the shepherd’s face for a moment. It was creased and leathery like the armchair in Peter’s study. Uncounted days on the hillside had given the shepherd a hide instead of the soft pallid skin of the townspeople. And set in that face were two dark green eyes, piercing Anselm kindly but firmly with the shepherd’s question.

“Because he’s not necessary to explain the world...the universe; and because people make some pretty unbelievable claims about him,” replied Anselm.

“Go on,” said the shepherd.

“Well the scientists seem pretty confident that the Universe could have just come into existence from....nothing, without any help. I don’t understand the argument fully, something to do with quantum theory and zero being equal to minus one plus one...negative energy and positive energy. Anyway , they reckon it’s theoretically possible that zero ...er nothing just split in two to produce positive and negative matter. Even if that’s not true, inventing God as the creator of the Universe just lands you with the question of who or what made God. You still end up with something unexplained.”

“I see your problem,” said the shepherd.

“And then the scientists are saying that maybe the physical laws of the Universe didn’t need any thinking about, they were...or are...inevitable, the only logical, consistent set of laws there could be. We haven’t gotten to the bottom of them yet but that’s because we’ve got limited brains. If and when we do it will be obvious this is the only way things could operate. So, another job for God is gone. We don’t need him to create the first stuff or to set the laws. He’s redundant.”

“A problem doubled,” said the shepherd.

“To make things worse we’re asked to believe God is good and can do anything; but then there’s all this suffering in the world caused by diseases, storms, earthquakes and things outside of our control. If God did decide the laws of the Universe then He’s responsible for natural disasters; not exactly the action of a good creator. If He didn’t decide the laws or can’t step in when something nasty is about to happen then He’s not exactly all-powerful is He?”

“Finally, He’s said to be omniscient...knows everything.” (Anselm thought four syllable words might be a bit much for a shepherd).

“If He is then it’s difficult to see how men can have free-will if He knows what’s going to happen. Peter came up with a compromise – but had to put God outside of time...making Him eternal to leave us still free. But I don’t buy it. That just puts God so far away. I can’t see how He could have anything useful to do with the world if He doesn’t get down into the days and hours with the rest of us.”

“Sounds like there’s some very serious objections there,” said the shepherd. “Doesn’t it make you wonder why so many people believe in Him or are still searching for Him if He’s a redundant contradiction?”

“Yes,” replied Anselm.

“Well, what’s your theory, young man?”

“I can only think of two explanations. Either people invented the idea of God because ‘whys’ always have to end up with a person. We’re just used to the idea that when something happens it’s because someone made it happen. Because our ‘I’ does that all the time and we think we know what an ‘I’ is. Problem is earthquakes or gravity needs a ‘super-I’ with a strange sense of what’s good and then you get stuck with all sorts of contradictions.”

“Or ?”

“Or, maybe man invented God to have someone who takes away our guilt.”

“How does that work?”

“Man invented God to be so all-seeing and all-powerful that we cannot truly be free to make choices. So ,we can’t be blamed...can we? I know in some religions there is a day of judgement. God has to do that because otherwise He’d be an accomplice in our wrong doings. But the fact is we’ve created God as someone who gets us off the hook of being really responsible for anything...because He’s in charge and nothing happens that He couldn’t have prevented or had happen in a different way. We’re just passengers, He’s in the driving seat.”

“Do you really think men invented the idea of God just to have a scapegoat Anselm?”

“I don’t know, really...but those who believe in God seem to be more comfortable with the world.”

“Like who?”

“Martha .....and Emily, when she was here.”

“And Peter?”

“Peter is an atheist...or he was last time I checked,” replied Anselm.

“So, the believers are better off you think?”

“In some ways. But perhaps they are both off the hook. If you believe in an all- powerful, all-knowing God; you lose the responsibility that comes with free will so there’s no defendant. If you don’t then there’s no judge.”

“Whichever way you look at it, inventing or disinventing God for one’s own convenience doesn’t seem a very noble act does it?” asked the shepherd.

The light outside was fading fast; little was now leaking through the dust encrusted windows of the cottage. Anselm could see the shepherd only by the flickering flame of the log fire. As the flame waxed and waned so did the outline of the old man.

The shepherd got up and threw on another log. He returned to his seat facing Anselm.
“So where does all that leave you Anselm?”

Anselm struggled to pull together the threads of doubt.

“The Christians believe that we each are an ‘I’, a self; with freedom of will, able to make choices; our choices between good and evil are important; that we...or at least our soul-self survives after death; when God judges us. But it seems just as possible,” said Anselm, “that there is no continuing ‘I’... that we change identity over time, like our body changes, and that memories are just handed on between succeeding ‘selves’; the world is clockwork and pre-determined; there is no ‘I’ after death and no final judgement; we are irrelevant, an accident of nature and no part of its purpose.”

“And what would you do different in the two cases?” the shepherd asked.

“Do good in the first case...and do as I like in the second?”

”Do those two things have to be different?” the shepherd asked.

Anselm fell quiet. Minutes passed.

“Well?” asked the shepherd.

“Maybe...I don’t know,” replied Anselm.

“Have you ever thought that God might need mankind and may just have to stand aside, to allow our futures to be open because only by doing that can the real purpose of our lives and indeed the world be fulfilled?”

"Why would that be?"

"Let's see if that becomes clear later," said the shepherd.

***

"I wanted to ask you something." Anselm finally broke the silence that had been gathering between them.

"What is it?"

"Can you tell me where I came from? I only remember you finding me that day on the heath, nothing before that. Don't know if I asked you then; everything seemed so strange."

"I was herding the sheep between pastures and ...suddenly...there you were."

"But I must have come from somewhere. I couldn't just have sprung up from nowhere....from nothing."

"Well that's what you said the scientists were beginning to think happened with the Universe or the stuff it all started from...just came out of nothing; so why not you?" the shepherd responded.

"That's different."

"Yes, you're right. The Universe is an altogether more complex thing; quite a challenge for nothingness."

"No; I mean people get born...as babies...from biological parents. I couldn't just arrive out of nowhere with an adolescent's body."

"Who says?"

"Well...it's like a physical law or a whole bunch of them. That's how the world works."

"But who says it has to be that way ?"

"The scientists do."

"Perhaps they are being a little inconsistent, don't you think. Something from nothing is okay for universes but not for fifteen-year old boys...eh?"

Anselm thought for a few moments.

"There's only one universe. ...There's lots of fifteen-year old boys...and they all got born as far as I know."

"So?"

"So, if it happens billions of times the same way, it must have happened that way for me too...mustn't it?"

"Perhaps there was no time to lose and things couldn't happen in what you have been taught to think of as the 'normal' way," said the shepherd.

"But things can't just happen like that."

“I thought we’d already covered that point,” the shepherd replied. “It seems to me, from what you have learned about the world, that it is a very mysterious place indeed. You are the least surprising feature...if I may say so without causing offence. A world that ranges from being purely an idea in the mind of God to one made up of undetectable, probabilistic strings depending on who you listen to should have no problem with the spontaneous generation of a teenager.”

This wasn’t the answer Anselm had wanted, or expected.

“Tell me,” the shepherd continued, “do Martha and Peter have any issue about ‘where’ you came from?”

“Well ...no, I don’t think so. They never seem to mention it unless I do.”

“And what do they say?”

“Martha says I was the answer to a prayer. They both say I am different...but good different.”

“Well that sounds a pretty satisfactory state of affairs,” said the shepherd. “Don’t you think so?”

“Yes, it’s good...but...”

“But what?”

“But having no memories from earlier makes me feel kind of ...incomplete, not a whole person...like something is missing.”

“Well maybe we could weigh in the balance what you lost and what you gained by just happening as you did,” said the shepherd. “What did you lose?”

Anselm thought ,then answered “Nearly fifteen years of learning, roast potatoes, Gull Cove visits, friends and ...love.”

“Hmmm.....a lot,” said the shepherd. “And what did you gain?”

Anselm paused again.

“Martha and Peter. I wouldn’t have been adopted by them if I’d come through ...er... the normal route. I guess some other people would have been my parents if I’d got born the usual way ......Martha couldn’t have babies.

“Anything else? ” A longer pause .

“Me...I wouldn’t have been ‘me ‘would I...if you know what I mean...like I wouldn’t have been the me here with you today. I would have been a different person with different experiences, memories, parents. I would have lost this version of me for another, I don’t know who. “

“So, how does that idea strike you?”

“Strange. I’ve been getting to like the idea of being me over the last few months. People seem to like this version...even if I am a bit different.”

"And what do you think it would have meant to Martha and Peter if you hadn't appeared?"

Anselm suddenly felt the stone of loss in his chest ...after so many months of absence. He realised it belonged not to him but to the Martha and Peter who inhabit that parallel universe of unrealised hopes and dreams...the Universe without an Anselm Swinbourne.

***

The room was dark now and Anselm could make out only the half of the shepherd's face which was turned towards the fire. It was strange to be talking to one ear, one eye and half a mouth.

"Tell me more about Martha and Peter. How they are...together. What was it like when you first arrived in their house?"

"They both seemed very glad I had come."

"I'm sure. But how were things between them?"

Anselm remembered back. "I don't think they liked each other much. Martha worked a lot and arrived home late and Peter used to sort of ...hide in his study. They both talked to me but didn't say much to each other...when they did the words seemed sharp."

"Go on."

“I remember the memory book with pictures of them from when they were at University and how they looked at each other. It was like they could almost fall into each other’s eyes. And their faces were soft. But then the looks seemed to stop and they didn’t look at each other for very long at all...a second or two and then they would look away. As if it was too painful to look; or like when somebody is embarrassed.”

“Has that changed?”

Anselm studied for a few moments.

“It started changing when we played the feelings game and made the calendar. They both started with stars mainly against the bad feelings, Martha more than Peter. Peter wasn’t too up to date on feelings. But over the last few months they’ve both been hitting some good ones, quite often.”

“Like what?”

“Happy...and Love,” replied Anselm. “The looks are coming back and I often hear the sound of them talking in their bedroom, and...”

The shepherd smiled.

“So how do you feel about that change?”

“Happy...and loved...and safer. They were both very nice to me from the start but when they were sharp with each other it made me feel tense...unsure of things. Like if two people married and living together are sharp with each other the whole world seemed shaky."

"And it was in enough trouble as it was with the philosophers and scientists eh?" said the shepherd.

"Now there seems to be plenty of love and warmth in the house, enough to go around, enough for the two of them and for me. Three people together seem to create more love than three people separately. It's like molecules reacting and giving off heat."

"Do you see what you brought for Martha and Peter, Anselm?"

"I...I never thought of it like that. I think they always loved each other, but they had forgotten or got out of practice."

"What do you think would have happened if you hadn't arrived?" asked the shepherd.

"I don't know."

"If you think about it a little more you will discover you do know. You asked me earlier why you are here in this world. Tell me more about this feeling of 'love'."

"Well it's like you always want to be with that person, the person you love; like they are the most wonderful person in the world; like they are a part of you.; you couldn't live without them, they give a meaning to the whole world; the one you love is the most important, most perfect one...like no- one else could be..."

"It's quite overwhelming then?"

"Yes, it is."

"And do you think that' s what Martha and Peter's love is like and the love they share with you?"

Anselm hesitated.

"Some parts are the same...but, no...they showed they could live without each other in a way and they lived without me...but with less smiles, with harder faces...with stones in their chests, I think. It's not as if the whole world depends on their love... it's just a better place because the love is there. And they do things for each other... and things for me."

"And sometimes they say 'no' when you want something?"

"Yes."

"They insist on you doing your homework?"

"Yes."

"They see your bad side as well as your good side?"

"Yes."

“Did this happen from the very start when you first arrived?”

“I think it took time. Just like it took time for them to find their love for each other.”

“And how strong do you think this love is now?”

“Like it could last until I die.”

“So, it seems that as they gave you more love then they took more and gave more to each other. And it’s a love that does, not one that just wants?”

“Yes...I think so...”

“So ,do you see now Anselm what you have brought to Martha and Peter? Do you see why you are here? And do you see that from ‘where’ is not the important thing but ‘why’ and ‘what’ are the answers we should seek? You said yourself Anselm that ‘whys’ always seem to end in a person. Perhaps your ‘why’ ends in two people...Martha and Peter and the love that your appearance has unlocked from such closely guarded hearts.

“It was only because of the potential for that love that you could be here and it was because of that love that there was no time to be lost. You are the watch upon the heath, Anselm, the work of the God of Love; a God who can break his own rules when needed through the miracle of a fifteen-year old boy who just happened...right on time.”

Their shadows played on the walls of the cottage, dancing to the fire's flames until the fire turned to embers and the shadows took their seats again in exhausted silence.

Anselm kept turning over in his mind what the shepherd had said. Surely there was more to it than that; but he couldn't imagine an answer to the 'where from' and 'why' questions that would be ...enough. What answers could the shepherd have given that would have left Anselm gasping...in awe; what answers would have left him amazed by the ingenuity of it all? He couldn't think of any that would have satisfied this hunger for a mystical purpose to the world and a mystical purpose for Anselm.

No. He came from God. Everyone does. But he came by special delivery. He, Anselm, was the exception that proved the rule. A 'miracle' the shepherd had called it. What more could he ask? And it seemed he had been sent as a gift to help Martha and Peter find each other again; to help them find a different kind of love; and it was working. If God hadn't broken his own rules maybe it would have been too late for Martha and Peter. Maybe if Martha had had a child the normal way things would have worked out like they had; maybe they would have been ready.

"So how do you feel about this?" the shepherd finally broke the silence.

"Special, and...important," Anselm replied.

"You are both of those things."

Anselm paused. “But is my work finished now? Martha and Peter have found each other; do they still need me? If I am here as a gift to help their love, isn’t that done now?”

“Love isn’t a task we finish and then move on Anselm. We don’t say ‘I’ve eaten once so there, that will do for the rest of my life,’ do we? Love is continually renewed and changing...it only persists if we do; if we put the work in developing our own soul life and that of our loved ones. Love is as love does and it needs the nourishment of our caring actions towards each other.

“You are not just the catalyst for Martha and Peter’s love for each other; not just there to light the blue touch paper and retire. No, you being there multiplies the love, as the third point of a triangle with three times the strength of the love between a couple. But also ,as you connect with other people in the world, so the love expands and multiplies. That is God’s purpose and your role in it is a life times’ work and more. Your work is not finished; it has only just begun. As you grow and learn the kind of love Martha and Peter increasingly show for each other and you meet others, so they will grow and learn too.”

The shepherd waited a few minutes for Anselm to respond.

“Then I think it’s time I got back to work, don’t you. It’s time I went back home... Martha and Peter will be missing me,” said Anselm.

***

They climbed the dirt track by the light of a full moon. The stream chattered and glinted in the moonlight. Anselm was tired. He looked at the stream. It seemed to be flowing up the valley side keeping pace with them as they climbed.

They reached a point where the path levelled out. Anselm recognised it as the place where he had heard his name spoken during his descent into the valley that morning.

"This is as far as I go, young man. You will find your own way from here," said the shepherd. He placed a folded piece of paper into Anselm's hand then closed the boys' fingers around it. "Only look at this when you have reached home."

With that the shepherd turned and disappeared into the night. Anselm hesitated for a moment then moved on. He remembered the water boatman again and, for a moment, felt as if he was pressing against the meniscus once more...pushing back into the world he had left that morning.

***

XII- EPILOGUE

"Anselm, Anselm....wake –up son. You're going to be late for school...it's eight o'clock...come on, time to get up."

Anselm woke like a drowning man reaching the surface...unsure where he was but lungs bursting and gasping for life.

Martha was shaking him by the arm.

“Come on...you’ve overslept. A quick shower then downstairs...you’ll miss registration...”

“What...where...how...?” There were too many jumbled questions to finish one before starting another.

“Shower! ” Martha issued the final, definitive command, then left him to it.

How did he get here? He couldn’t remember the walk back. Had Martha and Peter missed him? They must have done; he was away all day...must have been yesterday, Friday. But how come today was a school day?

He sat on the edge of the bed trying to regroup. He’d been asleep. It was a dream. No, it couldn’t have been it was too vivid, too real. He looked at the chair in the corner of his room where he usually left his clothes. His school trousers hung there. No sign of his denims.

He dragged himself to the shower, part in compliance with Martha’s order, part in the hope the shower might jolt him back to reality...whatever that was.

The hot water washed the night away and with it some of the vivid colours of the shepherd’s valley.

He dressed and stumbled downstairs still in a daze.

“Just time for a piece of toast and then we must go,” said Martha.

“Mum.”

“Yes.”

“Did you miss me yesterday?”

“What do you mean?”

“Well I was out all day, must have got back really late.”

Martha gave him a puzzled look.

“You were at school and back by five-o’clock. We played scrabble...don’t you remember?”

“No...I mean, yes...but that was the day before yesterday...wasn’t it?”

“Not unless my memory’s playing tricks. Now come on ,sit down and eat your toast!”

“I went to visit the shepherd yesterday...”

Martha stopped. “I...I don’t think so Anselm. Peter picked you up from school. You told us all about your day...no mention of the shepherd.”

She wondered what had brought this on.

“You’ve dreamed before about the shepherd. Do you feel you need to see him Anselm?”

“I don’t know, I’m confused .”

He must have been dreaming. There’s no way he could have been out of the house for a whole day, not missed, while the rest of the world stood still until he came back and then picking up where they had left off.

But such a vivid dream. If it was just a dream then did that mean that it didn’t count? He had felt happy with what the shepherd said. He liked the answers to his questions; the mystery solved and him knowing what he had to do. Did all that mean nothing if it was just a dream, not real? No, surely it didn’t matter; the truth’s the truth wherever you find it; and what the shepherd said sounded like the truth; but if it wasn’t the real shepherd how could it be the real truth; how could he rely on it?

Wait. The piece of paper.

Anselm leapt out of the chair and bounded upstairs. “Anselm, what...”, Martha’s words choked.

He opened the wardrobe door and tore at the hangars. His denims hung there... muddy stains around the trouser hems. He fished in the left-hand pocket...nothing; then tried the right hand...yes...his hand felt the folded parchment. He pulled it out slowly for fear it would turn into something from the wrong side of the meniscus.

Slowly he unfolded the paper...and read:

Don't look to the stars for your answers
They are too far from reach for your meaning

I hold in my mind all of the world
Reality depends on who is dreaming

What you see is simply a stage set
What you hear, just other people's lines

It's not there that you'll find your answers

They're not held in space or time

No, it's in the heart that I gave you
And the love eternal burning there
It's in the knowledge that you're here to grow

A love that doubles every time you share

So, let the scientists uncover forever
Puzzle- pieces and laws, on average, true
But remember He who makes laws can break them

A truth testified by the miracle that's you.

Your shepherd.

Anselm folded the note carefully and put it in his bedside drawer. He had the proof... but he didn't need proof any more. He would read that note many times in the years to come...to remember how to live his life.

THE END

www.ingramcontent.com/pod-product-compliance
Lightning Source LLC
LaVergne TN
LVHW091247150826
845673LV00006B/1352